Endorsements for *A Seat at the Table*

"This isn't just a policy book—it's a story of conviction, creativity, and the free market at work. Mitch Silk helped shape key areas of one of the boldest reorientations of US economic policy in decades, and *A Seat at the Table* captures the mission and the man."

—**Larry Kudlow**, Director of the National
Economic Council (2018–2021)

"Mitchell Silk was a trusted partner in strengthening the US-Israel economic relationship. Few people navigate both the highest levels of government and the deepest commitments of faith with the grace and conviction of Mitch Silk. This book is a rare blend of policy and personal mission—reminding us what public service can and should be."

—**David M. Friedman**, US Ambassador to Israel
(2017–2021)

"Mitch brought his brilliance as a lawyer, unique depth on China and infrastructure, and unwavering patriotism to our work at Treasury. *A Seat at the Table* captures how faith, intellect, and even a timely Yiddish proverb can strengthen the US in a complex world— whether in Beijing, Panama, or Kazakhstan."

—**David Malpass**, Former President of the World
Bank; Under Secretary for International
Affairs, US Treasury

"Mitch Silk was my law partner, Treasury colleague, and remains my friend. This book is classic Mitch—an elegant, candid, and courageous account of public service, full of stories where Talmudic wisdom meets hard-nosed financial diplomacy. *A Seat at the Table* shows how faith and intellect can guide a life of consequence."

—**Heath Tarbert**, President of Circle; Former Chairman, US Commodity Futures Trading Commission

"Mitch Silk was instrumental in launching the CARES Act program that saved the US airline industry and more than 600,000 jobs. He combined legal precision, policy savvy, and a steady stream of Yiddish quips that, while occasionally groan-inducing, we all learned to love. *A Seat at the Table* delivers that same blend of depth and heart."

—**Brent McIntosh**, General Counsel, Citibank; Former Under Secretary for International Affairs, US Treasury

"Mitchell Silk delivered real, measurable results for Panama. From the refinancing of our national utility ETESA—saving the country $60 million in debt service—to a $1.15 billion LNG project and rural electrification through micro-grids, his work under the US–Panama infrastructure framework has left a lasting legacy. *A Seat at the Table* is the story of how principled leadership and a home-cooked meal (with a little nip of home-infused vodka) can change the trajectory of a country."

—**Javier Enrique Carrizo Esquivel**, Gerente General, Banco Nacional de Panamá

"Thanks to Mitch Silk's leadership, Ecuador gained not just a friend in Washington—but results for Ecuador. His work on the US–Ecuador infrastructure framework and the $3.5 billion DFC facility provided an anchor for long-term stability and opportunity to our energy and infrastructure systems. *A Seat at the Table* tells the story behind that breakthrough—and many others like it."

—**Ivonne A-Baki**, Former Ambassador of Ecuador to the United States

"Mitch Silk played a critical role in establishing the US–Jamaica bilateral infrastructure finance framework—an initiative that catalyzes private investment, improves infrastructure resilience, and offers a new model for development in the Caribbean. *A Seat at the Table* captures his rare ability to pair policy vision with human connection."

—**Nigel Clarke**, Minister of Finance and the Public Service, Jamaica (2018–2024)

"Mitch has a truly unique perspective that comes from his experiences of different cultures and his scholarly approach to the acquisition of knowledge. I will always be grateful to him for how he moved the relationship between Taiwan and the US forward during his time in government. There is much to be learned from the experiences he shares in *A Seat at the Table*, especially about bridging cultures and how determination and professionalism can change the fate of nations."

—**Tsai Ing-wen**, President of the Republic of China (Taiwan), 2016–2024

"Mitch helped build our China practice at a time when it required bold thinking and nuanced diplomacy. From his groundbreaking work in Asia to leading multibillion-dollar infrastructure projects in the Americas, he brought unmatched skill and cultural fluency to every transaction. This book reflects the values he brought to A&O: intellectual rigor, authenticity, emotional intelligence and impact."

—**Andrew Ballheimer**, Global Managing Partner, Allen & Overy (2016–2020)

"Mitch Silk was with us on the ground floor of transformational power projects across China, India, and Latin America. Later, at the US Treasury, he advanced bilateral finance frameworks that directly supported the growth of US power companies, including AES, in countries like Panama, the Dominican Republic, and Vietnam. This book tells the story of a man who bridged the public and private sectors to accelerate sustainable infrastructure where it mattered most."

—**Andrés Gluski**, President & CEO, AES Corporation

"Mitch Silk can negotiate the technical guts of a 1,000 MW Chinese power deal in fluent Mandarin—then turn around and charm an airport official in Yantai into clearing us through an impossible and ever-present immigration jam just-in-time for our flight. His legal expertise is unmatched, but it is his appreciation of Chinese business culture, his grace under pressure—and a perfectly placed

Yiddish joke—that makes him unforgettable. *A Seat at the Table* is Mitch in full form: sharp, soulful, and very, very human."

—**James F. Wood**, Former CEO, Babcock & Wilcox; former senior US Department of Energy official

"Navigating China's infrastructure finance in the early days was high-stakes theater, and Mitch Silk was our leading man—precise in language, fearless in logic, and just irreverent enough to keep it human. His jokes were sometimes worse than mine—but his judgment never was. This book is a front-row seat to a great performance."

—**Ashley Wilkins**, Former Asia Regional Head, Société Générale

"Mitch Silk's dedication to public service had a profound impact on the aviation industry during one of its most challenging times. His timely pragmatism, clear understanding of the unprecedented challenges confronting the airlines as the result of the COVID-19 pandemic, and relentless efforts in navigating the economic and political complications, allowed the industry and its stakeholders to secure essential financial support that preserved jobs and ensured continuity of service. His book, *A Seat at the Table*, provides a compelling narrative of the behind-the-scenes work that safeguarded the future of air travel."

—**Stephen Johnson**, Vice Chair and Chief Strategy Officer, American Airlines

"In the face of a global pandemic, Mitch Silk's collaborative approach and strategic thinking were vital in securing financial assistance that kept Frontier Airlines flying and our employees supported. *A Seat at the Table* captures the essence of effective public-private partnerships and the importance of decisive action in times of crisis."

—**Jimmy Dempsey**, President, Frontier Airlines

"Moyshe Silk has long exemplified what it means to serve both country and community with unwavering integrity. His visionary leadership of Agudath Israel's pro bono legal services network helped thousands navigate complex legal challenges with dignity and support. *A Seat at the Table* is more than a memoir—it is a reflection of a life devoted to justice, compassion, and Kiddush Hashem."

—**Rabbi Chaim Dovid Zwiebel**, Executive Vice President, Agudath Israel of America

"In an era when public life so often compromises personal values, Mitchell Silk offers a different path—one of emunah, discipline, and quiet courage. *A Seat at the Table* is not just his story, but a call for Jews everywhere to rise to their mission with confidence, humility and grace."

—**Rabbi Moshe Hauer**, Executive Vice President, Orthodox Union

A SEAT *at the* TABLE

An Inside Account of Trump's Global Economic Revolution

MITCHELL A. SILK

BOMBARDIER

Published by Bombardier Books
An Imprint of Post Hill Press
ISBN: 979-8-89565-226-8
ISBN (eBook): 979-8-89565-227-5

A Seat at the Table:
An Inside Account of Trump's Global Economic Revolution
© 2025 by Mitchell A. Silk
All Rights Reserved

Cover Design by Cody Corcoran

This book, as well as any other Bombardier Books publications, may be purchased in bulk quantities at a special discounted rate. Contact orders@bombardierbooks.com for more information.

This is a work of nonfiction. All people, locations, events, and situations are portrayed to the best of the author's memory.

BOMBARDIER BOOKS   Post Hill PRESS

Post Hill Press
New York • Nashville
posthillpress.com

Published in the United States of America
1 2 3 4 5 6 7 8 9 10

CONTENTS

To my Zeyde, Max Friend z"l—
born Meshulam Menschenfruend in the shtetl of Nadvorna—
who stood five-foot-two but cast the moral
shadow of a giant and taught me that:

True justice demands action.[1]
Hard work redeems hardship.[2]
To serve with heart is to lead with purpose.[3]

Your legacy of perseverance, principle, steadfast
belief in providence and love for this country
live on in every word of this book.

[1] *Babylonian Talmud, Sanhedrin 98a* (citing *Isaiah* 1:27) and *Bava Kamma 30a; Mishna, Avos 1:17.*
[2] *Kedushas Levi, Parshas Beshalach (commenting on Exodus 16:4.)*
[3] "A Rebbe must carry his flock on his shoulders with joy," attributed to the Rebbe R' Mordchele of Nadvorna.

INTRODUCTION

Strategy, Strength, and a Seat at the Table

If you're holding this book, there's a good chance you're asking the same questions so many Americans are asking right now. From the moment President Trump took office for his second term, we've witnessed a flurry of executive orders and policy moves. The speed of change seems so dizzying and the scope so unprecedented that many Americans wonder:

Are all these changes truly going to make America great again—or will they jeopardize our future security?

What exactly is President Trump's idea of diplomacy—and what's his view on dealing with China?

Does President Trump really have a plan—or is he just winging it?

These are fair questions. After all, the world is volatile, the stakes are high, and the challenges we face today are deeper and more complex than ever before. But I can answer without hesitation:

Yes—President Trump has a plan. He knows exactly what he's doing. His approach is focused, strategic, and aggressive. From day one, his actions have *focused* on key campaign promises, such as government downsizing, foreign policy realignment, reduction of the trade deficit, energy independence, and border security. His approach to the problems that face us, particularly China, is not only serious; it's proven, pragmatic, and *strategic*, and it puts America first. And his use of executive orders is intentionally *aggressive*, issuing an exponentially large number of EO's with full knowledge they will face legal challenges.

This book is a story about returning to the table—not only in the diplomatic sense, but in the economic and strategic one. It's about how the Trump Administration, in its first term and now again in its second, reclaimed America's place at the global decision-making table. And it's about how I, a Chassidic Jew with humble roots in the Eastern European shtetl of Nadvorna, found a seat at that table—first as a lawyer, then as a senior Treasury official, and ultimately as someone entrusted to assist with implementing a vision that could restore American strength, growth, and influence.

The Trump Doctrine: Order Beneath the Boldness

Many commentators mistake President Trump's diplomatic style for a lack of strategy. The President Trump that I know does anything but improvise; rather, he games out. He moves on instinct, yes, but his instincts are grounded in a lifetime of negotiation, risk-taking, and above all, results. He approaches policy like a grandmaster playing three-dimensional chess. Every tariff, every handshake, every tweet—it's all part of a broader, calculated effort to reshape the global order in a way that benefits the American economy and restores national sovereignty.

I saw this approach first-hand when I served in the Trump Treasury. Take charting a course to liberalize our overly complicated system of financial regulation, including optimizing the rapidly changing landscape of the fintech and crypto-currency revolution. Trump aimed to cut through the jungle. Or, take navigating the unprecedented double-crisis of a worldwide pandemic and economic shutdown. In both areas and many more, President Trump steered our country confidently towards ever-greater prosperity, freedom, security and opportunity. At Treasury, we followed his lead. The mission: make markets freer, make the economy and workers stronger, and reduce the red tape.

Nowhere was this clearer than in our approach to China.

The China Challenge—and the Trump 45 Response

By 2017, the US-China economic relationship had become highly unbalanced. Worse, it was unsustainable. For decades, the United States had tolerated intellectual property theft, cyber intrusions, unfair subsidies, forced technology transfers, and a growing $500 billion trade deficit. The conventional wisdom was that engagement would liberalize China. That engagement would modernize China. That engagement would pacify China.

That conventional wisdom was wrong.

President Trump understood what others refused to admit: China wasn't converging with the liberal world order—it was systematically undermining it. And, so, he chose a different path.

He imposed tariffs—not as an end, but as a means. A means to bring the Chinese to the table. And they came.

I was there for those negotiations. I helped craft and deliver the tools of economic pressure and strategic opportunity that made them possible. Our efforts culminated in the 2020 Phase 1 Trade Agreement, a milestone that secured real commitments from China on purchases of American agricultural, energy and other goods and commodities, provided greater US access to China's vast services markets, and ensured protection of US intellectual property and currency practices. For the first time in recent memory, America didn't blink. We didn't cave. We led—and we won.

Rolling Back the Belt and Road

But tariffs were just one dimension. We also knew that China's influence wasn't only about trade. It was about infrastructure. Through its Belt and Road Initiative, the Chinese Communist Party was flooding developing countries with opaque, state-directed capital that locked governments into unsustainable debt dependency and handed Beijing control over ports, power generation plants, and key minerals.

The Trump Administration's answer? Build something better.

We launched America Crecé in Latin America and AsiaEDGE in Asia, and then adopted similar programming elsewhere in the world, including in the Middle East. These transformative programs delivered healthy growth through impactful energy and infrastructure projects capable of being financed with private capital solutions. They employed strategic partnerships built on US private capital, technical excellence, and transparent and competitive tendering. They provided a market-based, transparent alternative to Chinese debt traps—enabling our partners and their utilities to stand on their own two feet financial, delivering profitable, more efficient, and more accountable infrastructure, energy security and regional stability across the world.

In Panama, we mobilized $2.455 billion in private investment, helping refinance utility debt and catalyze new energy projects. In Vietnam, our work helped promote the $1.4 billion Son My LNG terminal, which will feed a 2.2 GW gas-fired power plant. These weren't pipe dreams—they were pipelines, power plants, ports, and growth.

Leveraging US Capital Markets and Regulatory Common Sense

We recognized something else: The United States has the deepest and most sophisticated capital markets in the world. Why not use them to advance our foreign policy and economic goals?

Under Trump 45, we integrated infrastructure finance with trade, diplomacy, and investment promotion. We worked across agencies to reduce red tape and led the private sector to support projects aligned with American strategic interests.

Another critical facet of President Trump's vision for America-first growth involved our paradigm for fintech and financial regulation. At Treasury, we adopted a hands-off, innovation-first and technology neutral approach to fintech and digital assets—encouraging breakthroughs while maintaining security and consumer protection. Rather than regulating with a heavy hand, we promoted an ecosystem where technologies like blockchain, tokenization, and decentralized finance could thrive. This wasn't deregulation for its own sake—it was a recognition that leadership in financial innovation is a 21st-century national security imperative.

Trump 47: A Vision Reaffirmed

Fast forward to 2025. President Trump is back—and he's wasting no time.

With the stroke of a pen, he signed executive orders to reignite American energy independence, expand US LNG exports, and remove artificial constraints on production. New directives support the revitalization of coal as a reliable, baseload energy source for domestic use and international demand, unlocking jobs and reinvigorating entire communities. These moves restore competitive energy pricing and secure long-term supply chains for industrial growth.

He also issued new Executive Orders promoting fintech and cryptocurrency development, aimed at reducing regulatory burdens, clarifying digital asset classification, and promoting blockchain-based infrastructure. These policies are designed to foster capital formation, streamline compliance, and ensure the US remains the global hub for financial innovation. Together, they promise to enhance market stability, expand economic inclusion, and accelerate domestic growth.

And yes, he's returning to tariffs—again, not as punishment, but as leverage. He's not winging it. He's setting the 3D chessboard—and moving first.

We are now witnessing the early execution of a long-calculated strategy. America Crecé 2.0 is being reactivated. A whole-of-government approach to global infrastructure finance is taking shape again. And the President is focused—more than ever—on reducing China's influence, restoring American competitiveness, and protecting US interests in every theater: energy, trade, finance, and diplomacy.

A Personal Lens, A National Moment

My journey from washing dishes in a Chinese restaurant to negotiating trade agreements in Beijing gives me a unique lens. I've seen the subtle art of Chinese diplomacy. I've studied the nuances of Confucian hierarchy and face-saving. I've watched as America gave away its leverage piece by piece—and I've had the privilege of helping take it back, in a manner informed by my heritage and delivered with a personal touch. Throughout my work, I have been guided by what I call "the Four Ps": Providence, Personal touch, Perseverance, and Progress over perfection. These four values have helped me overcome seemingly insurmountable obstacles with humility and humor. Along the way, I learned the importance of leveraging the power of a seat not just at the negotiating table, but also at the dining room table over a home-cooked meal.

President Trump gave us the mandate to do things differently. To use every tool available—strategic tariffs, capital markets, bilateral investment frameworks, private-sector leadership, and regulatory reform—to pursue peace through strength and prosperity through partnership. Not all of it made headlines. But it made a difference.

Although I share many of my personal experiences and stories, this book is not a memoir. It's a roadmap and a call to action. It's an inside look at Trump's economic principles and strategies through the lens of my Treasury portfolio, to help illuminate what Trump really stands for. It's for skeptics who think our country can't compete anymore. It's for believers who want proof that the vision is real—and working.

You will read about how America clawed back leverage from China and how we brought allies closer by treating them as partners rather than charity cases. I will recount how we rewired the global conversation around fair trade and healthy, impactful infrastructure finance, leveraging private capital in place of public subsidies. You'll also read about the political courage it took to take on these fights—and the moral clarity it required to win them.

So, does President Trump have a plan? Absolutely. And this book will show you how it was developed, how it was battle-tested in Trump's first administration, and how it is currently unfolding, step-by-step.

As for China, you will read exactly why and how President Trump believes it must be challenged, constrained, and ultimately countered with something better.

Trump 45 set the stage for a global economic revolution. Today we're at the beginning of a new chapter—Trump 47—and the global 3D chessboard is once again in motion. As Americans, we can either step back from the table—or pull up a chair and lead.

President Trump has chosen to lead. And I was blessed to have a seat at that table.

CHAPTER 1

THE GOOD LORD SENT ME TO
A CHINESE RESTAURANT

The movement of a single blade of grass in the depths of a
forest, on a stately mountain, or in a deep valley where man has
never passed...is determined according to Divine providence.

—Baal Shem Tov

The military plane carrying the official American negotiations
team to Beijing felt like a Marriott with wings. Steven Mnuchin,
secretary of the Treasury and the head of our delegation, had
his own private suite, which featured a bed, a couch, and a large
conference table. Other senior people, such as Secretary of
Commerce Wilbur Ross and Director of the National Economic
Council Larry Kudlow, enjoyed their own designated area, with
large and sumptuous chairs facing each other, separated by tables
and a long couch. The rest of the entourage, including the Secret
Service, sat in the back, waiting patiently as we stopped first in
Anchorage and then at Yokota Air Base in Japan to refuel before
heading to China.

It was, to put it mildly, a bit of a tense flight. Our trade deficit
with China had hit $500 billion, an unfathomable number betray-
ing an imbalance that was wreaking havoc on the American econ-

omy. We were losing jobs, losing productivity, losing our ability to compete. If that wasn't bad enough, the Chinese government had shown an abysmal record on respecting foreign intellectual property rights that another member of our delegation, Ambassador Robert Lighthizer, the US Trade Representative, had just detailed in a highly critical report published shortly before the trip.

Add to that a slew of cyber threats and non-tariff barriers that were making it very, very difficult for American investors to penetrate the Chinese market, and you'll begin to understand the magnitude of the challenge that awaited us when we touched down in Beijing. These were not going to be easy negotiations: The financial and security conflicts between the US and China were profound, and President Donald Trump had taken a stance. His position was simple: He wasn't having any of it.

With such tensions simmering, it did not come as much of a surprise to anyone on board that security for the delegation was extremely heightened. Even before departure, we received constant security briefings and were subject to rigorous security protocols, and once we were on board the flight, a large and high-level detail was looking after us, with senior members of our security detail holding ranks equivalent to military generals and yet treating all of us civilians with respect. I felt very safe.

We spent the flight going over myriad details and talking strategy, and by the time we finally landed, everyone on board was exhausted. Thankfully, the Chinese made things pleasant enough by offering not only a red-carpet welcome on the tarmac but also expedited arrival formalities at a diplomatic terminal. From there it was on to a motorcade, featuring a very rare full police escort. We zipped out of the airport and made our way to Beijing.

The scenery we saw out of the car window could've sucked all of the immense and nervous energy out of the air. The best way to describe what Beijing looks like near its massive airport is "nondescript." Large highways. Lots of trees on each side, with housing and commercial developments dotting the landscape and absolutely nothing changing from season to season, from year to year. But as we hit the Ring Roads, the seven massive highways encircling the city, the urban action began, with buildings and developments and more highways sprouting from the ground like weeds. Not that we had much time to admire the view. The drive to our hotel, normally an hour or so in snarled Beijing traffic, took all of twenty minutes. In my thirty-five years of traveling to Beijing, I had never seen anything like it. I was impressed.

The festivities continued at our hotel, where management had cordoned off a walkway for us in the lobby, keeping the throng of reporters already gathered there behind ropes. I did my best to avoid the constant flashes of cameras, as well as the barrage of questions being shouted at us: "How are the talks going?" "What is the US position on trade?" "What is your comment on the negotiations?" None of us dared to set foot in the lobby for a drink, though all of us could certainly have used one.

After a too-short stretch of getting settled in our rooms, we were on the move again, this time to the US embassy to prep for the first round of meetings. Given the size of the delegation and the senior ranks of some of its members, every single logistical detail was highly coordinated and meticulously orchestrated. And, given the tense nature of our relations with our hosts, everyone was walking on tiptoes, and every mundane turn felt urgent.

After a short and extremely tense meeting at the embassy, we left for Diaoyutai. The ancient royal garden has graced Yuyuantan Park for more than eight hundred years, when Emperor Zhangzong built himself a fishing shack there. By 1774, a lake had been added to the site, which then became an official imperial hangout.

When the Communists took over China, they turned Diaoyutai into a guesthouse for dignitaries, briefly running the Cultural Revolution from one of the compound's buildings. It was there, in Chairman Mao's favorite old haunt, that we would meet our adversaries.

The Chinese are no newcomers to playing hardball, and they made sure to gain the upper hand even before we arrived at Diaoyutai: At the very last minute, just prior to our arrival at the embassy, they had delivered a lengthy draft agreement—in Chinese—for us to consider. It was a ploy to rattle us a bit since we had agreed to use the US draft delivered to the Chinese long before we boarded our flight, but we were determined to keep our cool. I was instructed to get into the car with Secretary Mnuchin and translate the document as we drove.

I barely had time to make it through the first few pages, however, before our car sailed through the entrance to the largest and most ornate meeting compound in Diaoyutai. By the time we arrived, negotiators and subject matter experts, administrative people, drivers, translators, and protocol people from both sides already filled the cavernous greeting area. In addition, no fewer than ten Chinese ministers and a slew of vice ministers awaited us, matched by a goodly number of secretaries and under secretaries from our side. As state affairs went, this Beijing opera was the big leagues, with the highest levels of diplomatic protocols enforced. This meant that everything was carefully considered, mutually discussed, and begrudgingly agreed upon, from who gets to attend which meeting to who should sit where. That last detail, in particular, was crucial: In a meeting like this one, each person is assigned a chair according to his or her rank, making it clear who's who in the hierarchy of each side. And so, when the doors of the meeting room opened, all of us, Americans and Chinese alike, filed in, quickly finding our designated spots. And then, suddenly, our diplomatic dance came to a screeching halt. Something was wrong. There was nervous movement in the back of the room. It took us a moment or two to figure out the problem: One member of our delegation was missing a seat.

How, some of my colleagues muttered under their breath, could this happen? I half-smiled to myself, because I knew the answer: It couldn't. Unless, that is, it was done on purpose.

Surveying the members of the American delegation that chaotic day in Beijing, you wouldn't necessarily pick me as the resident China expert. I am, after all, an Orthodox Jew, and was dressed in a dark suit and a black felt hat—the same traditional style my zeyde, "grandfather" in Yiddish, favored when he moved to Chicago from the little shtetl of Nadvorna, in what is today western Ukraine. He, in turn, dressed just like his grandfather, a Talmid Chacham, a notable Torah scholar, and a follower of the town's renowned Chassidic master, the Rebbe Reb Mordechai. After watching Cossacks brutally murder his grandfather, my zeyde escaped to America, where he raised his family and became a community leader fighting for justice and human dignity. He taught his family to always do what's right, no matter the consequences; so, when his daughter, my mother, found herself with three children in a marriage that wasn't working, she picked up and left for a new start.

We had moved to Florida not long before the separation, and for my mother—an only child of first-generation Americans, Eastern European Jews from the shtetl—striking out on her own back in the early 1970s was virtually unheard of. But my mother was an independent and strong-willed woman, and so I found myself, a little boy from a rather homogeneous Jewish community in Chicago, in a sprawling secular school, fending for myself while my mother worked double shifts most days to make ends meet.

Being away from the nurturing, warm, and tightly knit Jewish communities I'd known as a small boy in Chicago was hard, and I missed my zeyde and my other family members terribly. My loneliness was somewhat relieved when I met two brothers who came from a very similar background to my own. They, too, were the children and grandchildren of newly arrived immigrants. They, too, believed that family mattered most, which meant everything from respecting your elders to taking every possible meal together. They, too, were unremitting about getting the best education possible. That I was a Jew whose ancestors hailed from Eastern Europe and they, Chinese who'd recently arrived from Hong Kong, mattered very little. Before too long, I was a permanent fixture at the Cheng household. There, I learned my first profound lesson about Chinese culture.

In my own Jewish tradition, food is very much at the heart of everyday life. We sanctify virtually all our religious observances—the Sabbath, festivals, and major life events—through the sharing of wine and various foods that we bless reverentially and eat joyfully. Indeed, according to Jewish tradition, since the destruction of our holy temple two thousand years ago, our dining room table was transformed to take on the role of the temple in so many different dimensions. "Every home a temple," the Talmud teaches us, "every family a sanctuary; every table an altar; every meal an offering." The Chinese, I soon realized, had similar ideas. Nearly two thousand years ago, Confucious' *Book of Rites*, one of China's Five Classics, outlined intricate and ornate rules and strictures on food ingredients, seasoning, and presentation.

The Chengs loved to eat, and they loved to cook, and they took food very seriously, an emotional and cultural touchstone rather than a mere means of sustenance. They soon taught me a few choice facts about their native Cantonese cuisine: What flies in the air that the Cantonese do not eat? they asked. An airplane. And what has four legs that the Cantonese do not eat? A table. I chuckled at these aphorisms and felt grateful for my new friends and their culture, so similar to, yet so distinct from, my own.

The family's father, whom I referred to as "Yi Sok"—literally, "Uncle"—had been an acclaimed chef back in his native Hong Kong. His cousin, who owned a Chinese restaurant in Florida, sponsored Yi Sok to come and cook at his kitchen. You didn't need to watch him work for more than a few minutes to realize this was a very good decision: Like a painter carefully choosing the precise hue on the palette, Yi Sok was a true culinary artist. He'd spend a long time fretting over his ingredients, washing and prepping with care, cutting and trimming with meticulous patience and astonishing precision. And he cared as much about how a dish looked as he did about its taste, serving intricately wrapped dumplings, large and gorgeous steamed fishes, and other delights. Though the kitchen was a hot, hectic place, Yi Sok neither yelled nor criticized. He always kept his cool.

His wife, whom I called "Ah Ma," or "Mom," was the exact opposite. She was a small woman, but she was fierce and unwavering; she had opinions about everything and the vocal range to make them heard loud and clear. If you messed up even slightly, Ah Ma would let you know.

The Chengs had four boys, three of whom were around my age. They started school immediately upon landing in America, and we met because the school administration asked me to shadow them and make sure they learned both the lay of the land

27

and the English language. Meeting the Chengs changed my life, but back then, in the moment, it felt more like arbitrary proximity brought us together, not divine providence. Now I know better.

I soon became close friends with Ko Ming, who went by Ricky, just a few months younger than me and a real live wire. He appeared to be perpetually in motion, always moving and always working. So when the Chengs asked me if I'd like a job at their restaurant—named, ironically in retrospect, Wuhan—I happily agreed. The job, I thought, would let me spend more time with my friends, and also earn me a few extra bucks my family direly needed. If I could buy my own clothes—and, maybe, someday, my own car—it would be a big help to my mother. With that in mind, I showed up for my first evening shift at Wuhan.

My first job—could it have been otherwise?—was washing dishes. When I close my eyes, I can still see the dishwashing machine, a large and powerful contraption with gleaming, stainless-steel counters where the busboys would pile pans full of dirty dishes. It had a four-sided door that I would push up and down, up and down, countless times during each dinner shift, each time releasing a huge puff of white-hot steam into the already impossibly hot and humid Florida-in-summertime torpor. It was hard and tedious work, but it taught me a few valuable lessons I still reflect on regularly. It taught me that everything in life takes hard work, and that preparation is key for tasks large and small. It also taught me the power of seemingly small things to have much larger consequences: The Chinese phrase 小处不可随便 means "one may not be lax with small details," but it becomes 不可随处小便 (one should not pee just anywhere) by moving just two characters around. Similarly, if I missed just a tiny spot in my dishwashing duties, then no matter how delicious the dish that Yi

Sok prepared, the customer was going to send it back and complain about the dirty plate.

But if washing dishes was hard, helping with prep was downright Sisyphean. Each afternoon, Wuhan would have hundred-pound bags of onions and cabbage delivered to the restaurant's back door, and because we were turning out Chop Suey by the metric ton, my job was to chop them by hand, work that left me tired and teary-eyed. So when I was offered a promotion to the front of the house, I was thrilled. For one thing, it was a testament to my hard work and dependability. For another, it had air conditioning.

I soon learned, however, that while the physical labor was much easier out in front, the emotional labor was tenfold more demanding. I had to wear a uniform. I had to deal with the customers, many of whom were retirees who delighted in complaining about each small imperfection. I had to deal with Ah Ma, who was watching my every step like a hawk, and with the cooks in the kitchen, many of whom were the temperamental sort and did not take kindly to a dish being sent back. And when a cook felt slighted, he could easily express his simmering resentment by making you wait forever for your plates to come up. In short, I was getting an advanced degree in international protocol.

I was also learning Cantonese. Without it, I could hardly do my job, as most of the restaurant's staff spoke little or no English. But no sooner had I started my studies than I realized that I was grappling with one of the most linguistically complicated of the Chinese dialects, with almost twice as many sounds as Mandarin. With no internet to turn to or official teacher to instruct me, I drove the Chengs crazy, pestering them to tell me how to say different phrases and then repeating those phrases, again and again and again, until I got the pronunciation just right. I would also ask any Cheng I could corner to show me how to write things, and practiced whenever we had downtime. I was fascinated by each and every nuance.

I was just as fascinated by the customers. Working in the front of the house taught me that most people are pretty easy to deal with as long as they don't feel ignored. Sure, some people can be difficult, and a handful are outright rude, but most of the customers were reasonable enough, and even if the problems they complained about didn't really exist—which, alas, was the case most of the time—they were perfectly satisfied once I catered to their needs. If they complained the food was too cold, I rushed it back to the kitchen and had it reheated. If they complained their drink was too warm, I'd add some ice. It wasn't rocket science. All it took was acknowledgment, a little attention, and accord, a lesson I later put to good use when dealing with countries that lodged diplomatic complaints on my watch.

The difficult, downright rude customers were another story, because each was unique, and there was no universal method guaranteed to confront extreme rudeness. The situationally difficult were far more specific than the chronic complainers, and required personalized care. I once waited on an old woman who was ready to go to war over a take-out container and a ten-dollar lunch special. When I failed to wrap up her food the way she wanted, she got so offended she launched a tirade at me and then stiffed me on the tip. This is the incident that caused me to recognize my inherently very low threshold for unfairness and injustice, a trait I'd inherited from my zeyde. It's also when I learned to recognize petty tyrants, even when they appear in the form of seemingly sweet old ladies.

Respect. Reassurance. Food. A place at the table: It all came together in Beijing the day of the trade negotiation. As China's

Vice Premier Liu He offered his formal welcome, and as Secretary Mnuchin responded in his usual impressive and compelling style, the talks in the hallway were on the verge of chaos. The deputy chief of mission at the US embassy in Beijing and his senior protocol officer got into a very heated discussion with the Chinese Ministry of Foreign Affairs' head of protocol and his team just outside the entrance to the meeting room, shouting about chairs. Our side pressed for the number of chairs that had previously been agreed upon. The Chinese stonewalled, insisting that they had set out the agreed number of chairs for both sides. One chair, our team requested, just one. That's all we needed. The Chinese said no. Our protocol negotiators were getting furious. Decibels were getting high. And, chair-less, one poor soul from our delegation, having traveled all this way and put in all the work, was effectively barred from attending the meetings. He loitered in the hallway, nervous and angry.

It took some poking around, but we eventually learned that the Chinese were miffed about a perceived diplomatic slight that they claimed their vice premier had been forced to endure when visiting Washington a few weeks earlier. Apparently, President Trump had not received Vice Premier Liu during his visit, and this was taken as a grave insult. It was all about saving face. This made sense to me: Public honor and respect, I knew, are paramount in Chinese culture. In retaliation, they had shorted us a chair on our visit. It was an international tit-for-tat in the midst of one of the highest-stakes and contentious negotiations between the US and China in recent history. It was almost farcical. I might have laughed if matters hadn't been so deadly serious.

When we took our first break more than an hour in, the chair debate was still in full swing. At this point, I walked over and asked our embassy team what the problem was. They brought me up to speed, and I went over to the chief protocol official from the Chinese Ministry of Foreign Affairs and asked him very politely in Mandarin whether all this fuss was really necessary.

He stonewalled me. I appealed to his sense of fairness, then to his common sense—it was only one chair, I said, come on now. He stonewalled me a second time. I considered diving into a full-blown argument, but then I remembered the wise words of my rabbi: "Never get into a debate with an imbecile, because he will drag you down to his level and then beat you on experience." And so I tried cajoling the man, and then insisted some more, but nothing seemed to work. He simply would not budge and deliver the required seat. It was then that I saw Yi Gang walk by.

The governor of the People's Bank of China and my friend from years of working with the Chinese, Governor Yi, a US–educated PhD, was most likely the only person who could help to sort out this petty diplomatic scuffle. He'd visited Washington shortly before the talks, and we received him warmly at the Treasury Department. I explained our predicament to Governor Yi, and asked if he could please somehow intervene.

I was hopeful for a short spell, but it didn't seem like the governor of China's central bank much impressed the men of the Protocol Department of the People's Republic of China's Ministry of Foreign Affairs. Obviously, the diplomatic umbrage the Chinese took to their perceived wrongs in Washington ran deep. They felt slighted by President Trump, they were doing their best to embarrass us right back, and if Governor Yi intervened on our behalf, he, too, would be slighted.

With that, I felt it was time to end the conversation.

The first, and most obvious, option would have been to come out swinging, to march right over to Mr. Protocol and inform him, Wild West-style, that this was now a showdown and that he'd better deliver a chair or else. But I'd had enough years of dealing with Chinese people, starting with those hot-headed cooks in the kitchen of the Wuhan restaurant, to know that such an approach was doomed to fail. If attacked, Mr. Protocol would only dig in his heels deeper.

I could also ignore the situation altogether, pretend that it was all just an annoying but inevitable part of doing business, and leave my poor, unseated colleague out to dry in the hallway. But that wouldn't be right. For one thing, we'd come to Beijing to stand up for American interests. For another, my zeyde always taught me never to let injustices, great or small, slide. There was another option, I realized, and, like so many things Jewish and Chinese, it involved talking about food.

I turned to Governor Yi and addressed him in the most honorific and polite Chinese possible. "Mr. Governor," I said, "allow me to invite you to my house, Palazzo Seta" (the playful Italian name "Silk Palace" I used for my home in Washington, DC's Kalorama neighborhood), "for dinner the next time you are in Washington." I knew full well that Mr. Protocol could hear me loud and clear. "I will prepare a feast of delicacies especially for you. And you know what? You can have as many chairs at my table as you like." I shot one more pointed glance in the direction of Mr. Protocol, then walked away.

After the break, the missing chair magically appeared, just as I expected it would. The damage had been repaired. The perceived diplomatic slight had been made right through a diplomatic honor, and the Chinese could go back to meeting us on equal terms. We may not have prevailed on *all* of our substantive points that morning, but at least we all had a seat at the table.

CHAPTER 2

TRAVELING THE WORLD TO
FIND A NEW HOME

If you've read this far, you're probably asking yourself one key question: Just how did I get into government in the first place? I am, I'm proud to say, the first Chassidic Jew ever confirmed by the US Senate for a senior administration position. How did I get here?

It's a question I still ask myself, and frequently. And when I do, I think back to a warm spring day in 2017.

I was just heading out from a very long meeting in the conference room of the law firm Allen & Overy, where I was a partner. Our offices were in Manhattan's legendary McGraw-Hill Building, and as I sauntered back to my office, I could see Sixth Avenue writhing with traffic and life beneath me, and the sun casting its rays like long, divine fingers, caressing the Hudson River. I was working on closing a highly complex multibillion-dollar international transaction, and I was feeling the usual mix of excitement, exhaustion, stress, and gratitude that I'd become accustomed to over decades as a hard-working and handsomely rewarded attorney. I was just about to enter my corner office when I heard the phone ring.

Ros, my wonderful assistant, picked it up. I heard her recite the usual greeting—"Allen & Overy, Mitchell Silk's office"—

warm, yet professional and standard. Then, I saw the smile fade from her face and watched her grow perfectly still.

"One moment please," she told whoever was on the line. Then, she looked at me, and in a voice that was very slow and almost as quiet as a whisper—a wild departure from her usual fast clip—she said, "I have the chief of staff of the secretary of the Treasury on the line."

I wasn't entirely surprised. I'd been talking to people at Treasury for weeks, entertaining the possibility of putting my legal career on hold and going into government service. But it doesn't take a political scientist to realize that a possibility like that is, at best, remote, as there are only so many high-ranking positions in an administration and, hallelujah, no shortage of wildly competent, successful, and committed people eager to step in. And so, as I stepped into my office, shut the door, and picked up the phone, I had no idea what to expect.

"Hello?"

The person on the other end didn't waste any time on niceties.

"This is Eli Miller, chief of staff to Secretary Mnuchin at the Treasury Department," he said. "I understand that you've had discussions with several of my colleagues over the past few weeks about the possibility of coming to work here at Treasury. I'm calling to offer you the position of deputy assistant secretary in International Affairs. But—first—I must ask you a question."

At this point his already amplified voice became positively booming: "WHY ARE YOU DOING THIS?"

Good question.

I don't recall exactly what I told Eli that day—I was too nervous to be all that coherent—but it was probably some true yet not entirely eloquent explanation about wanting to serve the country I so deeply and truly love. But Eli's question stayed with me, because it is, really, an invitation of the sort we all can use, an invitation to think about my life, the choices I made, and the values that brought me to where I am. And in thinking about these values, four in particular come to mind. Call them the Four P's: Providence, Perseverance, Personal touch, and Progress over perfection.

It may sound corny, but the more I think back about my life, the more I realize that without these four virtues, things likely would have turned out very, very differently for me.

By the time I graduated from high school, I had several years' worth of experience in my friends' Chinese restaurant, and the benefit of being fluent in Cantonese. I loved Chinese culture and was a bit frustrated that I only spoke a dialect common with a small minority of Chinese people. There are about 55 million Cantonese speakers in the world today, which is not nothing, but it's a drop in the ocean compared to the 933 million who speak Mandarin. Without hesitating, I enrolled in an intensive summer course at Vermont's Middlebury College, and in just nine weeks had crammed in an entire academic year's worth of Mandarin pronunciation, grammar, syntax, and vocabulary.

When I graduated, the program's director, Dr. Ta-tuan Chen, a seasoned linguist and the head of Princeton's Chinese department, gave me some very good advice. It was 1979, and mainland China was just emerging from ten years of isolation after the Cultural Revolution. This meant that China would soon be opening up to Western partners seeking to do business; but it also meant that, for the moment, there were very few opportunities for any Westerner who wanted to spend time in China in order to hone his or her language skills. If you want to get serious about studying Chinese and understanding the culture, Dr. Chen told me, you have to go to Taiwan.

With Dr. Chen's wise guidance, I applied to National Taiwan Normal University's Mandarin Training Center, a university-level program that specialized in Chinese-language and China studies in Chinese for non-native speakers. I was fortunate enough to be accepted and soon found myself in Taiwan, not a place many nice, young Jewish boys frequented back then.

My academic year in Taiwan was exceptional. I was fully immersed in the language and culture and finished the program with honors, having completed a number of courses in Mandarin, Chinese history, Chinese philosophy, classical Chinese literature, and modern Chinese literature. I also took advantage of the great cultural exposure that Taiwan offered. Whereas mainland China was hard at work erasing the regional variations of China's rich culture in line with the prevailing policy of the Chinese Communist Party, Taiwan offered most, if not all, of China's vibrant regional variations of language and culture in one concentrated geographic area.

In the afternoons after class, I studied Chinese kung fu and lion dancing, a form of martial arts performed at various Chinese festivals. In addition, I was captain of the Mandarin Training Center's dragon boat team, which competes in a crew-like sport on *Duan Wu Jie*, the Dragon Boat Festival holiday. My year in Taiwan laid an excellent foundation for a career involving China. It also paved the way for one of the most important relationships of my professional life, with my future mentor at law school, Professor Hungdah Chiu.

I had learned and experienced so much during my year in Taiwan that when I returned home to Florida, I was sure the future was bright and the possibilities endless. I applied to Columbia University and didn't bother looking for backup options. I was, after all, motivated, talented, and hard-working; the Ivy League school, I thought to myself, would be fortunate to have me.

But when the long-awaited envelope from Columbia finally arrived, it was of the dreadfully thin sort, containing nothing more than a letter telling me: sorry but not interested. I was crest-fallen. I was hoping to spend the year studying with some of the brightest minds in the world; instead, I spent it right back in the Chinese restaurant, working long hours and, whenever I had free time, taking some classes at the local community college to earn college credits. I saved every dollar I could and realized as well that if I was going to have a better shot at getting into a good school, I needed some wise counsel. And so, I turned to one of my most beloved high school teachers and mentors, Mr. Ed Foley.

A real prince of a man, Ed listened to me patiently, and when I was done babbling about my achievements and my interests, he delivered his verdict. My international experience, he said, and my language skills, left little room for doubt: "You are going to attend Georgetown's School of Foreign Service!" he declared, and I didn't dare argue. I applied, and in the fall of 1981, I started my first year at Georgetown University's Edmund A. Walsh School of Foreign Service, known for its excellent programs in international relations and China studies.

As good as the university's undergraduate offerings in Chinese were, my year in Taiwan put me well ahead of the curve, and so I wound up taking one graduate course in Chinese dialectology and serving as a teaching assistant in the first-year and third-year Chinese programs.

Academia had its appeal, but my goal was not to teach; it was to play a consequential role in international relations. That path was made possible by the guidance and wisdom of my mentor at Georgetown, Professor Thomas W. Robinson, a recognized scholar in international relations and, particularly, in Chinese foreign policy. He was fluent in Russian and Chinese, and one of the few world-renowned experts at the time in Sino-Soviet relations. He fostered my interests in Chinese domestic politics and foreign relations, and he pointed me toward law school.

I will never forget our chat about my future when I was nearing the end of my junior year. I confided in Professor Robinson that I wasn't sure what I should do when I graduated. "Do you want to attend medical school?" he asked. "No," I answered, "I'm not good with blood." "Do you want to go to dental school?" he asked. I answered, "No, that's never been an area of interest for me."

"Well, then," he concluded, "you are going to law school!" And so it was. Where would I be without Mr. Foley and Professor Robinson? Their role in my life was the perfect illustration of divine providence combined with the personal touch.

During my thesis work, Professor Robinson provided another invaluable service: He introduced me to one of the very few scholars of Chinese law in the United States at that time, Professor Hungdah Chiu at the University of Maryland School of Law. Professor Chiu was a legend: Born in Taiwan to a noted legislator, he excelled in his studies in law at National Taiwan University. He was the first person from Taiwan to earn an SJD (doctor of juridical science) degree at Harvard; he then went on to found the East Asian Legal Studies Program at Harvard Law School under the renowned Professor Jerome A. Cohen. In the 1970s, Professor Chiu accepted a position at the University of Maryland School of Law and built one of the most vibrant programs in Chinese law in the US in the late 1970s and 1980s. Professor Chiu not only became an invaluable source in assisting with my dissertation, he also recruited me to Maryland law school.

At Maryland, in addition to my classwork, Professor Chiu hired me as assistant director of his East Asian Legal Studies Program. This position provided me with the chance of a lifetime: to research and speak on interesting topics in Chinese and international law, and to be exposed to leading experts in the field, including Dr. Ma Ying-jeou, who would later become a two-term president of Taiwan.

I loved every minute in law school, but as graduation approached, I began to ponder my next step. I was keen to pursue a career in corporate law with a China focus. Such jobs, however, were mainly in big law firms in New York, and, as I feared and expected, it was challenging at that time for a Maryland grad to break into a top-tier New York firm.

In addition, the one credential for a career in Chinese that I was missing was having spent any extended time in mainland China. I learned that the US National Academy of Sciences' Committee for Scholarly Communication with the People's Republic of China bestowed ten scholarships to postdoctoral fellows for a year of study and research in their field at a host university in China. I threw my hat into the ring.

Of the thousand applicants, I was pleased to be chosen as one of the ten fellows for the 1986–1987 academic year, and the only fellow in law. My sponsor was the International Law Institute at Beijing University, run by one of the leading international law experts in China at the time, Professor Wang Tieya.

Our foreign student housing quarters was a veritable United Nations of students. In addition to students from North America, Japan, and Korea, there were large contingents of scholarship students from a number of African and Middle Eastern countries, as well as from Russia and Eastern Europe. I was able to conduct research, teach two undergrad law courses at Beijing University, and teach a course at the Shanghai Institute of Foreign Trade at Shenzhen University.

Beyond the hours I spent each week on research and teaching, I was afforded a front-row seat to the practical implementation of foreign investment law through an internship at Coudert Brothers, one of the very few international law firms with a Beijing office. The firm's bread and butter was assisting foreign investors to penetrate the China market. Nothing was easy, even the most basic trade and technology licensing transactions, let alone complex, large, capital-intensive joint ventures. The highlight of that year was participating in China's first cross-border limited recourse project financing—the financing of the $650 million Occidental Petroleum coal mine, then the largest open-pit coal mine in the world.

My year in China provided all the "résumé-building" items I needed. But the single most valuable experience I had came completely by accident.

Or, as I prefer to say, by divine providence.

Being based in Beijing afforded me the ability to explore China with little field trips outside the city. One week, I went with two friends to Kaifeng, the capital of China during the Song dynasty and end point of the Silk Road in China. Kaifeng's rich culture and deep cross-border trading roots gave rise to a diverse population, including a Persian Jewish community that existed there until the late 1800s. I was keen to see the historic remnants of this community.

Upon arrival, as foreigners, we were required to register with the China Travel Service. We assumed, wrongly, that China's key travel service would be able to provide basic information on Jewish sites in the city. Foreigners did not frequently travel outside the major cities in China, and religion was constitutionally banned, so a visibly Jewish man asking in fluent Chinese about Jewish sites in a country emerging from the Cultural Revolution did not elicit much warmth—or any information—from the fellow at the China Travel Service.

Wholly frustrated, we left the grounds and ventured out on foot. My attempts, alas, were futile. An hour later, I was right back at the same office. Putting on the real schmaltz, and with the sweetest and most honorific Chinese that I could muster, I asked again if anyone had any idea where I could find any sites of interest to Jews. Again, the man there wouldn't budge. But then something happened that was nothing short of miraculous.

The manager of the Kaifeng Hotel dashed out of the entrance of the hotel and ran over to me, asking with desperation in heavily Henan-accented Mandarin whether I could speak English. With even greater desperation, he pleaded with me to follow him into the hotel to assist with a foreigner who was very ill.

The manager took us to a room just off the lobby where a young woman was sitting on the bed cross-legged, moaning and swaying from left to right. Her face looked pasty and had a light-green tint. She was obviously very ill.

I approached her and asked her name. Her voice was barely audible and she strained to whisper that her name was Emily Feigenson. She explained that she'd arrived on an overnight train from Xi'an, to the west. I also learned that she was a Reform rabbi from Los Angeles, and like us, she'd come to Kaifeng in search of remnants of its once thriving Jewish community. However, she suspected that she'd eaten something spoiled on the train. She was noticeably dehydrated, and running a high temperature. It did not take a Harvard-trained physician to see that she was suffering from food poisoning and badly needed hydration and antibiotics.

But getting them was no simple task for foreigners traveling in central China in 1987.

The hotel had summoned a "medical professional" from the clinic across the street. This was still a time when barefoot doctors far outnumbered properly trained medical doctors in this part of China, and this "doctor" ran a clinic that had recently been the recipient of a brand spanking new foreign-manufactured EKG machine. Naturally, then, the "doctor" wanted to hook poor Emily up to the machine, because, he insisted, she was clearly suffering some sort of heart attack, or why else would he have been given a machine that monitored the heart? His reasoning made absolutely no sense, and we finally convinced hotel management that Emily needed the attention of a real emergency room. This presented another problem: In those days, foreigners could only be treated in designated facilities and there was no ambulance to transport her.

After endless haggling, we convinced the hotel manager to arrange a taxi to take us to the nearest medical facility. The taxi turned out to be a Soviet sedan from the 1950s, and the medical facility was a neighborhood clinic some twenty minutes from the hotel. It was a struggle just getting Emily from the hotel into the car. She was weak, had trouble walking, and was disoriented and extremely nauseous. She was not able to sit up, and we ended up laying her across the back seat of our taxi. Heaving and out of breath, Rabbi Emily moaned all the way to the clinic. It was a very long and intense twenty-minute ride.

The "examination room" at the "clinic" was a small office that was one of many rooms in connected structures that formed a sprawling, old, one-story classic Chinese courtyard. There were several old wooden tables, and virtually no medical equipment. Welcome to Kaifeng, China, in 1987. The doctor, who appeared to be a trained medical professional, took one look at Emily and realized she was dangerously dehydrated. After taking her vitals and hearing my recount (in Chinese) of Emily's story, he formally diagnosed her with food poisoning and prescribed intravenous fluids and antibiotics.

The next challenge that confronted Emily was whether to hydrate and take the antibiotics orally or intravenously. We explained the pros and cons. Drinking water and taking antibiotics orally would do the trick, but slowly. Also, Emily wasn't holding anything down. The intravenous approach would be much faster but would require a needle. Personally, I was rather concerned about a dirty needle or a negligent poke. We went back and forth in Chinese as poor Emily was lying on the floor. We finally put the question to her, and she chose the quicker route to recovery, notwithstanding the risks.

In the most polite yet firm Chinese, I asked the doctor to prepare an intravenous injection with a sterile needle. Off his assistant went to sterilize the needle. Another assistant, perhaps the needle expert, dutifully returned holding what seemed to be a sterilized needle in a hand so caked with black grease that he looked like he had just performed a major tune-up on a 1964 Chevrolet! Nope, not happening. The doctor dispatched another assistant, who returned very proudly a few minutes later with another sterilized needle, this time in clean hands, only to put it down on a table caked with a thick layer of dust. I objected to the needle in the dust, and off went assistant number three at the insistence of the doctor. Assistant three returned with yet another clean needle, the doctor poked Emily with it, and in went the fluids, glucose, and drugs.

Within thirty minutes, Emily started to stabilize. She felt well enough to be transported, and we made arrangements for her to be taken to a room. Three issues immediately confronted us. Emily could not walk, there was no wheel chair, and it was raining out. Because the facility was housed in a series of old courtyard structures, Emily had to be transported in and out of numerous buildings and through countless alleyways to reach her room. The staff rigged up a stretcher made of two poles and a piece of canvas. They laid the canvas on the floor, Emily laid down on the stretcher, the assistants picked her up, and off we went in a manner reminiscent of the TV series *M*A*S*H*. An additional assistant held an umbrella over her head.

The scene went from comical to hysterical once we left the examination room. Emily was bouncing around on the stretcher, the assistant was struggling to cover her with the umbrella, and the attendants were knocking the poles of the stretcher on every corner we turned. In the middle of all this, Emily suddenly grabbed me by the arm, gathered all of her energy, looked me in the eye, and said, "Please, I don't know if I'm going to make it. Go back to the hotel and please bring me my *tefillin*. I must put them on to say *Shema Yisroel!*"

As you may know, tefillin are small leather boxes containing holy Jewish scriptures written by hand on parchment that are wrapped around the arm and placed on the head with leather straps, and used in morning prayers. The *Shema*—a declaration of a Jew's allegiance to the Lord—is recited, under normal circumstances, numerous time a day, but also by one who feels his soul leaving him. Clearly, Rabbi Emily was concerned she didn't have long to live.

It was a very poignant moment, but, in hindsight, so utterly comical—all the more so since in the traditions in which I was raised, only men don tefillin. Emily did indeed survive. The fluids, glucose, and meds kicked in within a few hours, and she convalesced for a few days at the clinic before carrying on. I never did get her tefillin, but Rabbi Emily became a lifelong friend, and I had my first exercise in high-stakes negotiations, Chinese style.

With such experiences under my belt, I felt ready to take on the real world back stateside. I returned to America in 1987 and quickly heard that the venerable Wall Street law firm of Hughes Hubbard & Reed had just recruited a large team of international banking and finance lawyers, one of whom had a thriving Japan-centered Asian practice. The firm needed a few lawyers in the junior ranks to support this team. Thanks to my international experience and China skills, they offered me a job. The position was exactly what I was looking for, a job in corporate and banking law where I could pursue my interest in Asia at the same time.

Hughes Hubbard was an old-line Wall Street firm dating back to the 1880s. Its strength and reputation grew out of its early named partners, including a chief justice of the Supreme Court, a solicitor general, and a secretary of state.

Like many of the Wall Street firms at the time, Hughes Hubbard was known to be a "white-shoe" institution. Culturally, that was a bit of a change for me. I was one of three Orthodox Jews in a large Wall Street law firm. Shortly before I started, a young black lawyer, Christopher Reynolds, joined the firm after completing Harvard Law School and a clerkship for a federal judge. We were in the same intake class. Chris and I became sworn brothers and are still in close contact today. At the time, I joked (and still do!) that we were the two ethnic hires of our intake.

My work at Hughes Hubbard laid the technical and legal foundation for my career. It also provided another providential connection: I spent an intensive period learning about regulatory law and practice related to foreign banks from a highly respected expert in the field, Michael Iovenko. Mike enjoyed a distinguished career in public service; he was also an accomplished classical pianist who had studied with Rachmaninoff.

I became a core member of the firm's newly established Pacific basin practice, led by Yasuo Okamoto. Yas was one of the most respected Japanese practitioners in the United States, and the son of a prominent Tokyo family. I did a considerable amount of work for Yas's Japanese bank clients entering the New York market. Around this time, Taiwan was experiencing significant economic growth and its commercial banks had begun a wave of foreign expansion. Equipped with my Japanese bank experience, I marketed our firm to the Taiwanese banks that were considering entering the New York market, and we eventually captured the lion's share of work for these banks in New York. My earlier Taiwan experience and contacts served me well.

By the early 1990s, I was a mid-level associate, and the China market was starting to open up in a real way. With China liberalizing foreign investment in many sectors, including energy and infrastructure, New York firms were canvassing the market for lawyers with China backgrounds and Chinese language skills. A headhunter reached out to me on behalf of Chadbourne & Parke, one of the firms with a premier international project finance practice, looking for someone with project finance experience, particularly in the power sector. I had only been involved in one project financing and knew very little about the power sector. Nevertheless, I formulated my interview strategy. When asked about my experience in energy, I quipped at my interview that I was highly experienced given that I had been dutifully paying my electric bills for a number of years. In the end, I secured the position and promptly moved to Hong Kong to assist in building the firm's newly opened office there, which would primarily represent power developers seeking to expand into the emerging markets of China and India.

Rigdon Boykin, the Chadbourne partner who brought me to Hong Kong, was an exceptional mentor during this period. Rigdon was, in personality and appearance, quite different from the typical Hughes Hubbard partner. He was short, stout, and spoke with the Southern drawl of his native South Carolina. At the negotiating table and internal strategy sessions, however, he was larger than life. He was an excellent lawyer and profoundly shaped the legal terrain of independent private power development in the United States.

Rigdon had a refreshingly entrepreneurial approach to the practice of law: He didn't wait for work to come in the door—he went out and got it. He would travel throughout China, identify power generation projects ripe for foreign investment, secure rights in those projects, and then bring clients into the mix. The client's quid pro quo was to retain Chadbourne for the legal work and also to grant the firm a carried interest in the profits of the venture. In addition to the education in the practice of energy and project finance law I received from Rigdon, I gained invaluable skills at the negotiating table. I was also learning some entertaining phrases that I used liberally throughout my career, including some that were not so kosher, like "pigs get fat and hogs go to the market," which means that a deal that is too rich for one side is doomed for failure. And—most important, though I didn't realize it at the time—my years in Hong Kong provided me with the experience in energy and infrastructure that would one day put me on the radar of the federal government.

During my first three to four years in Hong Kong, I was constantly on the road with power developers in China, learning the technical and financial dimensions of the energy business. The challenges were mainly in the backwaters of China—Gansu province in China's northwest at the edge of the Gobi Desert; Yingkou, Yantai, and Harbin in China's northeast; Heilongjiang, Shandong, and Liaoning provinces; Wuhan and Zhengzhou in central China; and Guangzhou, Shenzhen, and Xiamen in southeastern China. I gained a priceless education in the power and infrastructure business from some of the world's leading developers, engineers, and financial analysts.

I forged an especially close relationship with James Wood, then a senior executive at Babcock & Wilcox. Jim, who started his career at B&W as a boiler engineer and slowly worked his way up to CEO, showed me the ropes of power development and finance. He taught me all about the technical aspects of steam generation and power production, transmission, and distribution, while his financial analysts schooled me in the design and engineering of financial models for power projects. This detailed knowledge greatly enhanced my ability to draft and negotiate—in English and Chinese—long and technical agreements for power project financing. But negotiating giant energy projects was not the only Hong Kong experience leading me to the White House. There was also the small matter of the *Chevra Kadisha*.

When I arrived in Hong Kong, the Jewish community had not had an operating Chevra Kadisha—the volunteer group that performs the final rites for the deceased and prepares the body for burial—for decades. Soon after my arrival, there was a death in the community, and I had the privilege of participating in the *tahara*, the ritual cleansing and clothing of the body, and the burial. It struck me that in so many ways—respectful handling of the deceased; dealing with the family with appropriate sensitivity; logistics and regulatory compliance; and liaising with the local funeral homes, authorities, and medical professionals—

the Chevra Kadisha needed to be organized and staffed. Before I knew it, the Trustees of the Jewish Community of Hong Kong, who looked after the largest pool of Jewish communal assets in the world, then valued at more than $350 million, appointed me chairman of the Chevra Kadisha of Hong Kong, responsible for renovating and managing the community's funeral facilities and the cemetery.

I held that communal position for thirteen years, balancing the endless duties and responsibilities of end-of-life care for the members of my community with the demands of a young family and an aggressively growing legal practice in Hong Kong. Many years later, as I was sworn in as the first Chassidic Jew to a Senate-confirmed position, I reflected on the fact that work and public service had always gone hand in hand for me. Another legacy from my zeyde!

As chairman of the Chevra Kadisha in Hong Kong, sometimes weeks and even months would pass with little or no work. At other times, cases would literally keep me up around the clock for days on end. As a small group, we were involved in end-of-life matters, picking up the deceased from medical facilities or homes, transporting and storing them prior to burial, preparing the deceased for burial, conducting the burial, or helping to arrange transport of the deceased back to his home country. In addition, we were frequently called on to deal with Jewish deaths in China. In cases of close proximity, we would travel to pick up the deceased. In fact, I advised Chevra Kadisha organizations throughout Asia, including Japan and Singapore—even in the ironically named city of Christchurch, New Zealand.

After having surveyed and studied matters in Hong Kong, I concluded that we needed our own facilities, rather than relying on local funeral homes for transport and storage of our dead. I jumped into renovating and upgrading the tahara facility. Using both my legal and linguistic skills, I secured a funeral home license for our tahara facility at the cemetery, enabling the community to exercise care of and control over its dead without having to rely on local facilities or the dreaded government morgues. I worked with a number of medical, engineering, and hospital equipment experts, and we developed and adapted equipment and designed modern facilities that would enable our small Chevra to carry out our holy duties and ensure proper *kavod hameis*, upholding the late person's dignity. By the time we finished, we had a state-of-the-art and self-contained tahara and funeral facility.

I also cultivated strong relations with the local hospitals, the main funeral home that provided transportation assistance and coffins and assisted with gravestones, the clerks in the Births and Death Registry, and the officials at the Coroner's Court. All these parties were key to ensuring that we could handle our cases smoothly and, more important, expeditiously. A litany of issues confronted our work: Sometimes, we could not get a hospital to issue a death certificate, which meant we couldn't pick up the body; sometimes, the funeral home was unable to dispatch a vehicle to transfer a body; sometimes, the Births and Death Registry was not open to register a death, making it difficult to guarantee a speedy burial. And sometimes, Hong Kong law required a Coroner's Court inquiry, which could delay burial by days if not weeks. I never thought of myself as much of a politician, but I spent my early days as chairman engaged in intensive public affairs work with all these parties, explaining to them that Jews placed a very strong premium on burying the dead right away and educating them in the basic Jewish laws governing end-of-life matters.

I started by formulating a campaign targeting the hospitals, working through the Hong Kong Hospital Authority. I met the Hospital Authority's leadership, explained our point of view, and was delighted to find them receptive and attentive. Then, we made presentations to the senior management of a few of Hong Kong's larger public hospitals, and the Hospital Authority, in turn, committed to calling a meeting of all public hospital leadership to review our data sheet and requested that each facility under its jurisdiction launch an education campaign, to be refreshed from time to time, to ensure that hospital management and department heads understood our unique and specific needs. The process was time consuming but extremely helpful. Our relations with the local hospitals were greatly enhanced, resulting in a more efficient Chevra Kadisha.

And yet, the Chevra Kadisha was heavily reliant on one of the large local funeral homes for key services, such as providing a driver and a vehicle anytime we needed to transport a deceased person, providing a simple wood coffin, digging all our graves, and providing special services when we needed to ship a body out of Hong Kong. Our funeral home partner was most accommodating, though I couldn't help reflecting on the fact that they all spoke Cantonese, making me especially thankful that the good Lord had sent me to that Chinese restaurant in Florida all those years ago.

When I wasn't running the Chevra Kadisha, of course, I was busy working. I was a central member of the team tasked to expand Chadbourne's Asia practice, I assisted in building the firm's Beijing office, and I represented numerous foreign developers in the successful development of power generation projects throughout China and Taiwan in sizes ranging from 24 megawatts all the way up to 3,000 megawatts.

But by 1996, I was starting to feel that the practice was one-dimensional. I needed to expand my skill set, client base, and geographic and sector coverage. I had been focused almost exclusively on representing developers in power generation projects in China. I wanted to work for financiers and underwriters, to work in non-energy infrastructure, and to handle projects in countries other than China.

The bell of opportunity rang. The Hong Kong office of Allen & Overy was looking to expand its China and project finance capabilities. A&O was a premier global firm, had one of the best China practices in greater China, and was a global leader in project finance. I decided to join A&O in December 1996.

This decision transformed my legal career. I became part of one of the world's leading and best-managed global law practices. At various points, I led the firm's China practice, its Asia Projects Group, its US China Group, and I played a key role in its leading global projects practice, particularly in Asia and the Americas. The firm offered me immense opportunities in both technical skills and law firm management. During my nine-year tenure at A&O Hong Kong, I advised on numerous landmark and award-winning projects in the power, gas, water, and transportation sectors.

By 2005, I had achieved a significant portfolio of success, completing some of the largest and most challenging energy and infrastructure projects in China, including the Jingyuan Power Project in Gansu province (the first Sino-US joint venture power project); the Shandong Zhonghua Power Project (the largest foreign-invested power project in China); and the $6 billion restructuring of Guangdong Enterprises (including the restructuring of the Dongshen Water Project, supplying 75 percent of Hong Kong's raw water supply). At the time, I had no idea that my work saving a Chinese provincial investment company from bankruptcy would prepare me to lead a key area of programming in one of the biggest financial rescue bills in American history.

Yet I was starting to feel it was time to go home. Personally, I was ready to move back to New York. At the same time, the markets were shifting. China had initiated an aggressive outbound investment policy, and A&O wanted to establish a China desk in New York to capitalize on this work.

And so, I moved back to New York to create and run A&O's US China desk. My team was on the front lines of some of the largest and most noteworthy Chinese outbound investment transactions in history. These included two large pipelines in Brazil for Sinopec; the $850 million acquisition of a company with crude oil operations in Colombia that was China's largest investment in that country; all of China Vanke's (one of China's largest real estate developers) early investments in the US; and the first Chinese acquisition of a broker-dealer to be approved by US financial regulators. My group represented all Taiwan and mainland Chinese banks in New York in financings, regulatory matters, and major litigation, and also formed some of the largest and most novel private investment funds in the energy, infrastructure, and mining spaces, including J. P. Morgan's first China real estate and Asian infrastructure funds.

As a member of the Americas team senior leadership in Allen & Overy's premier global project finance practice, I also worked on some of the largest and most challenging project finance transactions, and regularly advised on major gas, coal, solar, wind, nuclear power, water, mining, and transportation projects, and real estate acquisitions and financings in the US, Asia, Latin America, the Caribbean, and Africa, as well as on the acquisition of companies developing and owning disruptive technology with applications in the energy and infrastructure sector.

When I returned to the States in 2005, in addition to diving into my new role at Allen & Overy, I wanted to find a way to continue serving my community. While the Orthodox community in Hong Kong was vibrant, it was tiny compared to New York's, which is one of the largest Orthodox communities in the world. So when I moved to New York City, I decided to focus on the area where I felt I could be of greatest service, and that meant legal assistance.

I was familiar with the pro bono legal services offered by Agudath Israel of America, which had been of great assistance when I was working on a case in Hong Kong. So I reached out to the group when I settled in New York, and started to assist it with some cases. Within a year, I was asked to spearhead its newly incorporated pro bono legal services network. The network was called Agudath Israel of America Legal Support Services, and I was named chairman.

At the time, about five hundred lawyers nationwide provided a variety of pro bono work through Agudath Israel. Most of the cases fell into four categories: end-of-life issues, workplace issues, helping charitable organizations, and family law. For example, we provided pro bono legal services to community schools whose food programs and busing relied on government funding, assisting them with eligibility and compliance issues. We did a lot of work on real estate zoning, because many growing Jewish communities were in places where the local neighborhood was not so welcoming to synagogues. Our team members frequently rushed into court with emergency applications in end-of-life cases where hospitals wanted to pull the plug on an elderly or terminally ill Jewish patient, which is absolutely not permitted under Jewish law. We also handled a heavy plate of custody disputes, where children's rights were at stake in matters of visitation, education, and medical care. There were workplace issues, discrimination, First Amendment, and religious freedom issues. We provided anything from a few hours of legal advice to legal representation of people or institutions that needed it. Sometimes we would prepare and file amicus briefs, in proceedings at all levels, from state courts all the way up to the Supreme Court.

As chairman, I ran some very complex corporate reorganizations and compliance programs for large communal and educational organizations, some of which served thousands of students. I also spearheaded work on improving the infrastructure of the network, setting up a database for our lawyers to track intake, measure progress, categorize precedents, and so on. We also provided state-of-the-art training programs to lawyers in the network. We took a really creative approach to our training, including mock trials, bringing in judges and litigators, to make sure that our attorneys understood the practical applications of the laws at issue in our community. For one of our mock trials, we had a New York State Supreme Court justice come in to explore end-of-life legal issues.

Many of the cases we handled involved child custody, child kidnapping, and religious placement. For example, the US Constitution, as well as the constitution of most of the fifty states, says that when the state is placing a child in adoption or foster care, it must, whenever practicable, place the child with the same religion as his or her family of birth. Yet there were many instances where Jewish parents were trying to adopt a Jewish-born child while Jewish kids were going to non-Jewish families, an issue we fought both in the courts and via lobbying in New York State.

In one instance, a couple who couldn't have children had been trying to adopt for a long time. They learned that a Jewish child had just been born and the hospital was going to allow one of the nurses to adopt the child, even though the nurse was not Jewish. We wrote a very firm letter to the hospital, setting out the relevant laws and pointing out the Jewish parents ready and eager to adopt. That couple ended up adopting that child. I was at his bris, and I am looking forward to attending his bar mitzvah later this year. These cases provided a level of satisfaction far greater than even the largest and most complex of cross-border financings!

Perhaps my largest pro bono case involved the reorganization of seventeen different religious and not-for-profit educational entities and the establishment of a complex, multifaceted compliance program to protect the students and save the school system for all the families who depended on it. All my corporate law training came into play, as well as close to half a million dollars in time costs pro bono. In the wake of that matter, we created an entire compliance program, along with substantial training, in the hopes of avoiding a similar problem in the future.

My years in New York law, from orchestrating major finance transactions in the private sector to arguing a child custody case in Brooklyn's family court, were rich with challenges and discoveries. I learned from every case, whether triumph or defeat—and I felt that divine providence had led me exactly where I was supposed to be. What I didn't know at the time was that I was building a portfolio uniquely attractive to a future president.

CHAPTER 3

BUILDING A BETTER MOUSETRAP

It was January 2017, and the country had a new president who called China America's enemy. After spending my entire career helping Chinese companies and building Chinese-American partnerships, this didn't seem to bode well for me. What I soon discovered, however, was that my deep knowledge of and success with complex Chinese relations and infrastructure finance were exactly what President Trump needed—and, thankfully, wanted.

In almost every way imaginable, the Trump 45 administration inherited a dangerous and unstable world that presented multiple threats to America's prosperity and security.

Economically, the tectonic plates of global power were shifting, and America had yielded far too much ground to other countries. The US was confronted with overwhelming trade deficits with many key trading partners, the loss of US jobs to low-cost manufacturing centers abroad, and a decline in American manufacturing. Russia and China each presented multidimensional security and economic challenges to the US and the rest of the world. US relations with Russia were fractured and conflict loomed in Ukraine. Trade relations with China, the newly signed Trans-Pacific Partnership, and the future of the North American Free Trade Agreement (NAFTA) were all squarely in the crosshairs.

Virtually every region in the world also presented its own unique set of grave challenges undermining our national security. The Middle East was extremely volatile and had become radicalized. Jihadist terrorist organizations calling for the downfall of the United States were penetrating our country and carrying out frequent terrorist attacks in the United States and Europe. Conflict in Afghanistan and Iraq was bleeding outside of those two countries' borders. Syria posed grave threats of terrorism and spawned a serious refugee problem. The Iran nuclear deal challenged regional and global stability. And then, of course, there was the never-ending conflict between Israel and the Palestinians.

Asia, too, was highly unstable. North Korea was a serious nuclear threat and defied predictability. The Chinese regime presented a Pandora's box of risks, ranging from its predatory economic behavior to its overt manifestations of military expansion, including threats to Taiwan and a buildup in the South China Sea. The instability stemming from China's aggressive posture in its own backyard reverberated throughout the region and indeed around the world.

Meanwhile, the Western Hemisphere suffered from neglect and festered with danger. The US had lost control, influence, and value in international organizations, ceding dangerous power to China. The list goes on.

President Trump's approach to this plethora of issues was bold, even radical, to the traditional foreign relations establishment. Critics, of course, lambasted his rhetoric and his tactics. Yet his policies, dealmaking, and programs were designed to revitalize the United States' security, prosperity, and stature, while providing a path to world peace. Perhaps his solutions were unconventional. But, to borrow from the pragmatist Deng Xiaoping:

"It doesn't matter whether a cat is black or white, as long as it catches mice."

President Trump's goals were straightforward yet grand. He promised to "protect the American people, the homeland, and the American way of life"; to "promote American prosperity"; to "preserve peace through strength"; and to "advance American influence." Every one of these objectives required a fundamental repointing of approach, mindset, and policy in the one department tasked with financing our national agendas, the US Department of the Treasury.

My years of experience in global finance, cross-cultural negotiations, energy, and infrastructure lined up perfectly with those goals. Many of my mentors and colleagues turned out to form the ideal network of contacts and resources I needed. I was one of the world's experts in China dealmaking. And as much as I would like to attribute my fluency in Yiddish as a key to my success, the fact that I was fluent in both Cantonese and Mandarin didn't hurt.

Not, mind you, that government service was something I outwardly and actively craved. I enjoyed my law career immensely—the challenge of mega deals, the work with top clients, the rewards of delivering results that had an impact, and the benefits of working alongside friends who were really world class people and professionals. But I had always wanted to serve our great country, and I inherited from my maternal grandfather a very strong sense of civic duty and a profound appreciation of everything that America stood for.

My zeyde grew up in a small Ukrainian village called Nadvorna, in the shadow of Cossack terror. Along with his parents and seven siblings, he lived in dire poverty. He and his sisters would regularly collect sawdust, which their mother would mix with the porridge to bulk up their meager food. As a boy, he spent most of his days studying; his father and grandfather were respected *Talmidei Chochomim*, Torah scholars, as well as *sofrim*, ritual scribes. He was understandably blurry on details, but the stories he told me made it clear that he had witnessed his grandfather—a respected rabbinic scholar and scribe—brutally beaten to death by Cossack soldiers, leaving an indelible mark on his young heart. Throughout his life, my grandfather dedicated his considerable strength to deliver justice and safety for the defenseless.

Zeyde Friend arrived in the United States at the age of twenty—poor, willing, and eager. He was fluent in five languages before he landed in the US, but English was not one of them. He stood just five-feet, two-inches tall, but no obstacle was too high. Family lore has it that he sat in a closet all day for weeks after coming to America, teaching himself English.

What my zeyde lacked in physical stature, he more than made up for in his passion for what was right. Zeyde Friend led a movement against the city of Chicago to secure housing for lower-income families. I simply cannot fathom how this man, so small in height, for whom English was his sixth language, could successfully champion the working class in a battle against City Hall. In many ways, my own service to both my country and my community are simply a continuation of Zeyde Friend's legacy.

So, the table was set by my grandfather's commitment to service, and the perfect meal was created with a small serving of natural ability, a nice seasoning of valuable experience, a little dollop of unique skills, and a heavy dose of divine providence. Everything came together when I received that call from Eli Miller.

As they say in Washington, it's not always *what* you know, but *who* you know.

Back at A&O, I'd worked closely on Chinese and Taiwanese banking with the noted bank regulatory lawyer Heath Tarbert.

Prior to joining A&O, Heath had held senior positions in all three branches of the federal government. He was a clerk for Justice Clarence Thomas on the US Supreme Court, a senior counsel on bank regulatory matters in the White House, as well as counsel to the Senate Banking Committee.

In 2016, when the Ministry of Finance of Taiwan asked me to deliver a lecture to more than two hundred bankers on anti-money-laundering law matters, I suggested that Heath join me, given his expertise. And so, off we went on a fourteen-hour flight to Taipei for one day on the ground. We spoke for a total of three hours; I in Mandarin and Heath in English.

I know that Heath appreciated my fluency in both the language and the subject matter of our lecture. But what really made a lasting impression was our little side trip. You see, during our day in Taiwan, I also arranged to visit an old and dear friend of mine, His Excellency Mr. Ma Ying-jeou, who had recently completed his second term as president of Taiwan. I knew Ying-jeou from his time in the US, when he was completing his SJD at Harvard in the early 1980s. Ying-jeou had visited our law school many times and spent over a month with us before taking up a senior post in Taiwan, and we spent a lot of time together. He borrowed my car during his stay in the US, and I would cook dinner that we shared in the office while he was refining his PhD dissertation for publication. The fact that I was on such close personal terms with Taiwan's president blew Heath away, and he remembered that meeting when it came time to build Trump 45's Treasury team.

Fast-forward to late 2016: Heath joined President Trump's transition team and was subsequently appointed assistant secretary of the Treasury for international markets and development. Heath contacted me and introduced me to David Malpass, who had been appointed by President Trump as under secretary for international affairs. Both Heath and Malpass saw my proficiency in Chinese and accomplishments in China, as well as my expertise in energy and infrastructure, as important assets for Treasury's mission.

The actual interview process was an interesting one. After discussing my credentials and a potential role for me at Treasury's Office of International Affairs, David Malpass invited me to his apartment on Central Park West in Manhattan. I had a lovely chat with him and his wife Adele about China issues, global infrastructure finance, and a whole host of other matters. The meeting occurred just a few days before Passover. I had done my research and knew of the family's long-standing Passover traditions of extremely large (sometimes more than a hundred people) extended-family seders. I thus brought along a nice bottle of Israeli wine and some hand-baked matzohs for their Passover seder. This was the first time David was subjected to my attempts at humor. I handed over the package, and after explaining a little about the spiritual dimension of Israeli grapes and hand-baked matzohs, I reminded them that the central theme of the holiday was liberation. I hope, I said, that the wine would help to liberate his digestive tract from the impact of all those matzohs...

The joke went down well enough that David suggested I meet Adam Lerrick, who had been appointed assistant secretary for international finance. Adam had enjoyed an extraordinarily successful career on Wall Street and was a sovereign debt restructuring and special situations specialist. The conversation with Adam was fascinating. We spoke about international economic issues, many of them related to China. It was becoming clearer with each meeting that the position at Treasury was where I belonged.

The next milestone was my final vetting interview with Jim Donovan and Baylor Myers. Jim was, and still is, a senior partner at Goldman Sachs who was appointed to serve as deputy secretary of the Treasury, and Baylor was an integral member of the Treasury "landing team" for the presidential transition. Our meeting was scheduled at the Metropolitan Club in Washington, DC, and I took an early train down from New York for the meeting. I did a ton of homework on topics I expected they would want to speak about—China trade and investment, the role of the multilateral development banks, what the US position on the Asian Infrastructure Investment Bank should be, and many others. I was ready. But I couldn't resist another attempt at humor. And, as the Yiddish saying goes—*di beste lign iz di rayne emes* (the best lie is the absolute truth). At the end of their line of tough questioning on substantive issues, Baylor asked about my voting record. I told them I lived in a very conservative neighborhood in Brooklyn and that 86 percent of our district voted for President Trump. More impressive, I continued, was that 92 percent of my daughter's first-grade class at Beis Yaakov of Borough Park voted for President Trump in the class's mock election. I added that President Trump would have certainly carried 100 percent of the vote but for a certain appeal to a few girls of Hillary Clinton. Upon investigation, the teacher learned that it was not Mrs. Clinton's education proposals but her hairstyle that the girls liked.

Despite my corny jokes and lack of prior political posts, my years of experience in China, finance, energy, and infrastructure convinced everyone that I was the right man for the job. And though Eli Miller couldn't believe I'd leave my corner office in Midtown Manhattan to become a deputy assistant secretary, I was eager to embark on what became the biggest adventure of my professional life. And I was honored to serve my country and to help set its course on some of the most pressing matters of our time.

Detailing for you, my readers, those issues and challenges, it seems to me, is a much more productive use of time—mine and yours—than merely recounting more stories from the trenches. While there's much to learn from the lives of those who were fortunate enough to appear on our civilization's grandest stages, those stories (including my own) are only instructive insofar as they help others think about the questions that shape our culture, politics, and economy. And as these questions tend to be complicated and intricate, it is up to those who were tasked to grapple with them to explain them as cogently as possible. My definition of government service includes this responsibility to explain, so that friends and neighbors can be sufficiently well-informed to fulfill their own supreme democratic duty, the duty to periodically appoint the government, to the best of their ability. These issues are larger than any one man's life, and in the pages that follow, I shall present them not in a strict chronological order, but to make them as clear and as exhilarating for you as they were for me during my three plus remarkable years in the Trump 45 Treasury.

CHAPTER 4

THE WORLD IS UPSIDE DOWN: RESHAPING TWO DECADES OF THE US-CHINA RELATIONSHIP

Every incoming White House deals with situations it inherits from its predecessors. One of the Trump 45 administration's greatest inherited headaches was the state of the US-China relationship, the product of countless decisions made by multiple presidents over several decades. By the time Donald Trump took office in January 2017, the China situation was bleak: The US faced an enormous trade deficit, predatory economic behavior that affected global financial stability, and significant threats to intellectual property, the military, strategic security, and Western values.

For years, the West had been dedicated to encouraging and incentivizing China to become an equal partner in the global economic arena. We had hoped this would lead China to adopt and honor the generally accepted practices of fair and honest international trade and finance. By 2017, it was clear: Hope was not working.

The situation was perhaps best summarized in a refreshingly honest and pragmatic government document from 2020 called simply the "United States Strategic Approach to the People's

Republic of China [PRC]." The introduction confirmed what many insiders already knew.

> The PRC's rapid economic development and increased engagement with the world did not lead to convergence with the citizen-centric, free and open order as the United States had hoped. The CCP [Chinese Communist Party] has chosen instead to exploit the free and open rules-based order and attempt to reshape the international system in its favor.... The CCP's expanding use of economic, political, and military power to compel acquiescence from nation states harms vital American interests and undermines the sovereignty and dignity of countries and individuals around the world.

Ironically, China's attitude and the policies that supported it were strikingly similar to the status quo to which it had objected for more than a hundred years.

When China first began to engage in international trade, investment, and finance—during the nineteenth century—it was at the mercy of more powerful and technologically superior countries. For a hundred years, China endured invasion, occupation, multiple revolutions, and highly concessionary treaties with various powerful rivals. The Treaty of Nanking in 1842 imposed steep financial reparations, firm obligations to open trade, and eventually resulted in British rule of Hong Kong. Nanking and similar agreements came to be known as the "unequal treaties," giving rise to considerable resentment and anti-foreign nationalism in China. The mood was best summed up by reformer Zheng Guanying, who lamented, "Foreigners govern their own nationals in China, and enjoy unequal rights relative to us. This is a matter of extreme national humiliation."

After devastating economic experiments at the beginning of Communist rule and the decade-long Cultural Revolution, Deng Xiaoping ushered in sweeping domestic and outward-reaching economic reforms in the late 1970s. Deng's Open Door policies brought growth and stability. They also set the stage for China to go from insular and aggrieved to outward-facing and aggressive. Deng's policies encouraged a new global economic outlook. Initially, that took the form of export-oriented growth, leveraging China's cheap labor, strategic location, and increasing manufacturing expertise. China soon became the world's largest host to foreign investment, and "Made in China" became a ubiquitous tagline.

As its export-oriented domestic economy matured, China began to reimagine its role in the global economy, particularly with its accession to membership in the World Trade Organization (WTO). The world celebrated China's entry into the WTO, assuming it signaled the nation's next step in embracing global norms, such as open access to markets, adoption of a more transparent legal system, abiding by the rule of law, and respect for intellectual property.

But history took a different turn. Rather than pursuing growth in the global markets on a level playing field, China persistently tilted the table at the expense of its partners and global market stability in the wake of its admission to the WTO. Chinese markets remained highly limited to the West, while China pumped unfair subsidies into its manufacturing and export sectors, contributing to significant trade deficits for all its major trading partners, including the United States. Improvements in the rule of law were sparse and disconnected. China actively pressured US firms to transfer their intellectual property, often committing outright theft (including cyber theft) as well as intellectual property theft through lack of enforcement and court rulings. By the late 1990s, China commenced its program to unfairly compete against weaker "partners" for natural resources and technology, with little or no regard for international norms that govern healthy and responsible global trade and investment. The transformation was complete: China was behaving in exactly the same manner as the "unequal treaties" it had so bitterly complained about for more than a century.

As the Trump team took office, the magnitude of the "China problem" was staggering. It touched nearly every aspect of the US economy and national security, often in complex and insidious ways. China's refusal to operate on a level playing field affected virtually every area of global growth and stability—energy, technology, the stock market, banking, manufacturing, healthcare, agriculture—the list was nearly endless. An investigative report by the Office of the United States Trade Representative (USTR) documented the key aspects of the China problem, detailing Chinese subversion of Section 301 of the Trade Act of 1974. The scope of this three-hundred-page report revealed the extent to which China and the CCP had ignored, thwarted, and manipulated global economic standards, and it sounded the alarm that something had to change—and fast.

One of the biggest problems that President Trump inherited when he first took office was a gigantic trade deficit with China. Despite US superiority in innovation, manufacturing, and free-market pricing, by 2017, we were importing roughly $350 billion more per year in Chinese products into the US than we were exporting to China. How did trade with our number-one partner get so out of whack?

For starters, thanks to its state-led, central-control approach to trade and investment, China had learned how to rig the game of international trade. The Section 301 report, an annual review of global intellectual property rights, detailed how the CCP props up Chinese exporters and manufacturers, subsidizing them with government cash and manipulating foreign exchange rates to artificially lowers prices, making Chinese goods inexpensive and competitive overseas. Meanwhile, China slaps all manner of tariffs, fees, taxes, and functional barriers on Western imports into China, depriving its citizens of Western-made goods and services and preventing Western businesses from enjoying any hopes of fair trade.

According to the 301 report, the Chinese government provides subsidized low-cost capital through a number of different credit tools, including unfairly subsidized export credit financings, below-market-rate development loans, and low-cost political-risk insurance. All this tips the competitive hand to Chinese businesses by lowering export costs and project costs, particularly in emerging markets where high political-risk premiums are common. By artificially lowering the capital costs of doing business, Chinese companies can consistently afford to undercut competitors.

China simply wants to have it both ways: It wants to play on the international stage where everyone else follows a standard set of rules to ensure fair and free competition, while it refuses to play by the same rules. It's like playing a game of football when the green team is penalized every time one of its players jumps offsides or commits pass interference, while the yellow team is allowed to break all the rules and never be penalized. One can guess who would win that game: Most green teams would simply refuse to play at all.

And yet, the West has seemed determined to use the carrot of international partnership as a way to persuade China to play by the rules. Unfortunately, despite China's entry into the WTO and participation in international organizations like the Organization for Economic Co-operation and Development (OECD), China refuses to play by their rules and the US (and all other trading partners, for that matter) has not gained reciprocal access to China's massive domestic marketplace. Though China is the world's largest exporter, it systematically protects its internal marketplace from foreign trade through a variety of tariffs and barriers. Furthermore, by pressuring foreign companies to make technology transfers, restricting their licensing privileges, and hacking, spying, or acquiring them outright, China makes it difficult and cost-prohibitive for foreign firms to operate there.

One major pillar of the CCP's programmatic favoritism was the selection of certain "national champions"—state-owned enterprises (SOEs) that benefit from a range of subsidies, tax breaks, special development funds, increased credit support, and other assistance not enjoyed by foreign-owned companies.

Gradual reform of SOEs has supposedly been on China's to-do list for decades, but the Chinese government's behavior tells a different story. Its standard procedure is to strengthen these entities, rather than weaken them. Today, SOEs account for one-third of China's gross domestic product (GDP) and an estimated two-thirds of outbound investment. The logic is clear: Funding SOEs leads to success with specific CCP goals, such as supporting the growth of megacities like Hangzhou and Shenzhen. Strengthening SOEs enables the Chinese government to keep a close eye on market forces while "reserving the 'intervention option' in critical situations." Beijing has little to gain from relinquishing control of these mega-conglomerates, and even less from tolerating free-market competition.

If you've got a steady stream of predictable revenue and an easy path to micromanage it from the top-down, why would you stop? It's clear that China views its SOEs as market incumbents that benefit from a legal and natural monopoly. They enjoy regulatory privileges, local protectionism, and preferential treatment that taint normal trade relations. This favoritism for the state sector discourages China's private sector, which is already suffering from a slowing economy. Globally, as the 301 report explained, SOEs do not play by the same rules as US companies, and the Chinese government refuses to respond to calls for reform.

In the arena of export credits as well, China held almost every card in the deck. By providing export credits in the form of direct subsidies and below-market-rate loans to Chinese manufacturers, while crying wolf anytime another country threatened tariffs, the CCP made sure that its exports were cheaper than domestically produced goods. The CCP's universal commitment to manipulating export credit rules led American consumers to equate "Made in China" with "cheapest price in town."

In 2018, China became the leading adversarial voice among the WTO's International Working Group, as the US sought to address the unfair export lending practices. Despite the numerous allegations in the USTR report, the Chinese seemed to understand that they could skate by, "promising without proving" their cooperation. Thanks to the toothless, nonbinding efforts of prior US administrations, all they had to do was keep talking, and our side would eventually give up. If we questioned their underhanded lending practices, they would cry foul about their "impoverished status" as a Third World country, and demand we show compassion. If we called that bluff, they'd switch tactics and exhaust our efforts through stonewalling: death by a thousand meetings.

As if the barriers to entry for American goods and American businesses were not high enough, the 301 report also exposed how China had ramped up its plans to reduce competition from the West inside China.

Shortly after General Secretary Xi Jinping took office, a new agenda emerged: Made in China 2025. It set ambitious goals for the nation to rapidly grow in technological self-sufficiency—from 30 percent in 2015 to 40 percent by 2020, and then to 70 percent by 2025. In categories such as new energy vehicles, domestically produced energy equipment, and renewable energy equipment, the plan calls for 80 percent or greater market share to be held by domestic Chinese firms by 2025.

Every country, China included, has the sovereign right to pursue policies to become self-sufficient, wealthy, powerful, and influential. That said, every American president has a duty to stop foreign countries from pilfering and abusing the US economy. The president has an obligation to prevent other countries from robbing Americans blind, or from putting the US in a position of global strategic disadvantage. Especially when the US embraces free, fair, and open trade with that same country.

The 301 report laid bare that the Chinese had made it their mission to implement laws, policies, and practices to harm the US, its economic interests, and the lives of its ordinary citizens. It detailed how China consciously seeks to obstruct US imports, steal US innovations, replace American workers with Chinese ones, and undermine America's manufacturing, service, and technology industries.

It doesn't take a seasoned trade expert to realize that's a big problem. Healthy international trade relies on each participant accepting and playing by a common set of rules. When one side ignores the rules and "goes rogue," it not only threatens to undermine the global economy—it also really ticks off my passion for fair play. Thus, I was well suited to tackle China trade: While I was perfectly happy to be flexible and find creative solutions to thorny problems, on more than one occasion throughout my career, I have dug in my heels and demanded justice. One of the most dramatic examples was a pro bono case I handled through Agudath Israel's Legal Services.

The case came under the Hague Convention relating to child kidnapping. It was a tragic story: A married couple living in New York who had two children, with the mother pregnant with a third, were walking home after a Passover Seder when the mother and unborn child were killed by a car in a hit-and-run. As the husband grieved, the maternal grandparents, who lived in Switzerland, offered to bring the young sisters to Switzerland for a two-week summer vacation. The problem was, they never sent them back.

What do you do when people simply ignore the rules, ignore what is right, and hide behind international borders? We swung into action, fighting in international court, and, after a long battle in two countries, we got those two little girls back from Switzerland to their father.

I reflected on that case often when dealing with China, as America's trade conflict with the Chinese is similarly rooted in a clash between two very different systems. One is open and transparent, subject to audits and limits, and errs on the side of fair play. The other is closed, secretive, unaccountable for its financial management, and comfortable using unfair lending practices. China happily uses any tactic necessary to stack the deck in its favor.

The sheer number and variety of ways in which the CCP created (and protected) this unlevel playing field was daunting. China has frequently offered to "help" weaker and poorer countries who are desperate for capital and infrastructure—especially when the US has ignored them. But that help often comes at the expense of their partner states and violates best practices of global governance. This game plan is repeated around the globe.

A perfect example is the impoverished country of Bangladesh, which badly needs power plants and grids, but has neither the financing nor the expertise to build them. China makes Bangladesh an offer that's difficult to refuse: a $500 million loan for a power plant project, at below-market-rate financing, plus the technical and engineering expertise to build the plant. But there are strings attached. You see, the Chinese have decided that the mouth of the Meghna River is useful as a strategic naval outpost, so that's where they insist the power plant be built—notwithstanding demonstrably greater port capacity demand elsewhere in Bangladesh. Of the $500 million budget, $350 million conveniently goes right back to Chinese companies for equipment and construction. China also becomes a shareholder in all revenue flowing from the power plant it builds, and gains unfettered naval access to islands at the mouth of the Meghna.

Meanwhile, Bangladesh is saddled with several problems. First of all, the mouth of the Meghna is not where it needs a power plant. It would have been much more efficient and helpful for that power plant to sit at the juncture of the Padma and the Meghna Rivers. But that's not where the Chinese wanted to build it. Second, Bangladesh doesn't really need 1,320 megawatts of power generating capacity where the Padma and Meghna meet, representing a walloping 10 percent of Bangladesh's total installed generating capacity. Projected local demand was considerably less. But the Chinese were only willing to "partner" with them on the bigger project. Third, all labor on the project is handled by Chinese firms and Chinese workers, depriving Bangladesh of much-needed jobs that normally would come with such a big project. In the short term, Bangladesh gets below-market-rate financing, and technical assistance, for a badly needed power plant. But Bangladesh is now saddled with much more debt than necessary or than it can service, there is no job boon, the power plant is in the wrong spot and too large for the intended purpose, and a foreign country has control over strategic territory.

Imagine seeking a small commuter car so you can start driving for Uber. Along comes a dealership that offers to lease you an exotic Italian sports car at a ridiculously low rate of interest—in exchange for a percentage of your sales. It sounds tempting—until you realize that the costs of maintaining your vehicle eat up almost all your income. You also discover that you can't park the car in the assigned space in your apartment complex; you must take a bus across town to retrieve the Ferrari from the dealership's showroom, just to get your work day started. As for the money you were supposed to earn, nearly all of it goes to the dealership (from sales) and the bank (in loan repayments).

Similarly, in this scenario, the Bangladeshis would receive a high-end power plant, in a poorly sited location, producing much more power than they need (which they cannot sell), disrupting local power market pricing. The Chinese, meanwhile, get a major stream of income—both as a shareholder and a lender. You might assume that many of these small, impoverished nations default on their loans—and they do—but Beijing doesn't mind. The Chinese then foreclose on the loan—and now they own the power plant outright, to do with as they see fit. Continue to run it and collect the income...or not. They regularly abandon projects like this once they've obtained their strategic foothold.

It's all part of China's One Belt One Road initiative (now called the Belt and Road Initiative). China's "help" burdens countries with projects that are not sized or sited to actual need, fosters corruption, and wreaks instability in developing economies through unsustainable debt burdens, all while advancing China's ability to project power throughout the world. China insists it wants to be a good global citizen, but its actions make clear that a different agenda is at work.

Perhaps the most alarming section of the USTR's 301 report contained the details of China's intentional and sophisticated program for infiltrating US markets in order to steal our technology. For well over a decade, the Chinese have been helping themselves to trade secrets, technical data, negotiating positions, and sensitive or proprietary internal communications.

One of China's key strategies was its National Medium- and Long-Term Science and Technology Development Plan. A mountain of evidence made it clear that China's intention was to acquire, replicate, and improve technologies invented in the West, through any means necessary. Rather than develop Chinese technologies, the development plan directed the government and Chinese firms to "introduce, digest, absorb and re-innovate" technologies developed in the US and other Western countries.

Under this approach, China would gather intelligence on innovations in the US, then invest in US tech firms and ruthlessly negotiate technology transfer agreements to access (or simply steal) our intellectual property (IP)—then "introduce" it by sending it back to China, where companies can develop their own versions to sell.

Meanwhile, foreign firms seeking a permit to sell in China were required to reveal every detail of how their product worked, so that the Chinese could "digest" it—study, analyze, and disseminate the information and technology. Then they'd "absorb" it—Chinese firms and state agencies would collaborate to create their own versions of the product. And finally, they'd "re-innovate" it—produce their own versions to sell at lower prices overseas. After all, you can afford to set your prices lower when you steal your competitors' innovations rather than develop your own.

If US firms want to license their IP for sale in China, they must do so on terms favorable to Chinese recipients. If those recipients are named in a lawsuit stemming from the IP, Chinese regulations indemnify the licensees, so that only the licensor may be held liable. If licensee firms make improvements to the technology, they enjoy exclusive rights to 100 percent of the profits, while the licensor gets nothing. When licensing contracts expire, Chinese regulations permit the licensees to continue using the IP indefinitely, without any financial obligations to the licensors.

Despite promises on at least ten different occasions from two successive Communist regimes to curb technology transfers, Chinese officials continue to pressure US firms to divulge their most closely held secrets as a condition of operating in China.

The depth of China's influence and ability to siphon useful information is difficult to fathom. In brief, these stem from a fundamental difference in worldviews, which finds its strongest expression in Beijing's Military-Civil Fusion (MCF) strategy. According to the US State Department,

> As the name suggests, a key part of MCF is the elimination of barriers between China's civilian research and commercial sectors, and its military and defense industrial sectors. The CCP is implementing this

strategy, not just through its own research and development efforts, but also by acquiring and diverting the world's cutting-edge technologies—including through theft—in order to achieve military dominance.

In other words, it's safe to assume that if you trade or do business with any Chinese company, you're also trading with the Chinese Communist Party, and likely strengthening the Chinese military. Your sensitive data and information are almost assuredly compromised—and will be used to help China achieve its stated goal: to develop "the most technologically advanced military in the world." So much for China's claims of being a good global citizen.

The story of Chinese corporations accessing the US public equity markets shows an equally troubling lack of regard for an orderly rules-based system, causing significant harm to US investors and capital markets stability. It is a tale of almost unbelievable numbers, seemingly taken from the pages of a Greek tragedy featuring meteoric rises, calamitous falls, and hopeful redemptions.

Let's have a look at the numbers. The PRC corporations first began to tap into the US capital markets in 1989, with roughly five issuers raising less than $100 million total. A mere drop in the ocean of the more than $2.8 trillion market capitalization in the US public markets. Activity picked up in late 1996 and 1997 when two of China's largest airlines—China Eastern and China Southern—raised multiple billions, respectively, through the issuance of American depositary receipts. By 2012, approximately 500 China-domiciled companies were listed in the United States, with 70 on the Big Board (the New York Stock Exchange) and 122 on the Nasdaq, and 259 over-the-counter (OTC) securities. On

June 29, 2012, the combined market cap for all China-domiciled companies traded in the United States was $107.9 billion.

The public offerings fell into three main categories: (1) mega-global offerings by major PRC banks and energy companies underwritten by global investment banks, (2) mid-market offerings by a variety of privately owned Chinese corporates underwritten largely by reputable investment banks, and (3) small to mid-market offerings conducted largely by reverse mergers, many of which were underwritten by small and aggressive underwriters.

All was humming along until it wasn't. The market cap of China-domiciled companies trading in the US showed healthy growth: 20.60 percent ($22.8 billion) from 2009 to 2010. From 2010 to 2011, the growth rate doubled to 40.13 percent ($53.5 billion). Then the bottom seemed to drop out. A large number of Chinese issuers lost an alarming amount of value the very next year when this group lost 42.20 percent of its value ($78.8 billion). The numbers were ugliest with the 103 issuers that came to market from China through reverse mergers: Twenty-eight lost at least 90 percent off their highest price, fifty-six lost at least 80 percent off their highest price, sixty-three lost at least 70 percent off highest their highest price, seventy-six lost at least 60 percent off their highest price, eighty-three lost at least 50 percent off their highest price, and eighty-nine lost at least 40 percent off their highest price.

This caught the attention of the US Securities and Exchange Commission (SEC), which on June 9, 2011, had already issued an Investor Bulletin outlining the risks of investing in companies that enter US markets through reverse mergers. Fraud allegations abounded. As a result of the uproar, equity holdings in US-listed Chinese companies, once highly coveted assets, became tainted and viewed with suspicion by the investor community, exchanges, and regulators.

One of the favorite tactics of Chinese corporate issuers was the "reverse merger." A "reverse merger," otherwise known as a "reverse takeover" or a "reverse IPO" (initial public offering), is essentially a shortcut to becoming a public company in the United States. Reverse mergers allow a company that has all its operations abroad to enter into the US capital markets to raise money from American investors while bypassing the relatively stringent regulatory requirements of the US IPO process. The steps for raising capital in such a manner were fairly straightforward.

1. A Chinese company purchases a controlling share in a publicly traded US shell company.

2. Using its controlling share, the Chinese company replaces the directors and officers of that US shell company with its own and causes that company to acquire or merge with the Chinese company.

3. After the merger is complete, the resulting US-listed Chinese company engages in the process of issuing additional shares for sale to American investors.

According to an investigation conducted by the Public Company Accounting Oversight Board (PCAOB) between January 2007 and the end of March 2010, it was estimated that more than one-quarter (that is, 159 companies) of the 603 reverse merger transactions in the US during that period involved companies from China. Moreover, the number of Chinese companies that became listed in the US through a reverse merger was nearly triple the number that did so through a standard IPO (159 companies through reverse mergers vs. 56 through IPOs).

The allure of US listings for Chinese companies of all sizes and levels of viability is easy to understand. Raising capital in China at the time was far more time consuming and costly and there was very limited market depth or capacity. Listing in China was a more difficult process than in the US, and was almost always entangled in politics. For instance, most private Chinese companies at the time had difficulty obtaining loans from state-owned banks because these banks largely restricted their lending to SOEs. Moreover, achieving a domestic listing in the Chinese capital markets required a minimum three-year application process, the outcome of which depended on whether the company was in a favored industry or whether its management had a good relationship with the Chinese government. Listing in the US completely sidestepped these challenges. Furthermore, in addition to the potential for capital infusions from American investors, the cachet of obtaining a US listing facilitated the acquisition of capital within China in the form of subsidies and other favors from local Communist officials, who would gain prestige from having such companies located in their jurisdictions.

Beginning in mid-2011, Chinese companies that entered the US capital markets through reverse mergers found themselves at the center of widespread fraud allegations by American investors and regulators, leading to dozens of suspensions and delistings from the New York Stock Exchange (NYSE), the American Stock Exchange (AMEX), and the Nasdaq.

At the crux of these fraud allegations was a revelation by the American investor community of pervasive deficiencies in the financial disclosures of small-cap, US-listed Chinese companies. Alarmingly, in the first half of 2012, more than twenty-five of these companies had disclosed accounting discrepancies or seen their auditors resign—with some of these auditors even accusing their former clients of fraud.

According to the PCAOB, these deficiencies in financial disclosures were due in large part to a combination of substandard auditing practices by the US-registered public accounting firms that serviced these companies (the vast majority of them being US triennial accounting firms) and the inability (read: roadblocks put up by China) of the PCAOB to inspect the work of the China-based auditors with whom these accounting firms coordinated.

The US capital markets reacted very negatively to this situation. By mid-2011, the Bloomberg China Reverse Merger index, which at the time tracked eighty-two US-listed Chinese companies that entered the markets through reverse mergers, fell 67 percent in value from its peak at the start of 2010. Moreover, the index was trading on a price-to-earnings ratio of just 4.6, compared to a ratio of 14.4 for the S&P 500. To further illustrate the extent of this market jitter, in 2011, a single investor-initiated report on a US-listed Chinese company that accused that company of committing fraud wiped out $3.25 billion in market capitalization in just two days (that's a loss of more than a quarter of the total market capitalization for reverse-merger US-listed Chinese companies at that time).

This marked the beginning of the end. There was a flurry of litigation and regulatory action by the SEC and the PCAOB. Yet for over a decade, the Chinese regulatory authorities thwarted regulator and investor access to Chinese-issuer audited financials. As the SEC and other regulators have noted, the bedrock of robust US capital markets is reliable and accurate financial statements and related disclosures. Without that, investors are at risk and market instability becomes likely.

The majority of the litigation cases and regulatory actions that cropped up against these Chinese firms since 2010 were from highly speculative investment deals. Unfortunately, on one level, US investors were lured by "easy money," and lots of it. Not unlike the greed that led to the 2008 subprime mortgage crisis. But at least the mortgage-backed securities that toppled the market back then were "known entities." You could see those numbers. That meltdown was a product of labeling a known "bad" risk as a good one. With these Chinese firms, their entire financial position was completely misrepresented, or not disclosed at all—and, rather outrageously, they were all hiding behind their government's stonewalling to prevent full and reliable disclosure of basic financial information to allow investors to make prudent and informed investment decisions. The first-day returns were irresistible, but the sale of their stock was based on thin air, without any oversight or scrutiny of their viability.

In sum, by the time the Trump team took office in January 2017, the China problem was huge—and immediate. China enjoyed a record $350 billion trade surplus with the United States. It had been on a long streak of poaching technology, IP, and sensitive instruments (like semiconductors) without accountability or oversight. At home, it maintained a complex web of licensing practices and permit procedures designed to discourage foreign firms from doing business in China. Abroad, it engaged in a wide variety of tactics and tricks to exploit the free-market system while ignoring rules and laws that were inconvenient to pursuing its end goal.

China has made no secret of what that end goal is. As General Secretary Xi laid out in a 2013 speech, "Capitalism is bound to die out and socialism is bound to win." Four years later, he stated that the CCP aims to make China "a global leader in terms of comprehensive national power and international influence." His party leaders perpetuate his vision under the banner of "building a community of common destiny for mankind."

To the US, China had become the functional equivalent of an abusive partner who steals from you and escapes accountability by whispering sweet nothings every time you question the behavior. One could say that China wants the benefits of marriage and the benefits of divorce at the same time. The abuse only stops when you stop tolerating it.

President Trump understood that a "carrot" doesn't work without a "stick." It was time to get tough. He outlined his new policy of "principled realism," codified in the 2017 National Security Strategy of the United States of America (NSS). He explained that this policy reflected a "competitive approach to the PRC," one that was willing to tolerate "greater bilateral friction."

The policy had two objectives:

- first, to improve the resiliency of our institutions, alliances, and partnerships to prevail against the challenges the PRC presents; and
- second, to compel Beijing to cease or reduce actions harmful to the United States' vital, national interests and those of our allies and partners.

The NSS, the Trump administration explained, is not an attempt to "change the PRC's domestic governance model," but rather to "empower our institutions to withstand the CCP's malign behavior and collateral damage from the PRC's internal governance problems."

This approach was a radical departure from previous administrations, both Republican and Democratic. Rather than waiting and hoping, we would deal with reality. "The United States responds to the PRC's actions rather than its stated commitments," declared the president. "Likewise, the United States sees no value in engaging with Beijing for symbolism and pageantry; we instead demand tangible results and constructive outcomes."

It was indeed a new day for this very important and contentious relationship. The specifics of the Trump policy were bold, clear, and wide-ranging. They addressed economic, energy, military, diplomatic, human-rights, and technology issues, including:

- significant resources devoted to identifying and prosecuting trade-secrets theft, hacking, and economic espionage;
- increased measures to prevent malign foreign investment in US infrastructure and supply chain threats;
- provisions to prevent companies connected with the Chinese government from accessing sensitive US government information;
- strengthening the Committee on Foreign Investment in the United States (CFIUS) to prevent Chinese companies from gaining access to US innovation through minority investments;
- ramping up seizure of counterfeit and substandard goods exported by China to the US;
- "rebalancing" the US-China economic relationship by supporting US exports and breaking down unjust barriers to US trade;
- new tariffs to protect US steel and aluminum industries ("in response to Beijing's repeated failure to reduce or eliminate its market-distorting subsidies and overcapacity");
- working with allies to ensure that "discriminatory industrial standards do not become global standards";

- prioritizing the modernization of the nuclear triad, including "the development of supplementary capabilities designed to deter Beijing from using its weapons of mass destruction or conducting other strategic attacks"; and
- multiple actions to promote Western values of free speech, individual liberty, free market capitalism, healthy and fair competition, and respect for human dignity.

It was a complete rewriting of the playbook. The Trump team expected a stiff response based on prior US negotiations with the Chinese. After twenty years of abuse with no consequences, we knew that Beijing would not suddenly reverse course and respect the rules. But the least we could do was insist that it play by the same rules as the rest of the developed world. President Trump has consistently opposed China's designation as a "developing country" within the numerous international organizations that accord significant benefits to a country that has the world's second largest GDP. "The United States has never accepted China's claim to developing-country status, and virtually every current economic indicator belies China's claim."[1]

With principled realism as our motto, the Trump 45 Treasury set out to chart a new course for US-Chinese trade and finance. And I buckled in for a long and bumpy ride.

---

1 "Memorandum on Reforming Developing-Country Status in the World Trade Organization," The White House, July 26, 2019, https://trumpwhitehouse.archives.gov/presidential-actions/memorandum-reforming-developing-country-status-world-trade-organization/?utm_source=link.

CHAPTER 5

TOUGH BUT FAIR:
RESETTING THE TERMS OF THE
US-CHINA RELATIONSHIP

After an exhausting month of prep work, I boarded our flight to Beijing with wary optimism. I had worked intensively leading up to this March 2018 trip, drafting a comprehensive framework document outlining a new trade deal with China, a proposal that would overhaul virtually every aspect of the US-China economic relationship. David Malpass wanted us to get in front of matters, and called on my legal drafting skills to get the ball rolling. The interagency process took over from there, notably led by the skilled team at the USTR.

The proposal was groundbreaking. It was comprehensive, concrete, and detailed, which of course meant it was also the subject of massive internal debate and horse trading within the administration before we could even present our proposal to the Chinese. I couldn't help thinking of the old saying, "Jews grow up learning to count by knowing that there is one G-d, two Jews, and three opinions." The same is true, it seems, for government agencies.

Everybody and their mother seemed to have changes to make to the document. The Department of Commerce, the Department of Energy, the Department of Agriculture, the National Economic

Council (NEC), the Treasury, the USTR, the US embassy in Beijing, and more. After collecting mountains of input and details, after several rounds of hitting "refresh," after incorporating the USTR's comprehensive, and wholly voluminous, list of issues to be resolved, we settled on the proposal. The meat had been put on the bones, but the basic framework was intact, covering seven core issues:

- Trade deficit reduction
- Protection of American technology and intellectual property
- Restrictions on investment in sensitive technology
- US investment in China
- Tariffs and other trade barriers
- Market access for US services providers
- Agriculture

We'd sent the proposal to our Chinese counterparts several days earlier, and now our high-level trade delegation was en route to Beijing to negotiate the largest change to trade relations in at least ten years. The cast of characters illustrates just how significant this trade deal could be. It included Secretary Mnuchin (head of the delegation), Under Secretary David Malpass and me (Treasury), Secretary Wilbur Ross (Commerce), US Trade Representative Robert Lighthizer and several of his deputies, NEC Director Larry Kudlow, Under Secretary Ted McKinney (Agriculture), and Peter Navarro (special assistant to the president and director of trade and manufacturing policy).

I could only hope that we would be able to build the kind of rapport with our Chinese counterparts that had been crucial to the success of my previous negotiations on high-stakes Chinese deals. As we cruised above the Pacific at thirty-five thousand feet, I thought back to one of my favorite moments from a past negotiation.

Back in the 1990s, I was engaged in the negotiation of the first US-China joint venture power project to fund equity—the Jingyuan Phase 2 Power Project in Gansu province. We had been negotiating the deal for well over a year with the Gansu provincial authorities, who held a majority of the Chinese participation in the project, alongside one of China's state investment companies. Negotiations went in fits and spurts—one step forward, two back, three forward. Part of the challenge was the level of sophistication of the provincial authorities—they were well versed in the power sector but had not done a transaction with foreign investors or ever dealt with foreign commercial banks.

In 1994, shareholding on the Chinese side of the joint venture shifted, and overnight we were dealing with the State Development and Investment Corporation (SDIC), a new dominant partner at the central level. With the change in composition came a distinct difference in approach to negotiation and position. The provincial parties would not move without the blessing of the SDIC, and the negotiations resembled a Chinese Communist Party congress more than a commercial negotiation.

I was unable to attend the beginning of a particularly critical negotiation because of a scheduling conflict. When I arrived, late, the negotiations were bogged down on a sensitive point with the Chinese side, led by SDIC representatives. I sat on the back bench and listened as the American side persisted rather persuasively through a translator. About forty-five minutes into a particular point, I could not sit back any longer. I spoke up in Chinese to the lead Chinese negotiator, who was a senior cadre in the Chinese Communist Party. I waxed on in native-enough

Chinese, and it appeared that I convinced the Chinese side of my position. Of course, the lead negotiator could not concede without some pushback. And so, after I finished, he paused, collected his thoughts and then began to speak. The first words out of his mouth were, "*Su Tongzhi*," translating to "Comrade Su" (my Chinese surname). Not Mr. Su, Mr. Silk, or just Su Qi (蘇騏), my full Chinese name, but Comrade Su, a title reserved for a member of the Chinese Communist Party. Not more than a second after the words left his mouth, he stopped and turned to his colleague with a look on his face that broadcast, "Did I just call him Comrade Silk?!?" He then turned to me with the same look on his face. I turned to my American colleague and translated, and the whole room simultaneously burst out laughing.

On reflection, I didn't think anyone would be calling me comrade at this meeting.

We arrived at the US embassy in Beijing with about an hour to review our plans one more time before we had to depart for Diaoyutai—the state guest house where Mao and every leader since has entertained foreign dignitaries. But there was a surprise waiting for us at our embassy: a brand-new proposal, drafted by the Chinese, which they were putting forth at the eleventh hour, and which we had never seen. It was about fifteen pages long—and *completely in Chinese*!

I was one of the few people in the room who could read it. After a quick scan, I told the group: "This is wholly unacceptable. This document doesn't say anything—they're just messing with us." A heated debate ensued over how to respond, and how the Chinese were likely to react. But there was no time to reach a consensus; it was time to leave for Diaoyutai.

There was a mass exit from the secure room where we met at the embassy, and, almost like a well-choreographed ballet with a hundred moving parts, we all shuffled to our designated cars. As Secretary Mnuchin stepped into the limousine to take us to the meeting, David Malpass insisted that I ride with the secretary and pushed me into the seat next to Mnuchin, saying, "We need to know exactly what this says—can you translate it on the way?" As we sped through the streets of Beijing, I sat in the back seat, literally *shvitzing* as a technical term in Chinese got the better of me, and furiously translated as I read out loud, in English, what the Chinese had dropped in our laps.

Even as we climbed the stairs into the building and entered the meeting room, none of us was quite sure how Mnuchin was going to handle this hot potato. After Vice Premier Liu He's flowing stream of diplomatic pleasantries welcoming us to China, the secretary calmly stated in response, "We received your draft. Thanks for sending it over—but we're going to use *our* draft for today." It wasn't the preamble they expected. But it was entirely consistent with the new tone that President Trump had set from the day he took office.

From the very start of his first term, President Trump had signaled that he was committed to a full reset of the lopsided US-China relationship. Early on, he put China on notice that there was a new sheriff in town, and this sheriff had very new messages:

- We are fed up with your unfair and one-sided approach to trade, and see no reason to continue the status quo.
- We are finished with meetings that produce nothing. We are only interested in serious, meaningful negotiations that produce tangible, measurable results.
- We are not going to back down, and we are not going to slow down.

Our new approach, we told them, was laser-focused on three significant goals:

- slashing the $500 billion trade deficit,
- eliminating barriers and increasing US access to China's markets, and
- ensuring proper respect for US markets, including intellectual property, technology, and companies.

The message was straightforward and unequivocal—as shocking as it may have been for the Chinese. It upended decades of habit that had produced lots of talk and zero results.

In the waning days of the George W. Bush administration, then-Treasury Secretary Henry Paulson instituted a monthly working group meeting with China, which perfectly symbolized the problem with US-China trade relations. Modeled on the G7 and G20 summits, these meetings required an entire committee from the Treasury to spend weeks prior to each set of meetings planning and attending to logistics. Committee members drafted preparatory material, talking points, and background papers. When the Chinese delegation showed up, the American side dutifully attended to ensuring equal representation and fair hearings of Chinese issues. When the meeting concluded, it was considered a win for US trade, simply because the meeting had taken place.

These meetings continued, month after month, for ten years, and throughout the Obama administration. But in ten years of monthly meetings, you'd be hard pressed to name even one tangible positive outcome. The cultural phenomenon of participation trophies comes to mind, as though the only thing we needed to do was hold meetings!

After all that time and energy, all we had to show for it was a $500 billion trade deficit, pathetically minimal market penetration in China, and an abusive relationship of theft and subterfuge in our market, particularly with respect to US intellectual property and capital markets.

President Trump instructed his team that those days were over. We were going to put serious, concrete proposals and demands on the table, and stick to our guns when the negotiations got tough. We had to not just talk the talk, but walk the walk—*thousands* of times, in a myriad of ways, with an adversarial negotiating partner trained by our predecessors to regard any tough talk from us as mere political posturing.

If you've ever tried to hold a confrontational posture against someone for an extended period of time, you know that it's exhausting. The Chinese knew how little appetite Americans have for protracted discussions and lengthy cultural protocols. They'd played that card for two decades, and it worked like a charm. Now, we had to convince them we were all playing an entirely new game.

One of the simplest ways was changing how we interacted with them. US negotiators were used to being drawn into protracted discussions, pondering abstract hypotheticals or splitting hairs over cultural nuances. But starting in 2017, we took a new approach. We advance-planned our interactions with them in detail—beginning, as author Stephen Covey would say, with the end in mind. We rehearsed a litany of Chinese objections, questions, and diversions, and practiced steering the conversation back to the original agenda. We analyzed their stall tactics and the methods they used to keep negotiators talking in circles, dragging out discussions with no end in sight. The Chinese were experts in the "slow roll."

We also stopped sacrificing our long-term goals in the interest of a "harmonious" relationship. Instead of politely allowing the Chinese to wear us down and whittle away our demands so as not to appear overly aggressive, we simply stood our ground. Over and over and over again. After Secretary Mnuchin and Ambassador Lighthizer had set the tone for future meetings, Lighthizer handed day-to-day meetings over to Deputy US Trade Representative Jeff Gerrish. From moment one, Jeff faced his Chinese counterparts and rebuffed one objection after another, never deviating from the script. They would pummel him for the better part of an hour, another hour, a half day, and then a full day—but he never took the bait. He simply restated our demands, over and over, until the Chinese either assented to his request, or tabled the matter for the next meeting. When the next meeting took place, they would raise their same objections, hoping to wear Gerrish—and other negotiators—down until he compromised. He refused to yield, repeating once again our position and our demands. (We also anticipated their next move; if they retaliated with tariffs, we'd raise our tariffs, and we told them so.) Gerrish was a rock.

Meanwhile, those monthly meetings hosted by former administrations which had yielded little to no tangible results? David Malpass abolished the practice and disbanded the committee. We were not interested in talk—we wanted action, and the Chinese were put on notice that we meant business.

Just three months after taking office, President Trump hosted China's President Xi Jinping at Mar-a-Lago for their first summit. While Trump had been quite vocal about his intention to reset the economic relationship with China, Xi may well have expected just a new version of the same toothless negotiations of the past.

But this tiger had teeth. President Trump used the summit to deliver a clear message: We expect results.

The summit was quickly followed by the release of a hundred-day plan detailing a series of rapid changes, requiring immediate cooperation from Beijing. Issues ranged from agricultural imports to energy to regulatory barriers in the financial services sector. The opening salvo of the US-China trade war had been launched.

While the Chinese gave ground on some of the smaller, less consequential points, they stalled, dithered, or retaliated on most of the major issues. It was disappointing, but not surprising. We had "trained" China to view our demands as mere wishes, and our conditions as empty threats.

The Trump 45 administration quickly demonstrated that we were serious. In August 2017, the Office of the US Trade Representative announced the beginning of its Section 301 investigation. Through hints and allegations, formal and informal, and some leaks to the press, we also put Beijing on notice that restrictions, tariffs, and reforms were on their way, unless they made some meaningful changes. It caused an immediate spike in chatter and speculation, both from China and the global media—just as we had anticipated. Many American economists and experts took to the airwaves to denounce the administration's stance, lambasting the investigation as needless provocation, and fretting about the impact that tariffs would have on the US economy.

China's government, as well as its media, expressed equal alarm and outrage. But behind the scenes, they were starting to pay more serious attention to our demands, the essential first step toward any meaningful reform.

During one of my visits to Beijing, for example, two senior team members of Chinese Vice Premier Liu's (the counterpart to Secretary Mnuchin) team asked to meet with me over lunch. Alarmed by the confrontational posture and tone from Washington, they peppered me with questions, probing for details on what we hoped to achieve. Word had trickled down that we were planning a special action under the authority of Section 301 with far-reaching implications for Chinese investment in the US, and that we were at the advanced stages of strengthening our investment security statute. What was likely to happen? they wanted to know. Would the president follow through on his threats to impose tariffs? Doesn't he realize, the canny pair argued, that doing so might be cutting off our nose to spite our face? How could President Trump face our voters if we cut them off from inexpensive Chinese goods? It was a masterful attempt at feigning concern for our own political welfare while trying to extract information and prepare their own response.

My replies were a twist on Taiwan's "Three No's" policy.

In an attempt to build rapport between the mainland and Taiwan, the PRC developed in 1979 the "Three Links" policy, proposing to Taiwan to establish cross-Straits postal, transportation, and trade links. Then-Taiwanese President Chiang Ching-kuo less than ceremoniously declined, retorting with his Three No's policy of no contact, no negotiation, no compromise. An acerbic political commentator in the 1990s coined his own Three No's policy to describe Chinese bureaucrats of the day, which worked well for me in the context: *bu zhidao*, *bu qingchu*, and *bu haoshuo* (I don't know, it's not clear, and it's hard to say).

Between Xi's visit to Mar-a-Lago and President Trump's state visit to Beijing in November 2017, the US and China took part in a number of "comprehensive dialogues." Meanwhile, tremendous work was going on behind the scenes. President Trump had proclaimed a total reset in US-China relations; now the complex and laborious process of White House decision-making proceeded. We had to decide which policy options were feasible, along with forecasting their impacts and likelihood of success. Agencies gave input, and my buddy Tim Fitzgerald, chief international economist of the Council of Economic Advisers, analyzed mountains of trade data, consulted with countless experts, and conducted numerous meetings—this was the hard work necessary to turn around a decade of inaction, frustration, and failure.

By early 2018, it was clear that China was not going to act on any of the substantive issues we'd put on the table or correct any of the abuses outlined in our 301 report without some stiff "encouragement." Which wouldn't happen overnight.

One of the many lessons I learned from my Zeyde Friend was that meaningful change takes time. You cannot give up as soon as you meet resistance; when you are on the side of justice, you have to be willing to stick to your guns and persevere. As we faced the prospect of a long tug-of-war with the Chinese, I was reminded of a ten-year fight I had waged to save a young Jewish boy.

As chairman of Agudath's Legal Support Services before joining Trump 45, I assisted with many legal cases involving the Jewish community. One such case involved a young mother caught up in a custody dispute with her ex. The couple were originally from Kansas. When they divorced, she was awarded custody and came to New York with the children. She wanted to raise them Orthodox, but the father no longer agreed. The father was extremely litigious and appealed to the courts incessantly until the case was transferred to a Kansas court, which gave the youngest child back to the father. I drafted a brief that supported the boy's right to live with his mother and as an Orthodox Jew, and then I lined up ten of the most influential children's law professors and children's advocacy organizations in the US to sign on as amicus brief participants. I knew we would be best served if we could find a Kansas lawyer to file the brief, but none of the Agudath's network was admitted to the bar in Kansas. So I started digging.

First, I approached a firm that had been involved in a similar case in the past, but the firm turned me down. Then I looked up all the big firms in Kansas City with offices near the court proceeding, and I approached any lawyer who had a Chinese-sounding name. I introduced myself as the head of the China department from Allen & Overy, which got me in the door, and then I presented the problem and asked for help. That's how we found Eugene Balloun, the ideal litigator for this case. Although he was not an Orthodox Jew (he wasn't a Jew at all!), he had a heart for children and a passion for pro bono work. Together, we pursued this case for the better part of ten years, ultimately winning so that the mother could bring her son back to New York.

Fast-forward to negotiating a massive China trade deal, and I saw the same long road ahead of us. Yet at the core of the trade question was simple math: Why should the US keep buying China's exports if it was so unwilling to purchase ours? President Trump had a simple objective: We buy less of what they sell, and they buy more of what we sell. Our job was to obtain concrete, time-measurable, dollar-specific commitments from China to increase purchases of US goods and services. The teeth of this proposal lay in our power to *decrease* our purchases from China, through tariffs, until Beijing saw the wisdom of cooperating. At the same time, we hammered home our demands for reducing the high and often illogical barriers the Chinese had erected to keep our products, services, and businesses out of China.

The Chinese offered a proposal for reducing the trade deficit, but like so many aspects of Chinese negotiation, the targets were both underwhelming and laden with caveats. They proposed increasing US exports into China by $200 billion over two years, but then came the fine print (I paraphrase): None of these numbers represent firm commitments. First, the US must ensure its supply capacity; then it should improve the quality and price of its goods; then it must meet our regulatory requirements; and finally—the results may vary.

Oy vey! Talk about gaslighting! Really?! The most powerful, productive, and resource-rich nation on earth has to ensure its supply capacity and improve its quality and prices? What they gave with one hand, the other hand took away.

President Trump wasn't having any of this. Accordingly, we drew up our own proposed targets for the first two years of the relationship reset. Raising China's $200 billion stake to $362.1 billion, we demanded immediate increases in Chinese imports of American-manufactured goods (machinery, pharmaceuticals, aircraft, vehicles, iron, and steel); agricultural products (such as oilseeds, meat, grains, and seafood); energy products (crude and refined oil, coal, and liquefied natural gas); and services (uses of intellectual property, business travel and tourism, financial services, and cloud computing).

Our trade deficit demands were bold, but the Chinese were dragging their feet. It was time for the next chapter in this battle of wills.

In January 2018, President Trump fired the first shot. Dipping into Section 301, he levied tariffs on China's exports of washing machines (20 percent for the first 1.2 million machines imported, and a 50 percent tax on all imported thereafter) and solar cells (30 percent).

Beijing fired back in February, announcing duty investigations on more than $1 billion of US sorghum imports, just two days before the first US tariffs took effect. The battle was on. In

March, we announced $2.8 billion of Section 232 tariffs on steel and aluminum imports from China. The US media went to great lengths to downplay China's response, describing it as "muted" and "indifferent." China itself, however, responded by publishing a list of 128 proposed US products, valued at $2.4 billion, to target for retaliation. The very next day, April 3, the USTR announced a fresh round of investment restrictions and 25 percent tariffs on $50 billion worth of Chinese goods, under Section 301.

The temperature continued to rise. China published a list of $50 billion worth of newly proposed tariffs. We doubled down, announcing the possibility of *another* $100 billion in tariffs of our own. Just how far did the Chinese want to take this? A week or so later, Beijing announced preliminary duties of 178 percent on US sorghum imports.

As the tariff wars intensified, meetings continued between US and Chinese representatives. From February 1 to June 3, seven different bilateral meetings were held, four in DC and three in Beijing, involving trade delegations and high-level cabinet members on both sides. These meetings had all the hallmarks of the old Chinese attitude: stall, delay, deflect and—when concessions were finally agreed to—slow-roll the implementation. The difference this time, however, was that the US was no longer waiting patiently. We warned our counterparts that tariffs and other consequences were coming—*and they came*. Through this rapid round of meetings and imposition of tariffs, our message was clear: We want results and we intend to get them.

After a lengthy round of meetings in Beijing from late May to early June produced no results, the tariff war kicked into high gear. The USTR published a revised list of tariffs in June, to the tune of 25 percent on $34 billion of Chinese goods. It went into effect in July. President Trump kept up the heat, announcing the possibility of a further 10 percent tariff on $200 billion of Chinese imports. Beijing retaliated in July by imposing a 25 percent tariff of its own on $34 billion of US goods. Undeterred, on July 20, we announced the consideration of across-the-board, universal tariffs on the remaining $262 billion of Chinese imports. We were ready to go as far as they wanted to go.

This fistfight lasted the rest of the year. Our 10 percent tariff on $200 billion from July? We raised it to 25 percent. The Chinese didn't blink, so it went into effect at the beginning of 2019. They tried to hit back with tariffs of 5 percent to 25 percent on $60 billion of our goods, which took effect in September. Meanwhile, the USTR came back with tariffs on another $16 billion, and the Chinese mirrored them. Back and forth it went—the irresistible force meeting the immovable object.

The US media and academic economists bombarded the public with cries of disaster. They wailed that tariffs and other trade sanctions would only hurt Americans, raising prices on all kinds of goods that average consumers wanted and needed. No doubt higher prices squeezed some consumers (though it also rescued many US producers), but the larger point was this: The only way to force China into serious, meaningful changes to its trade and investment policies and to reverse decades of its unfair, dangerous, and illegal behavior was to demonstrate that we meant business. Not just to warn of consequences, but to impose them—and stick to them.

China, on the other hand, kept its slow-roll going, including by tying up US exports in red tape and bureaucracy. In February, the Chinese Ministry of Commerce announced "environmental duty investigations" on more than $1 billion worth of US sorghum imports, accusing the US of "dumping" the sorghum on the Chinese market (a move it rescinded three months later). US fruit, seafood, and pork rotted in Chinese ports as the result of inexplicably longer and more demanding Chinese import process and inspections.

One of President Trump's longest-running grievances with China's economic warfare was its habit of currency manipulation. Because of the trade imbalance, the Chinese found it useful to artificially depreciate the renminbi—which made the problem worse. Like so many of their tactics, this was intentional rather than accidental, just one more strategy for unleveling the playing field.

Another favorite Chinese tactic was the classic "moving the goal post." Agree to benchmarks, and then walk back from the agreed-upon numbers. For example, in mid-2018, China had agreed to increase imports of US agriculture, energy, manufactured goods, and financial services to the tune of $127 billion over two years. Then, in December, Beijing came back with an altered offer. Now it would only buy $200 billion total over *six years*—and the Chinese purposefully left certain categories blank! This was a classic Chinese slow-roll technique: Negotiate, make us wait, and then come back with a lesser offer, hoping we'd agree, just so we could say we accomplished something. "Sorry guys," we told them. "First, you told us two years; now you're saying six. We need numbers and timelines in two years, or there's no deal. Repeat: *no deal.*"

While tariffs and other restrictions were aimed at lowering China's flooding of our markets, we were also continually offering the Chinese proposals that would benefit their economy, their markets, their industries—and their people. Virtually all of the policy changes we proposed during these extensive (and exhausting) trade negotiations were demonstrably mutually beneficial, improving revenue and growth for both partners. We were committed to putting practical, actionable, market-tested solutions on the table.

For example, I worked specifically on solutions to the trade shortfall in energy, where one of China's retaliatory tariffs caused sales of US liquefied natural gas (LNG) to China to decline precipitously in 2018. We made up the difference by selling those exports to Europe, the Middle East, and countries in other regions, but China's obstinacy caused unnecessary headaches for itself and for US producers, who needed long-term contracts to secure financing for construction of expanded export facilities and their operations. Domestically, China's demand for all forms of fuel—coal, oil, and gas—was going through the roof, and we were among the top sources for imported LNG. Yet, to the extent that China wished to snub us in LNG sales, it could easily enough divert gas purchases to suppliers from countries with which it wished to curry favor, including Qatar, Nigeria, Russia, and Australia.

It was in everyone's interest for China to back off on its tariffs—not only on LNG, but on crude oil (where demand had doubled) and refined oil products (where it was expected to double by 2020). The only thing stopping both the US and Chinese economies from the progress and profits of this explosion in demand was the Chinese Communist Party. We were prepared to sell China all the energy it needed—energy that could fuel enormous economic growth *inside* China—if only the Chinese would let us.

Their massive need for coal gave them yet another reason to cooperate with us on energy trade. I conceived of a plan that I thought was sure to appeal to them involving high-efficiency, low-emissions (HELE) coal technology. At the time we were negotiating, at the end of 2017, China had (and has) one of the largest and dirtiest coal-fired power generation fleets in the world—more than 945 gigawatts to be exact, enough to power roughly 80 percent of the total electricity needs of the whole United States—and was pumping out more than 10 million kilotons of carbon dioxide into the atmosphere, making it the largest carbon emitter in the world. What is more, China was projected to create an additional 50 gigawatts of coal-fired power-generating capacity by the end of 2020.

My programming involved retrofitting pilot Chinese coal-fired power plants with US-manufactured HELE boilers and US high-thermal-efficiency coal. Based on the technical diligence and math, these projects would have cut operating expenses materially, even after taking into account the capital expenditure required for the retrofit, and would have reduced each plant's carbon footprint by not less than 25 percent. We proposed to help the Chinese to source suitable raw coal (either from us or from Australia), advanced machinery and technology to generate cheaper and cleaner power using a small part of their coal fleet they were (and still are) not seeking to decommission. We would help them with the retrofit, lower their energy prices, and create new jobs—all of which were vital to their economic engine. Not to mention they could reduce emissions materially and curry favor with the global community's demands for cleaner energy. For a nation determined to compete with and surpass the US as the global leader, you would have thought this was a no-brainer, but it was the exact opposite. For reasons known only to the Chinese, trade in energy commodities ultimately contributed only a very small piece toward reducing the trade deficit.

The massive trade deficit between the US and China grabbed the headlines, but it was not the only way in which the playing field was decidedly tilted in China's favor when President Trump first took office. Another major focus of our trade negotiations was on securing greater access to the massive Chinese financial services market for US banks and financial institutions. In this area, it was not the import and export of products and goods that suffered lopsided treatment, it was the ability of our banks, investment houses, asset managers, insurers, and credit rating agencies to market and sell their financial services and products in China. In short, while we had opened our arms to Chinese banks, Chinese investors, and Chinese participation in our markets, the Chinese had kept their arms firmly crossed and tightly locked.

Our goal was simple enough: Make sure everyone plays by the same rules of market access and open competition that we, and all of the G20, had accorded Chinese banks and financial institutions when entering our markets. Getting China to agree, however, was far from simple.

In our first discussions (and many others after that), the Chinese argued that they were unfairly accused. They were more than happy to welcome foreign banks and brokers into China, with just a few, "perfectly reasonable" conditions. Pull back the curtain, and you can see that these conditions were often impossible to fulfill. For instance, foreign banks were required to have multiples of the minimum capital requirements to operate in China compared to the requirements in any other free-market country. The US firms wishing to operate in China, of course, also faced a web of limitations on the types of business they could engage in and where in the Chinese market they were permitted to do business.

When we pointed all this out, the Chinese's next tactic was to complain that we had not allowed their banks into the US, so why should they allow ours into their country. We politely presented them with the facts, which told an entirely different story. Before 2005, China might have had a sliver of a case about its banks; only two Chinese banks had ever operated in the United States. But in 2005, the US banking authorities started approving Chinese banks at a brisk clip. Tracking the growth of loan assets of Chinese commercial banks operating in the United States told the whole story. In each year of the following decade, these loan assets grew exponentially—751 percent to be exact—from $17.3 billion in 2010 to $130 billion in 2015. This hardly smacks of regulatory limitations or market discrimination.

Our banks and financial service providers had plenty to offer China's financial market—product development, treasury management, system strengthening, operational efficiency, tons in the area of compliance and market building. The list was never-ending. The Chinese banking system had grown in leaps and bounds since market-opening reforms began in the late 1970s and early 1980s. But there was so much more ground to cover. Asset management was one good example where US (and other foreign) asset managers had much to offer the Chinese. The numbers at stake were off the charts.

At the time, the Chinese asset management industry had more than $15 trillion of assets under management, with the National Social Security Fund, China's national pension fund, representing a not small chunk of that total. With an aging population highly reliant on these retirement funds, effective asset management was (and still is) of paramount importance. Our asset managers, with more than a hundred years of relevant experience, could assist with much-needed industry reform, including asset class and manager diversification, as well as much-needed policy and regulatory reforms to ensure that China was meeting the great challenges of its rapidly aging society's increasing reliance on pension holdings with the most current and de-risked products, systems, and services. The same was true of every facet of banking and financial services.

Our proposals would have created greater market opportunity for our banks and financial services providers and would also have been highly beneficial to the Chinese market. We laid out numerous proposals for using our cutting-edge technology and know-how in the banking and financial services sector to help China. Let some of our firms be lead bond underwriters, and we can help to build more market depth and inject more competition into the market. Let us have licenses to be mutual fund custodians, and this will spur growth and efficiency in your mutual fund industry. Let us engage in a joint venture with one of your credit rating entities—and we can help you!

But the Chinese were simply unwilling to allow foreigners greater penetration into their state-owned economy. Everyone would have benefited, but overcoming centuries of protectionism was a daunting task.

While we went head-to-head on trade issues directly, we also pushed forward on three fronts outside of the trade negotiations. In all three venues, our message remained the same: We are done with endless meetings and hollow promises—we want results, and we mean business. So while our team of negotiators hammered out a trade deal, we also tackled:

- a complete overhaul of the US investment security regime operating under the Committee for Foreign Investment in the United States (CFIUS), and the Department of Commerce's actions against Chinese tech giant Huawei to protect telecom networks from national security threats;

- designating China as a "currency manipulator" and renewed US leadership in eliminating unfair export credit subsidies; and
- meaningful reform of Chinese issuers' access to the US capital markets.

In each case, our message was: It's a new day in this relationship, and we mean to do business in a very new way. And to win, we needed to think creatively.

Which is something that my life as a Chassidic man observing ancient traditions in an all-too-modern world had taught me to do. Consider, for example, the sardines.

The Silk home has always been open to everyone, from unaffiliated Jews to *heymishe* travelers. Our week revolves around Shabbos preparations, where everything is homemade—homebaked challah, gefilte fish, herring, overnight chicken soup using Bubby Friend's recipe, broiled chicken (with many different variations), two types of kugel (including an Asian-inspired kugel made of taro root), vegetables, and various baked desserts. But when I lived in Hong Kong, my family had to make accommodations. For example, I had to give up on the herring. *Oy!* In the beginning I'd ask friends to bring herring when they visited from New York or London. But that led to a most unfortunate event. A friend had arranged to bring a nice quantity of special herring from London. Imagine the consternation of neighboring passengers in business class on British Airways when one of the containers in my friend's hand luggage broke and started leaking in the overhead! After that I decided to improvise, and I started grilling locally sourced sardines in place of herring. You guessed it—sardines are still a staple at the Silk Shabbos table. And if we could substitute sardines for herring, surely we could find a new solution to the intractable problem of China trade.

New solutions were direly needed. China's game of artificially lowering prices on exports through government subsidies was a huge issue in both our overall trade imbalance and how China behaved in the international trade, investment, and financial markets. It was a stark violation of the letter and spirit of its obligations to the World Trade Organization. To add insult to injury, China stonewalled us through a record number of meetings of the international working group set up to address unfair subsidies of export credits, where the US and other countries raised objections to China's behavior. No matter how much we pressed the Chinese negotiators for transparency of the terms and conditions on which they provided export credits, no matter how strenuously we argued for a comprehensive application of export credit rules to financing of both goods and services, as well as adherence to basic rules of debt sustainability and oversight, the most they ever gave in reply was noncommittal rhetoric. They provided no details or timelines for any cooperation they pledged, and refused to abide by accepted rules setting out the limits to export credit subsidies.

An international working group had been trying to tackle the issue of unfair export credit subsidies for more than eight years through twenty in-person meetings. Europe and the rest of the developed world were equally sick of China's approach. Like us, they also suffered imbalances in trade and diminished exports. Several other countries joined our chorus to protest China's abuse of accepted norms in government subsidies of export credits. It was a big issue. At the time, China was the largest provider of export credits to benefit its exporters (and, as a natural consequence, to the detriment of its competition), of a magnitude of around 75 percent of all export credits provided by the G7 combined. With tiresome predictability, the Chinese contingent complained we were "singling them out," and repeated the accusation ad nauseam.

No one had ever stood up to the Chinese on export credit subsidies before. When it became clear that the working group discussions weren't going anywhere, we called their bluff. We simply stood up and said, "Fine. No more meetings." We caused a suspension of the group and cut off further meetings. The silence was deafening.

Our arguments for seeking more access to China's markets were based on sharing our experience and know-how to help both sides. But when it came to the naughty behavior of Chinese companies in US commercial and capital markets, it was no more Mr. Nice Guy. There were two serious issues at hand: first, the bad habit of Chinese companies stealing sensitive data and technology from their US partners; second, the nondisclosure and false disclosure of material financial information by Chinese companies listed on the US markets.

China's blatant disrespect for US intellectual property and cybersecurity was alarming—and legion. It was fond of hacking through firewalls, snooping on innovations, and stealing trade secrets and sensitive information—all so it could copy and sell them at a profit (or worse, such as feeding information to its military-industrial complex). Merely thinking about it aroused President Trump's indignation.

If the Chinese couldn't hack sensitive technology online, they seized it when those firms tried to offer their products to the Chinese market. Their policy on technology transfers made any attempt by a US firm to do business inside China a venture of extraordinary exposure and risk. The Chinese Communist Party fully intended, as it indicated in its Made in China 2025 economic agenda, to rob the West of its own innovations, and then compete (unfairly) in the world export market.

When we challenged the Chinese negotiators about technology transfers, they flatly denied it. I always admired Secretary Mnuchin's ability to keep his cool and be calmly assertive with them. At the 2018 trade meeting in Beijing, he told them, "You need to learn to respect our intellectual property. Our country has values and laws for it, and it's time you respect them and stop with the cybersecurity intrusions." Given half the chance, some others in the room might have turned up the thermostat by a few hundred degrees.

In numerous discussions and meetings, we warned our Chinese colleagues that this behavior would not be tolerated any longer. We signaled that the president was preparing to issue an executive order on the authority of Section 301 to restrict Chinese investment in sensitive US industries in order to stop the technology and IP theft.

As usual, the Chinese dragged their feet and bogged down negotiations. They argued that we were unfairly targeting them with limits on investment in sensitive sectors, limits we would not place on other foreign investors.

Rather than using an executive order, we found an even better way to combat the problem. In a rare display of bipartisanship, the House and Senate came together to pass the Foreign Investment Risk Review Modernization Act (FIRRMA) in August 2018. With the new reforms, CFIUS could now block any non-US firm from investing in US firms with sensitive data and IP. These rules applied to *all* foreign investment—not just Chinese—thus robbing the Chinese of any argument that they were being unfairly targeted or excluded. *Everyone* must play by the rules; that was the message—and now it had teeth.

As for the problem of backdoor listings on our market exchanges and circumventing disclosure requirements, all of which put our investors at unreasonable and needless risk, the president threatened to delist companies who didn't follow the rules.

The Chinese claimed their hands were tied—that revealing the data we sought was a violation of their "state secrets" laws, exposing them to punishment, imprisonment—even torture and death. "We respect your laws and your system, but you must understand that we have our own in China," they said. "We are not at liberty to disclose the financial footings of Chinese companies, and we cannot allow foreign accounting firms into China to audit them. Nor can we provide access to audit papers or reports prepared in China. If we do, we can be imprisoned or executed."

We were unfazed. "Sorry guys," we responded. "You can do whatever you want in China, but this is America, and if you want capital market access, you'll play by our rules, or you won't play at all." If they refused to comply—if the rules in their country forbade that—then they could pick up their marbles and go home; we weren't having it.

President Trump convened President's Working Group (PWG) to address the issue of nondisclosure and false disclosure by Chinese companies seeking to be listed on US stock markets. The PWG ultimately produced a report with far-reaching impact.

Issuance of the PWG report followed on the heels of passage of the 2020 bipartisan Holding Foreign Companies Accountable Act (HFCAA), which focused on the same issue of inadequate or false disclosure of foreign issues in the US markets, and was particularly focused on China. The HFCAA called for enhanced disclosures and a prohibition on trading of listed securities by issuers who flaunted the HFCAA's rules for three years running.

The PWG report was far more pointed than the HFCAA and covered all so-called non-cooperating jurisdictions (NCJs), of which China was a major offender. The PWG called for all NCJs to satisfy enhanced listing standards (including access to audit papers) and issuer disclosures. It recommended delisting more than 200 Chinese companies for failure to meet these new standards, removing them from the US stock market and protecting investors from undue harm. It was a rather large and blunt instrument, covering 195 companies with more than $1.7 trillion in global (US and non-US) listed stock market capitalization. The US view was that the policy approach was appropriately calibrated to the market disruption in 2011 from the precipitous drop in value among so many Chinese issuers in the United States.

With the passage of FIRRMA, the threatened delisting of problematic Chinese companies, the suspension of the international working group on export credits, President Trump's multiple volleys of tariffs, *and an entire year of tough trade deal negotiations*, the Chinese "ice" finally started to break up and the trade rivers to flow. For instance, we achieved significant progress with financial services. China dropped some of its restrictions, particularly on credit rating agencies and lead bond underwriters, as early as mid-2017, and started approving more of our banks and financial services providers to do business in China. We also saw bilateral trade starting to trend in the right direction.

The Chinese have a saying, *daqi wancheng* (大器晚成), "it takes a long time to build a big vessel" (think aircraft carrier!). There was no immediate transformation, and the improvements that did emerge were skewed by the COVID-19 pandemic. However, we were successful in righting the ship by creating the foundation for a more balanced relationship benefitting both sides, and encouraging China to be a more responsible member of the global trade, investment, and financial markets.

The capstone of three years of tough talk and tough action was the major new trade agreement we reached with China in late 2019. Like any comprehensive agreement, the final details represented a lot of horse trading, but the results were substantial. We finally convinced the Chinese to agree in writing to a large increase in US exports, which would slash the budget deficit in half over the next two years. We also successfully addressed several of our long-standing areas of concern—trade secrets, pharmaceutical IP, trademarks, and stronger enforcement against piracy and counterfeit goods—with meaningful, measurable reforms of everything from IP protection to technology transfers, to agriculture, to financial services and currency, to trade and dispute resolution.

The new trade agreement opened huge opportunities in banking, data, electronic payments, distressed debt management, insurance, securities, and fund management. With the new agreement, the process for dispute resolution improved. Instead of the onerous, often unenforceable process of WTO complaints and resolutions, and the seasonal indifference of other nations, we could now deal with imbalances and asymmetry directly. If China wanted to continue trading with the US, it would have to allow vigilant US oversight of its cooperation in resolving disputes or risk further US retaliation.

We were well on our way to a completely recast relationship that would have been favorable for all, including China, when the chaotic year of 2020 brought the agenda to an abrupt end. In my view, we succeeded on several fronts: First, we got China to take us seriously and show up to the negotiating table. Second, we forced the Chinese to forsake pageantries, pleasantries and puff pieces in favor of meaningful, concrete, and measurable agreements to protect and honor both nations. We reformed and passed our own laws, with wide bipartisan support, and enforced them rigorously. We experienced record economic growth and reduced inflation and unemployment, all despite the media brouhaha over the efficacy of tariffs and protectionism. We restored the president's role as head of state, *in the service of US interests* rather than foreign ones.

Unfortunately, the COVID-19 pandemic wreaked havoc on the global economy, and then the Biden administration decided to take us, and the world, in a decidedly different direction. With President Trump returning to the oval office, I am hopeful our work in the Trump 45 administration will serve as a blueprint in the Trump 47 administration for standing up to China in ways that are vital to guaranteeing America's national interests, and those of the entire free world.

Of course, Trump 45 faced diplomatic and trade issues much closer to home as well, in countries that sorely needed our help after years of neglect. The president tackled those with a similar America-first pragmatism, as you are about to read.

CHAPTER 6

RETAKING OUR PLACE IN THE WESTERN HEMISPHERE

It was 2018 and our second meeting with the delegation from Panama. The first meeting had not gone well.

Our intentions were noble: We sought to address the infrastructure and energy crisis facing emerging markets and developing economies across the globe. Our work would help to repair a landscape marred by crumbling bridges, roads, and tunnels; crippled by weak, inefficient, unreliable, and polluting power sources; and stunted by severe lack of private capital funding, overreliance on constrained government spending, and rampant government corruption.

We envisioned partnerships of a new kind, with any willing country. The US would provide expertise, advice, and best practices to redraw the landscape. Starting with countries in our own backyard, we would transform their approach to infrastructure; inaugurate a new era of clean, sustainable, reliable, and plentiful power sources; create and deepen markets; close the multitrillion-dollar funding gap; and restore vitality and independence to the local people. Along the way, we would unseat the bad actors who filled the funding vacuum over the previous eight years, shackling poor countries with burdensome debt and stripping them of their minerals and raw materials.

In short, we simply wanted to help Latin Americans raise expectations for life in their own countries. You turn on the tap, and out comes clean, potable water. You plug in a lamp, and it works. You need enough groceries to feed your family, and the shelves are stocked. You need to get to work, and fast, efficient, and cheap public transportation gets you there. We wanted a "new era" of sorts, similar to what we enjoy every time the US makes significant breakthroughs in areas like technology and medicine. We wanted them to enjoy clean, sustainable, reliable, and plentiful power sources; new and expanded markets; lots of private investment; and a renewed sense of vitality and independence at the local level.

Neglect during the previous administration created a vacuum in the Western Hemisphere, which left the door open for China and Russia. When we analyzed the trade agreements and partnerships they formed, it was clear: Our neighbors in Latin America got the short end of the stick when they did business with those countries. Our intention was to outperform them—to make the burdensome debt and win-lose deals offered by Beijing and Moscow unattractive compared with what we could offer.

President Trump saw a *huge* problem and charged us with fixing it. The Summit of the Americas in Argentina was approaching rapidly, and it was an opportunity for the United States to regain its place as the leading partner in the region. We could reverse eight years of neglect and make it difficult for China and Russia to operate in our neighborhood and form relationships that threatened our security and hobbled the countries they purported to help. We could help dozens of countries to become stronger, healthier, wealthier, energy independent, environmentally conscious, productive, and safe for all their citizens. And, of course, we could serve important US interests. We could increase exports of energy and equipment. We could create new and attractive environments for US developers and financiers—who would, in turn, create new American jobs to move their projects forward. It was a win-win-win. If you've heard the saying "Everything comes in threes," this was a fine example of it—and so was our strategic outline, at least when viewed at the thirty-thousand-foot level. I could clearly see three pillars to the stool of a revitalized, cooperative, and allied Western Hemisphere.

- Capital pipelines—the sum total of shovel-ready projects. With the right amount of up-front homework, stronger regulatory oversight, and the correct "packaging" of the deals, we could put a lot of people and money to work very quickly by creating robust pipelines of bankable infrastructure projects.

- Capital bridges—developing economy debt markets with greater depth and liquidity and longer tenors (repayment time frames) that were accessible to US investors with a clear pattern they could recognize easily, along with bells and whistles to protect against the ordinary risks of emerging markets. Fortunately, we had the blueprint for this—we had already been doing it in the US for a long time.

- Capital enablers—stronger state-owned utilities and energy providers. The spread of civil, industrialized, and competitive nationhood rests on these two categories. Water, power, high-speed internet, and natural gas all require competent management and operation, as well as adequate funding, to keep pace with the times and expectations of the people they serve.

If we could create growth and positive outcomes in all three of these areas, our partners would not bother answering when Beijing and Moscow came to call.

I had only been on the job a few weeks when Mauricio Claver-Carone, counselor to Under Secretary for International Affairs David Malpass, asked me to join a meeting. It was there that I met John Rader, who'd been sent to us by Jared Kushner. Jared was spearheading key parts of the Western Hemisphere plan, and dispatched John to Treasury to explore options for the Summit of the Americas. That led him to me. With thirty years of experience structuring, planning, negotiating, and financing energy and infrastructure deals worth billions of dollars around the world, I was Treasury's point person on infrastructure finance. I'd already pitched David and Mauricio on the advantages of using infrastructure finance at Treasury, and Mauricio saw this as the perfect opportunity to test the strategy.

We sat around a large table in Mauricio's room with a huge Rand McNally map of the world that took up most of the wall. John framed the request: As the Summit of the Americas approached, President Trump wanted to announce a bold new program for the region, led by the United States. "So," John asked, "what's the plan?"

I glanced at the map of the world on the wall behind us, and it immediately came to me.

"It's simple. We go for global domination."

I was joking, of course. And I wasn't. As we say in Yiddish, *In yeden vertl ligt a bisel emes* (In every joke, there is a bit of truth). My overstated, flippant response contained more than a bit of truth.

Capital-intensive infrastructure is a game changer, especially when financed by private capital. We assist in building infrastructure that is key to economic growth and stability, and unleash US capital markets—the deepest in the world—to achieve that task by ensuring that the projects we bring along are in line with market requirements. At the same time, we also help our friends build their own markets for the future. If the growth side of a new infrastructure finance program led to widespread increased prosperity, keeping the bad guys out would take care of itself.

Easier said than done. We faced a long list of multidimensional challenges. Which policies and programs are currently effective? Why? What's not working? Why? What are the current policies or programs that promote private sector investment infrastructure? What are the energy and infrastructure goals in the market? Once we identify the appropriate investment projects and programs, which do we prioritize?

To update a country's infrastructure is, in some cases, like updating your computer from the early DOS operating system to the latest version of Microsoft Windows. There's no developing just one link in the chain unless it can function with the others; it's a giant web of interdependence. What happens to one link affects the next, and improvements must follow a sequence. It's easy, despite the noblest of intentions, to cause more problems than you solve.

No man is an island in the grand energy and infrastructure value chains. Without pipelines and oil and gas export terminals, you can't convert resources into energy. If there's no facility to convert them, like power plants, investors will shy away because the runway to returns is too long and littered with obstacles. But even if you can generate energy, you need the wires and relay stations to transmit it to population centers, often across miles of countryside.

On it goes: You need trucks to provide goods, services, and construction equipment to lay the wires and build a station to bring energy to an underserved area. Those trucks require solid roads, bridges, and tunnels on which to travel. To build (or rebuild) the roads, bridges, and tunnels, you need quick access to large amounts of money with small amounts of red tape. In turn, that triggers the need for an advanced banking system, a stable currency, and social and political order.

Inside their own borders, our partner countries lacked the speed and funds to improve their infrastructure. Their governments couldn't finance projects of this size and scope, and the banking systems lacked the maturity and sophistication to support debt for more than a few years. Most of the infrastructure and energy projects we identified would require debt tenors of twelve to seventeen years.

Reading this, do you estimate *decades* to successfully complete it? The task before us was daunting.

That's probably why the first meeting with the Panamanians hadn't gone so well. Mauricio and colleagues in the West Hemisphere office at Treasury had paved the way for the meeting, calling Dulcidio de la Guardia, Panama's minister of finance, to tell him we had a new program that we'd like to discuss with his team. He agreed to chat during the spring meetings of the World Bank and International Monetary Fund, where you can find every foreign government finance minister and his grandmother twice a year. Dulcidio enjoyed a distinguished commercial law career prior to joining government. He was well connected and well regarded. I expected him to jump at the opportunity with open arms. It didn't go quite as I'd hoped.

Our first meeting was with Dulcidio and two members of his delegation—relatively small and low key. After a brief exchange of pleasantries, I had the stage. I launched into my shpiel about how we could cooperate to pour US investment into Panama and create win-win-win outcomes. I explained the big-picture vision for seven key areas of Panama's infrastructure that could attract as much as $15 billion in investment over a five-year period.

I looked up from my notes to a sea of disbelief and unease. They were polite, but the faces of Dulcidio's younger colleagues said it all:

"Did he just say what I think he said—that he can fix our country's intractable funding problem?" "What is this guy talking about?" "This is way too complicated." "This is not going to be good for my job." "Is this guy speaking Martian?"

Ever so politically astute, Dulcidio was thinking: "This is a great idea, but it's going to kill some other political initiative. The president will not like this."

We had our work cut out for us. The Panamanians were still expecting the hollow, discarded promises of the previous administration. We had to make clear that we could be trusted to follow through. One of the best ways to do that was by explaining the stark differences between the philosophy and methods of the Obama and Trump teams.

We launched into the PR stage in earnest, talking to friends in the Presidencia and the energy secretary's office in Panama. We showed them what we had in mind, how we could help them and how we could work with local businesses and government officials. We walked them through the private investment concept and assured them we could bring in deep pools of billion-dollar funding, at reasonable rates and terms. At every turn, we took pains to show how private investment was a more stable long-term approach, rather than relying on raw deals from China and Russia that left them debt-ridden and poorer.

The programming spoke for itself; we just needed to get back to basics and explain how, at every stage, this would benefit *everyone* involved. But if it was to be a deal between friends, we would need a more intimate setting than a sidebar chat during a World Bank session. What could be better than a lingering discussion over a quiet home-cooked meal? I organized the first of many dinners for the Panamanians at my residence in Washington, a truly beautiful landmark home in Kalorama. The food was home cooked, well presented and plentiful, as was my home-infused vodka.

Slowly, the ice began to thaw.

"Food first" was one of my favorite mottos for diplomacy. I even treated Secretary Mnuchin to my food-first approach. Each year, I would bring a number of my wife's homemade honey cakes to friends at work just before Rosh Hashanah. I would usually bring more than twenty in all for distribution in the Treasury Building and at the White House. Distributing a large number of honey cakes at the White House was a bit tricky given logistics and tight security! As time went on, the folks at reception at the main door of the West Wing got to know when the Jewish holidays fell.

One year, David Malpass and I had a small meeting with the secretary in his small conference room, directly off his office, just a few days before Rosh Hashana. At this particular meeting, one of the regional deputy assistant secretaries attended with one of his senior economists in order to provide expert views on the issues that we would be discussing. David and I were on one side of the secretary; the other two flanked the secretary on the other side. The staff economist was going to be doing most of the talking since he had prepared the bulk of research and analysis for the meeting.

We waited for the secretary to enter. After he did, and after all the formalities, he looked up and signaled that he was ready for the meeting to begin. Under all other circumstances, David would have introduced the topic and the staff economist would have commenced the report. But this was not just any day. It was the day that I'd brought my wife's honey cake for the secretary. Before David had the opportunity to start, I jumped in and said, "If there is no objection, I would like to start with a very important matter of state." And with that, the eyes of the secretary, David, and all others focused straight on me. I went on to say, "My wife has instructed me to deliver this to you." I then took the very nicely wrapped honey cake and pushed it toward the secretary. He immediately lit up. I was expecting a kick under the table from David, which thankfully I did not get, and our colleagues across the table chuckled with no small bit of relief.

We commenced the meeting. The economist started to provide a detailed report of his analysis and findings, but it soon became abundantly clear that Secretary Mnuchin was wholly focused on the honey cake in front of him and not on the report. The economist persisted with his report. After a few rather long minutes, the secretary said, "This cake looks so good that I would really like to take one of Andrew Johnson's knives and tuck into it." We chuckled a bit, I got a few stern looks, and my colleague continued with his report. After another couple of minutes, the secretary interrupted and said, "You'll have to excuse me. I must go get a knife from my office so that we can enjoy this cake." He left the room, walked into his office, and returned with a knife in less than a minute. Everybody got a slice.

Only after we had all eaten did the staff economist get his chance to present his report—and not surprisingly, the report went down even better on stomachs full of honey cake.

Persuasion takes many forms, and I used all the spices in the cupboard to sell our America Crecé (Growth in the Americas) initiative. Our second meeting with the Panama delegation took place in the majestic Main Treasury Building. It's the oldest functioning federal office building in the country, and so rich with history that author Pamela Scott wrote an entire book about it.

I don't recall whether the Panamanians were impressed or not, but I like to think that the process of entering the building made an impact. It took time to simply get them all through the front door. Security was tight, and one tiny error in a passport number or birthdate could cause a delay of up to an hour. Once they were in, I took them for a quick tour of the Cash Room, a grand hall meant to resemble an all-marble traditional Italian palazzo. It's more than sixty feet long and more than thirty feet wide, with vaulted ceilings rising above thirty feet. The room made its debut as the venue for the inauguration of President Ulysses S. Grant in 1869.

On the way to our meeting room, the Panamanians viewed exquisite artwork made of old bills and coins printed by the Bureau of Engraving and Printing, and portraits of all the former Treasury secretaries. We met in a large office with a very large conference table. Everything took place according to strict protocol, with a little bit of political theater. Everybody had assigned places and seats and their talkers—except for me. I just presented great opportunities—simple, basic, truthful, practical.

I could see the wheels turn and heads begin to nod as I discussed the details and parameters of our plan. The Panamanians began to engage, asking questions about how we would choose which initiatives to pursue. They were curious about how we could estimate the value of a certain project and forecast in dollars how much investment it would attract. You could tell—they had moved from distrust to hope.

When we broke for coffee, Jennifer La Rocca approached me. She was one of Panama's senior officials from the Ministry of Economy and Finance. I said to her, "I'm glad to see so much enthusiasm today, after our last meeting. I felt like I was talking to a brick wall last time we met."

"Well," said Jennifer, "you know what they were all thinking? It's the same question I have for you today: Where the hell have you guys been?"

She was right. We'd turned our backs on our western neighbors for eight long years. In his 2009 address at the Fifth Summit of the Americas, President Obama spoke of "dynamism," "equal partnership," "our common prosperity," "a new partnership on energy," and "security and liberty."[1] The words sounded inspiring, but they turned out to be empty promises.

Not surprisingly, China swooped in, offering to "help" many of these smaller, poorer countries to rebuild and modernize. Unfortunately, most Chinese "cooperation" involved pillaging the country's natural resources and raw materials. China focused only on infrastructure that was strategically valuable to Chinese military access, and offered financing that crippled the country with unsustainable debt loads and terms. It was a redux of the days of the Soviet Union's "client" states, such as Cuba and East Germany: A handful of elites got rich; average citizens got raped, pillaged, and plundered; and the country was in worse straits, economically and militarily, than before.

The Panamanians had good reason to be wary.

---

1   "Remarks to the Summit of the Americas in Port of Spain, Trinidad and Tobago," in *Administration of Barack Obama, April 17, 2009, https://www.govinfo.gov/content/ pkg/PPP-2009-book1/pdf/PPP-2009-book1-doc-pg511.pdf.*

To regain trust, we had to convince Central and South America that our goal was to empower and uplift them as partner countries. We also had to demonstrate that we could do it in an honest and sustainable way. Only then could our partners become powerful economic players, valuable allies, and sound trading partners. The true path to a strong Western Hemisphere lies where it always has—in healthy economies, strong financial markets, and strategic cooperation.

After months of presenting, discussing, revising, and fine-tuning, we were ready to publicly unveil the plan. David Malpass, then Treasury under secretary for international affairs (who went on to serve as president of the World Bank), would give the speech. As the day of presentation drew near, one issue remained: What would we call it?

I remember walking into the under secretary's reception area, just as David and Mauricio emerged from David's office, still engaged in a heated discussion.

"I'm not sure," David said.

"Why? It's perfect!" replied Mauricio.

David held the paper copy of his speech out to me and said, "Read this. What do you think of the name?"

A few lines into the speech, I noticed the name for the plan: America Crecé. It's Spanish for "Americas grow."

I was worried that some people wouldn't understand the Spanish. I looked up at David, and then at Mauricio. Eager to find agreement, I innocently asked, "Why not *Amerika vakst*?"

Flabbergasted, they looked at me as if I'd just sprouted antlers and exclaimed in tandem, "What?!"

"That's how you say 'Americas grows' in Yiddish," I explained. "It's my favorite language in the world."

I made my point—only people who spoke and understood the language would grasp the meaning. But since the majority of people whom we sought to persuade were native Spanish speakers, we agreed that the cultural significance of a Spanish name was worth the risk. We stuck with America Crecé.

David formally introduced the initiative on February 2, 2018, in a speech at the Center for Strategic and International Studies. He explained:

> Growth in energy and infrastructure, both in the US and abroad, is a high-priority Administration objective, and critical to broader growth. With that in mind, we are developing a multi-part approach that will promote US exports of energy and energy infrastructure; attract investments in the region in the areas of energy and infrastructure, with new opportunities for US businesses to participate; and catalyze private capital for the financing of these exports and investment projects....
>
> The purpose is to build open, competitive, resilient, reliable, and efficient energy markets, while expanding US exports of energy and energy infrastructure. Affordable energy will stimulate economic growth and strengthen regional political and energy security. Country frameworks within this initiative will vary with the host economy and the opportunities. Some countries are net energy exporters, but could benefit from a framework agreement that would expand US investment in power generation, transmission, refined products, and energy infrastructure, as well as other infrastructure.

We launched America Crecé to great fanfare in the palatial Indian Treaty Room of the Eisenhower Executive Office Building on December 17, 2019. Afterward, we held a private-sector event with more than three hundred senior business leaders hosted by the US Chamber of Commerce. Several senior US officials addressed the audience, including senior representatives of more than twenty governments in the Latin American and Caribbean region. The US speakers included Treasury Secretary Mnuchin, Secretary of Commerce Wilbur Ross, National Security Advisor Robert O'Brien, National Economic Council Director Larry Kudlow, and Senior Advisor Jared Kushner. Secretary Mnuchin summed up the program in his remarks:

> This initiative is a whole-of-government effort that expands upon work Treasury has been leading over the past two years. We are working with many of our allies and trading partners in Latin America and the Caribbean to institute pro-growth reforms, and to foster private sector investment in energy and infrastructure. The United States' economy was built on the strength of open, competitive markets that stimulate private sector investment. Competitive markets can deliver the same growth and strength to our partners today. We estimate that the infrastructure needs in Latin America and the Caribbean are $1.1 trillion over the next five years. While the need is great, the supply of private capital willing to invest is now at an all-time high globally.
>
> America Crecé seeks to focus that capital for infrastructure and energy investments where there are tremendous opportunities. We will share our financ-

ing market expertise to identify critical infrastructure investment opportunities and propose enabling reforms that will attract private sector investors. We are drawing on all of our tools—technical assistance, financial market structuring, commercial advocacy, and private capital formation—to support private sector solutions. Our model will enable private capital markets to create growth and reduce government and taxpayer burdens. Unlike projects that rely on subsidized lending through state-controlled policy banks, we are proposing a more sustainable path that avoids burdensome public sector borrowing, increases transparency, and drives down costs through competition. We are already seeing results for our partner countries. With today's launch, we reaffirm our commitment to the America Crecé vision and build on our progress. We look forward to developing even more partnerships to deliver greater economic growth throughout the region.

From the outset, the two guiding principles for America Crecé were growth and security.

Growth meant helping partner countries to grow by opening and expanding free markets, trade, and enterprise. We were confident we could spark meaningful progress within each of our partner countries—and growth for the US, through opportunities for US corporations and financiers.

We could also look forward to stronger *security* benefits: vibrant local economies and infrastructure would help every country (including ours) to protect itself against outside aggressors and predators. It would build the foundation for the Western

Hemisphere to remain a stable and formidable presence from a geopolitical perspective. It would discourage ambitious leaders in places like Beijing and Moscow from pushing the envelope.

We targeted energy and infrastructure because they are the two primary engines for growing an economy. If you have energy and infrastructure, you can build markets, commerce, and industry, and create jobs. Additionally, they require huge amounts of capital to kickstart, which is why they're such bottlenecks for development. Our financial help was essential.

Infrastructure, to put it mildly, is capital intensive. The global funding gap between current growth requirements and actual spending trends to meet global energy and infrastructure needs is a staggering $1.6 trillion a year. Emerging markets and developing economies, which have the hardest time attracting private capital, require more than half of this eye-popping amount. The good news? We have the money to meet that demand. If you combine the total net value of global institutional assets like pension funds, insurance companies, foundations, and sovereign wealth companies, as much as *$120 trillion* is available. There is, simply put, a mismatch between where the money is and where it needs to be. When you look at where those giant institutions invest their wealth, foreign infrastructure represents a pittance—only 0.44 percent—of total debts held. If we applied just 2 percent of North American pension funds, we could reduce roughly a quarter of the present gap. If we applied 20 percent of those assets, we'd bridge the gap completely by 2030.

In other words, private capital markets have more than enough money to solve this problem.

It looked, to paraphrase Bogey, like the beginning of a beautiful relationship. Not only did we have the money, but our partners needed it more than ever. Projects need financing, investors need projects. Why the gap? Essentially, the structure and terms of most projects simply do not meet the investment criteria of these huge capital pools. Ironically, there was not only a financing gap—there was a shortage of bankable projects. Furthermore, the woeful condition of most state-owned utilities usually left them prone to nonstarter status in the eyes of US investors. To add to the irony, most of these countries' SOEs also function as gate-keepers and controllers of *all* energy and infrastructure projects. You couldn't have one without the other, nor could you have the other without the one.

Reluctance is natural, if you don't know how to look under the hood and solve underlying problems. Almost every country south of the US border had a track record of instability, which we knew would be a concern for any educated investor or fund manager. The most literate among them would quickly point to a host of risks. The money was devalued. It was difficult to convert to and from US dollars. Prices were inflated. The supply chains were primitive. Logistics (such as delivery) were challenging. Local laws were inconsistent, or applied inconsistently. Political upheaval was common. On and on it went, which is why the institutional groups we wanted to involve developed the habit of shying away in the first place.

For the average person, the situation might have looked bleak. But if you've spent decades mastering all the different ways to put these kinds of deals together, you relished the opportunity. I was excited. I *knew* we could make this work.

Most people's eyes would glaze over if they heard the term "limited recourse project finance." If Joe Homeowner agrees to finance terms, he risks losing his shirt if he can't repay the loan. If he defaults on his mortgage, the bank reclaims the house, and he's on his own with a bad mark on his credit score. In my world, we call that "*full* recourse project finance."

With limited recourse lending, the borrower and lender negotiate an acceptable level of risk for both parties. Usually, this includes long-term project contracts with a long-term revenue stream. They work according to a firm budget, control against cost overruns, and set benchmarks for timeliness and quality of delivery. Wherever there's more control and less risk, both parties benefit—and the project can move forward.

To bridge both the funding gap and the project pipeline gap, we had to do three things: help our partner countries build robust and attractive pipelines; create wider, more accessible paths for investors to bankroll them; and strengthen or revitalize their state-owned utilities. America Crecé used project finance principles to multiply on-ramps for partner countries while broadening the base of opportunities for institutional investors.

By way of example: In just two years, America Crecé catalyzed more than $2.455 billion in private-sector investment in Panama, providing more than thirty-five thousand jobs in a relatively small country. We helped the country to secure $1.2 billion for a gas-to-power project, plus another $500 million to refinance its electric utility, Empresa de Transmisión Eléctrica SA (ETESA). That saved the Panamanians more than $58 million in debt service. We supported an ambitious micro- and mini-grid development program, and two gas-to-power projects critical to the transition to clean energy for the region. As a result, we displaced the Chinese from two huge projects and supplanted them with American companies.

And yet, once the groundwork of strategy and foreign PR began to resonate, there was another daunting task: marshaling, coordinating, and mobilizing authorities in ten separate US agencies to implement the program. If you think of constructing a sky-scraper, the "foundation" of America Crecé was rebuilding trust and confidence with our partners and coming up with a plan to encourage substantial investment by large institutions. Now, we needed to deploy federal agencies as consultants to help with the dizzying array of tasks and challenges in the actual construction of the building.

Our team was a well-oiled and effective machine that served as a trusted financial advisory "firm" to foreign government partners. This firm drew specialties and skills from the Departments of the Treasury, State, Commerce, Energy, Transportation, and Interior. We also incorporated the US Agency for International Development (USAID), the US International Development Finance Corporation (DFC), the Export-Import Bank of the United States (EXIM), and the US Trade and Development Agency (USTDA).

It was definitely in everyone's interest to improve infrastructure "in the moment." If your local bridge is about to collapse, it's comforting to know that civil authorities have the money and the manpower to repair or replace it. However, we didn't want to stop with short-term fixes. We took the view that one hundred years from now, the Western Hemisphere will still have rival and competitor countries as well as shared security objectives. Our program, therefore, had to address issues of long-term financing as well as large-scale project viability. At the same time, we had to address the specific, often unique, challenges and limitations of the partner country itself.

Fortunately, I had plenty of experience bringing new concepts to wary recipients. Just consider the complicated task of building a *sukkah* in Hong Kong.

Autumn in Hong Kong is quite different from fall in New York, but one thing never changes, no matter where we Jews live:

Five days after the highest holy day of Yom Kippur, we celebrate a weeklong festival called *Sukkot* (*Sukkos* in Yiddish). The word can be translated as "booths" or "tents," and hearkens back to the Exodus of the Jewish people from Egypt, when our ancestors camped in tents on their journey to the land of Israel. For most Jews, that means it's time to build a sukkah, an impermanent outdoor structure. On one occasion, my family had recently moved into a new apartment building in Hong Kong. Virtually no one has a backyard in Hong Kong, and our balcony, like all others in high-rise apartment buildings, was directly under the balcony of the floor above, rendering it unfit under Jewish law for our sukkah since it was not open to the sky. I had to get creative, so I built our sukkah in a swapped car space. The slot was completely hidden from plain view and tucked in a space only accessible to the one car that could be parked there, with nothing at all on top of it. I crossed my fingers and hoped that no one would bat an eyelid at it.

Well, that didn't last very long. People noticed immediately, and I felt more like Noah building the ark: "What is this thing?" "What are these strange religious observances next to the parking lot?" "What are these oddball Westerners doing, holding food while looking pensively at the rain?" It never occurred to anyone that we were simply waiting for the rain to abate. We explained everything to one of the elders of the building, who ultimately prevailed on the opposing tenants to be more understanding of our position.

The following year, however, it got a little more serious. I submitted a request to maintain the sukkah, and proposed a swap of car spaces for ten days so that the sukkah would be hidden from plain view. The management seemed indifferent and complacent, and my request prompted a noncommittal letter to the managing agent. The letter said there was no objection per se, but referred the matter to the building committee. The other parking-space tenant did not respond to our request at all. The managing agent later told us that one of our neighbors had expressed vehement opposition to another sukkah.

Meanwhile, the clock was ticking closer and closer to *yontif* (Yiddish for "the holiday"). I made calls to the managing agent and held meetings with each member of the committee. Then I made *more* calls to the managing agent, and we had more meetings. No one could give a straight answer or offer guidance, and no one seemed remotely interested in humanitarian, societal, religious, or just plain neighborly kindness. Finally, at 8 p.m. on *eruv Sukkos*, the day before *Sukkot* began, we received a letter rejecting our request and threatening legal action if we proceeded. There was one ray of hope—the committee might reconsider if we delivered a written promise to refrain from filing lawsuits if anything went wrong with the sukkah. We submitted what they wanted—but still did not receive a reply, favorable or otherwise.

The moment of truth arrived. A few hours before Sukkot, I started to build our sukkah. I finished well before it was time to light the candles and start the celebration. We began our Sukkot observance not knowing if or when the building might remove the sukkah. After all, you can't really "hide" them—look up YouTube videos of sukkahs in Brooklyn apartment buildings, and you'll see what I mean. We proceeded with the evening and daytime meals on the first day of yontif—albeit with a heightened feeling of spiritual and physical bonding to our sukkah.

Then another threat emerged—the weather. Two weeks prior, Hong Kong had been ravaged by the worst typhoon in sixteen years (a Number 10 typhoon signal—the most severe weather signal). Word arrived that another typhoon was set to hit us

Saturday night. What could we do? I imagined the *schach* (our sukkah roof made of bamboo mats) being ripped off and the sukkah itself spinning through the air, perhaps with us inside it, and landing on some poor, unassuming pedestrian on the road below. *Oy ve!* We passed the night on pins and needles. Thankfully, the sukkah proved stronger than I thought, and the typhoon was not nearly as treacherous as predicted. We did not find anyone pinned under the sukkah the next the morning, and the building management also stayed at bay, allowing us to complete our holiday in peace.

If I could build a sukkah in Hong Kong that withstood suspicion, opposition, apathy, building committees, and mistrust—not to mention a typhoon—I reasoned that we could gently push through the mistrust and disconnect that the Obama administration had fomented in the Western Hemisphere. I also had no fear of the differences in infrastructure or economic climates between countries like the US and Canada and emerging economies like Panama or the Dominican Republic. We knew we could overcome bad blood *and* bad conditions. It would just take a little more effort than previous administrations had been willing or able to exert.

We gave the multifaceted plans we helped each country to create a name: Framework to Strengthen Infrastructure Finance.

A typical framework focused on five key goals: (1) using "limited recourse" financing to attract private capital, (2) streamlining the red tape and timeframe of securing approvals and start-dates funding, (3) advising government partners on how they could make their state-owned utilities stronger financially, (4) improving and implementing bidding and procurement processes, and (5) developing domestic financial markets.

At the same time, we kept our eye on providing beneficial outcomes for US investors and businesses. America Crecé was a boon for American energy exporters and financiers, who supplied natural resources and financial management and oversight. We tapped American technology companies to deliver expertise and outfit the partner countries with modern tools. The loans that paid the freight of these projects, in turn, appealed to US asset managers, who purchased them to add to other investment portfolios.

In a nutshell, America Crecé exported to Latin America the financial principles that made North America financially strong and independent. It taught public utility managers how to run their agencies in a balanced, growth-oriented way. It structured infrastructure and energy projects in ways that encouraged substantial institutional and private investment. It aimed for independence and long-term sustainability—for everyone, not just the US. By conservative estimates, we expected to unleash as much as $100 billion in Latin America and the Caribbean, and more than $500 billion in Asia-Pacific, over the next three to five years. With even a modest rate of return, we had reason to be optimistic.

CHAPTER 7

PRAGMATIC SOLUTIONS IN ACTION

As we embarked on implementing America Crecé we dove into a multitude of technical, legal, and logistical details. Not surprisingly, given the international flavor of the work, there was also a healthy serving of political theater, with an occasional dollop of humor. One such memorable evening occurred in the Dominican Republic.

I was part of a small US delegation to South America, led by Adam Boehler, who served as chief executive officer of the DFC. Adam joined the government after a successful career in venture capital and healthcare. He initially held a senior position at the Department of Health and Human Services. Later, he led the newly reconstituted and recapitalized DFC, the US development finance arm, as well as Operation Warp Speed during the pandemic.

It was close to the end of the term, but there was still a ton of work to do, especially in the wake of the worst of COVID-19. Adam invited me to join him on a mission to the Caribbean and Central America in October 2020. We were to visit five countries in three days: Guyana, Suriname, Jamaica, Haiti, and finally, the Dominican Republic. On the first day, we covered Suriname and Guyana, ending in dinner with Guyana's President Irfan Ali and Vice President Bharrat Jagdeo. We left Guyana in the early morning for a short hop to Jamaica, where we met Prime Minister Andrew Holness and several members of his cabinet, including my good friend, Finance Minister Nigel Clarke. Our leg in Haiti was very pressured. We touched down in the early afternoon, had a formal event at the US embassy, did a factory tour, and rushed back to the airport to make it out before the sundown takeoff curfew.

And so we arrived in the Dominican Republic, our final stop, where US embassy staff immediately whisked us away in a motorcade to a grand dinner with President Luis Abinader.

The Palacio Nacional came into view. Designed by Italian architect Guido D'Alessandro, it looked every bit of the neoclassical European palace that Rafael Leónidas Trujillo Molina meant it to be. Trujillo was the Dominican Republic's not-so-kind ruler for more than three decades. One of the Dominican Republic's architectural treasures, the national palace houses the offices of the president and vice president, as well as a number of palatial ceremonial halls. It is topped with a dome more than 110 feet high supported by eighteen columns, and boasts nearly 200,000 square feet of usable space. As we approached, rich and radiant pink lights—signifying Breast Cancer Awareness Month—cast a majestic glow on the huge stone steps that led up to a portico lined with big marble pillars. It was grand, regal, and ostentatious—designed to impress. As we pulled up, torrential rain began. Just pouring down in buckets. Before we could get out of our cars to race inside, an entourage of palace staff with umbrellas rushed down the steps to escort us into the building.

We entered the palace, and the president greeted us. He proudly led us on a tour through highlights of the building, including the Hall of the Caryatids, where a scene from *The Godfather II* was filmed. Then we attended a formal state dinner in the most majestic hall. The ceilings were vaulted, thirty to forty feet high, dripping with beautiful marble. There was a long table in the middle of the room, which seated more than thirty people on each side. On one side sat the president, vice president, minister of foreign affairs, minister of finance, and a slew of other ministers as far as the eye could see. On the other side was our delegation, including Adam and me.

Everyone made speeches—President Abinader, then Adam, and then the ministers of foreign affairs and finance. Our ambassador spoke. It's all part of the ritual. I turned to Adam, and asked, "Would you mind if I said a few words?" I was not slated to speak and thus did not have any remarks cleared. But Adam knew that I had crafted the program, negotiated the terms, and made the deal that he would sign the next morning, and he was very easy with protocol. To the consternation of State Department colleagues, Adam gave me the green light.

I took the microphone and delivered the following short remarks:

> Mr. President, our Jewish sages teach us to thank our hosts first, and I must thank you for the extraordinary reception, in this majestic room, and for arranging a kosher meal for me. Mr. President, we've just finished our Jewish high holiday season. There are four festivals in this season. The period begins with apprehension, introspection, and a fear of the judgment that occurs on the first two festivals. And we go from an overwhelming feeling of repentance or fear into a series of two holidays which mark relief of the judgments that have been sealed and executed in the celestial spheres and end with joyous celebrations.

At the very end of all four holidays, we recite the prayer for rain. Since we started as an agrarian society, rain is meant, in our tradition, to be a sign for growth and for wealth. Mr. President, we are here to sign an agreement between our two governments under our programming called America Crecé, "the Americas Grow," which will assist our two countries to realize growth together. So not only do I commend you for the room and the reception and the meal, but I gotta tell you, you really pulled out all the stops when you arranged for all of that profuse rain that greeted us on our way in. Well done, Mr. President!

Each country we partnered with presented a unique set of challenges based on its energy and infrastructure landscape. No matter where we looked, we found problems that needed solutions, and every reason to provide the support the countries needed. To simplify this "capital pipelines" part of our strategy, we identified three main categories of projects in virtually every country that could—if properly structured—attract private capital and meet each partner's economic and security needs.

In each country, you could spot the opportunity to improve efficiency and reliability in their existing, *conventional* energy system. We found plenty of inefficient thermal power plants that we could convert to modern gas-fired or high-efficiency, low-emission coal. Countries with ambitious renewable programs and electricity shortages were prime candidates for utility-scale, natural-gas-fired power plants. We helped countries lucky enough to have a surplus of fossil fuel resources to explore for and produce upstream oil and gas. We also helped them build receiving terminals, pipelines, and storage facilities necessary to support production and demand.

The investment potential for some of these projects was huge. Take Vietnam: Based on the potential of its conventional energy programming, we projected as much as $9.25 billion in energy trade, and $20 billion to $29 billion worth of shovel-ready opportunities over a two- to three-year period. Those numbers would shrink the trade deficit with Vietnam and stir plenty of market activity. Moreover, every time we found a good investment opportunity, we also found an average potential of 25 percent reduction in carbon emissions.

Even small Caribbean countries held promise for return on investment and reduction in carbon footprint. Most of the region relies on diesel as a primary source of energy. But diesel is expensive, inefficient, and dirty (it has a relatively high carbon footprint). If we could help the Caribbean market transition to natural gas, it would be cleaner and it could total as much as $3 billion in investment opportunities.

There were some obstacles. The geography of island countries made it challenging to share infrastructure costs like on the mainland. The technological and political hurdles of displacing entrenched diesel economies and supply chains are formidable, but they're certainly worth a try in the interest of long-term, environmentally friendly growth. As we saw it, America Crecé offered two unique benefits to small island countries. First, it alleviated a major constraint to growth: the world's highest electricity prices. Second, and of greater importance, it enhanced energy security, stability, and resilience for countries under constant threat of extreme weather events, like hurricanes. The Caribbean countries embraced several of the proposals we put forward.

One of the reasons why America Crecé was so successful was our ability to tailor each framework to suit the partner country. Our team was pragmatic and resourceful. When we saw an opportunity, we grabbed it, and when there wasn't an obvious one, we created it. My background had prepared me extensively for maximizing projects right in front of me, and finding new solutions when the landscape looked barren. Like, say, a Hong Kong prison.

During my twelve years in Hong Kong, I often assisted members of our Jewish community, using my experience negotiating with businessmen and politicians in Asia. These negotiation skills came in handy in a variety of contexts that benefitted our community, including navigating the maze of administrative hoops of the Hong Kong bureaucracy surrounding death and burial in my role as chairman of the Chevra Kadisha, the Jewish burial society of Hong Kong. When one of our community members was sentenced to serve prison time in Hong Kong, the circumstances stretched the limit. The sentencing hearing was a bleak day. The defendant was taken away unceremoniously, in complete shock, wrenched from his family. We had to circle the wagons to confront the numerous delicate personal and family matters, including issues of Jewish observance. We wanted to ensure that our friend had kosher food, access to *tefillin*, prayer books, and Jewish reading material, and was able to perform ritual observance. In our traditions, Jewish men above the age of bar mitzvah wear tefillin during morning weekday prayer.

After our friend's formal sentencing, our community rabbi, Rabbi Mordechai Avtzon, and I worked night and day to secure prison exceptions for kosher food, tefillin, and a prayer book. The initial request was not welcome, particularly for a new inmate. Our first meeting with the prison warden and his staff was as you would expect it—he was gruff and firm, and frequently referred to prison protocol, which we could understand. It's all about uniformity. And, as our friend learned, no inmate wants to be accused by others of favoritism.

The warden initially vetoed the tefillin. He cited concerns of personal security, since inmates are known to harm themselves with shoelaces. The authorities saw leather straps as an even greater danger. After a lengthy exchange and our explaining in detail what tefillin were all about, with the proper assurances, the prison warden approved the tefillin and one prayer book.

And then there was the question of food. There were two key issues: sourcing food supplies, and food preparation in the kitchen. To our knowledge, this was the first time that the Hong Kong prison system had to deal with a request for kosher provisions. At first, the prison warden allowed deliveries of kosher food from the Jewish Community Center (JCC). That fix had a short shelf life. We knew we only had a limited amount of time relying on delivered food—there were issues of favoritism—before we had to find a long-term solution. The warden and his prisoner-welfare staff agreed to a meeting with us to explore alternatives. In advance of the meeting, we outlined the needs and requirements of keeping kosher and the issues we foresaw, so that the prison could consider matters in advance.

By the time we arrived for the meeting, the prison staff had indeed done their homework. They outlined their plan. The prison would put out a bid for kosher food supply. The quantities and prices for their set menu were highly regulated. They were exacting, down to the ounce of meat to which each prisoner was entitled every week. They had identified a few spaces where the prison could install a small facility for kosher food preparation. The bid went out as anticipated. There was only one bidder in town—the JCC. The gap between the prison price guidelines and the JCC costs was significant, but the prison and the bidder managed to agree on terms. We inspected all proposed kitchen sites and decided on one—a large closet that was not in use—that was centrally located and provided adequate space for the preparation of the food.

Lastly, the prison outlined two options for preparation: Our prisoner could be assigned kitchen detail as his official "jail job" and prepare the food himself, or the prison would assign a cook from the existing kitchen detail. Our prisoner opted to work off-site, in a detail that worked weekdays only, thereby avoiding the potential of breaking Shabbos, the Sabbath. The prison, therefore, assigned another inmate for kosher food preparation. This particular prisoner was serving a five-year sentence for robbery but had previously been a chef at the five-star Peninsula Hotel, one of Hong Kong's most exclusive properties. Imagine that: Kosher food in a Hong Kong prison, cooked by a gourmet chef!

Experiences like this reminded me of the Bible's teaching: "In every sadness, there will be profit" (Proverbs 14:23). It's true that we did not transform the Hong Kong prison into the Peninsula Hotel, but what we did accomplish there was certainly outside the norm. I saw a parallel, as I thought about helping our partner countries. I didn't think of myself as trying to alter their ways of life, by turning them into smaller versions of the United States. I wanted to help them find the *profit* in simply being themselves— so that they, too, achieved beyond the norm of the Western Hemisphere.

If kosher food prepared by a gourmet chef in a Hong Kong prison was a huge departure from an inmate's routine, then so was the idea of cutting-edge energy sources powering some of the more undeveloped countries in our orbit.

Change seems to be the only constant in the energy supply landscape. Overnight, the US became energy independent with the introduction of fracking technology. Solar and wind installation costs dropped precipitously in the early 2010s, which spiked their growth. Battery technology became commercially viable, sparking progress on electric vehicles and more.

Thus spawned the wealth of opportunities in *transitional* energy. Each of our America Crecé initiatives came with robust programming in midstream and downstream energy projects suitable for US liquified natural gas, micro- and mini-grid projects, municipal street-lighting projects, district heating, municipal water, renewable energy projects of all sizes and technologies (including hydro and geothermal power, small nuclear reactors and solar and wind power) and rural electrification. Put them together with modernized banking systems, and we could indeed find our way toward a healthier environment, stable access to energy, and widespread economic growth.

Transitional energy was the low-hanging fruit in every country where we worked. The sheer magnitude of the market is staggering. Latin America and the Caribbean will need as much as $200 billion in investment capital to fuel transitional energy growth through 2030.

Two of our most impactful wins in the energy and infrastructure finance space were in the liquefied natural gas (LNG) sector, where US policy, technical expertise, and private capital converged to deliver transformative results. Through targeted technical assistance, regulatory and policy guidance, and risk structuring support, we helped enable the successful completion of two large-scale LNG receiving terminals—the $1.15 billion AES Colón project in Panama and the $1.4 billion AES Son My

LNG terminal in Vietnam—each fueling critical downstream applications, including baseload power generation.

Both facilities have concluded long-term US LNG supply contracts, benefitting and supporting US domestic midstream LNG infrastructure. These projects are backed by US private capital and developed in alignment with President Trump's strategic objectives: expanding American energy exports, strengthening US energy independence, and supporting the growth of free and fair energy markets abroad. These projects serve as flagships of America's capacity to deliver market-based, high-impact solutions that replace opaque, state-driven alternatives promoted by adversarial nations.

In addition to expanding the global market for US LNG, these projects supported President Trump's policy agenda by enhancing energy security for key allies, diversifying regional energy mixes, and laying the foundation for industrial development and economic resilience. They provide stable, lower-emission power to fuel manufacturing, support grid reliability, and power hundreds of thousands of homes—while demonstrating how American energy leadership drives global prosperity and strategic alignment.

In tandem with the pursuit of large, capital-intensive projects, among the more cost-effective ways to solve our partners' energy needs were micro- and mini-grids. These offered many benefits, such as increased efficiency, reliability, and security, not to mention lower power costs and, perhaps most important, power to areas not serviced by the grid—in particular, rural areas and small islands.

Micro- and mini-grids are a model for the rest of the world. Mini-grids in particular could serve approximately half the world's population (an estimated 111 million households) by

2030. Financially, that translates to investment opportunities of at least $125 billion (though some estimates are as high as $400 billion). Micro-grids, meanwhile, increase grid resilience and improve power quality. The global micro-grid market was valued at $28.6 billion in 2020, had topped $50 billion in 2025, and is projected to exceed $100 billion by 2029.[1]

We knew that municipalities bear the burden of providing basic services to their populations. As in the US, you turn to your town or village for potable water, sewage and sanitation, surface transportation, street lighting, and gas. These projects are typically implemented and financed at the municipal level and subsidized mostly by taxpayer revenues. Our goal was to help countries reduce the costs while ensuring access to infrastructure and public safety. Public lighting, for example, fuels important economic growth after dark. It's also important for reducing crime and traffic accidents (by up to 20 percent and 35 percent, respectively).

LED lighting is the optimal way to provide high-quality lighting and reduced carbon emissions. Our Smart Streetlights Project in Jamaica, for example, facilitated an upgrade of the country's street-lighting by installing smart controls and metering for 110,000 streetlights nationwide. It saved taxpayers a boatload, used a fraction of the power, emitted very little carbon, and relied heavily on US technology. This groundbreaking work paved the way for numerous street-lighting projects worth between $50 million and 300 million.

The environmental benefits of the transitional energy projects we pursued under our frameworks were clear. For example, buildings account for almost 4 percent of global energy and

---

[1]   Precedents Energy and Power Experts, "Microgrid Market Size, Share, and Trends 2025 to 2034," Precedence Research, last modified January 27, 2025, https://www.precedenceresearch.com/microgrid-market.

process-related carbon emissions, and the large cost of heating, cooling, and powering these structures burdened building owners, including national and local governments. By helping our partners realize bundled energy efficiency, we were able to provide solutions that both reduced costs and fueled progress toward enviro-friendly solutions.

Transitional energy projects also came with setbacks and challenges. Distributed energy, municipal service, and energy-efficiency projects are small. They present technological risks, not to mention credit risks. To work around these risks, we grouped small projects together and standardized the siting and sizing processes. We introduced economies of scale for financing, procurement, and operation and maintenance, and the process for bidding within a certain timeline. This made projects more cut and dried, which meant we could do more of them, faster. As with any economic activity, the more quickly and efficiently you produce a desirable outcome with a solid financial return, the more investors, suppliers, providers, and customers flock to it.

Panama's micro- and mini-grid projects showcase the transformative nature of grouping small- to medium-sized projects together. Our US-Panama Working Group identified more than $750 million in generation and mini- and micro-grid opportunities. These included public-sector assets (such as municipal government buildings, schools, and hospitals), private-sector assets (such as commercial and industrial companies), and off-grid systems for more than 450,000 people in remote communities.

We enjoyed a robust program with our Panamanian counterparts. We hosted Panamanian experts on technical fact-finding trips and site visits in the US, where they met with industry experts and toured model facilities. We provided technical and legal advice on their rules for two-way trades in power, rational tariffs, and time-of-day pricing to make their projects work economically.

As with the US, every country in the Western Hemisphere badly needs mending and upgrades to core systems. There is a huge demand for roads, bridges, and tunnels; for port logistics, such as airports, freight, and passenger rail; for water (drinking supply and wastewater treatment); healthcare and social services; and for digital connectivity.

Unlike distributed energy or municipal projects, however, core systems can be very large. They often require significantly greater funding, have much longer runways to success, and they also come with growing pains—the unexpected consequences of their improvement. The financing is more straightforward and less nuanced, so we stayed busy with appropriate sizing and siting, removing barriers to delivery, debt structuring, and fair and competitive bidding and procurement. Needless to say, stronger core systems bring immense benefits to trade and international relations. That's not to mention meaningful domestic economic growth, environmental protection, and energy access and security.

As America Crecé rolled out, it became clear that the demand went way beyond our hemisphere. It wasn't long before countries in the Eastern Hemisphere took notice, and our phones began to ring. As I'd anticipated, several countries could benefit from our whole-of-government approach. Even some of the world's more sophisticated economies, such as Japan, South Korea, Taiwan and Singapore, were eager to partner with us. One very successful relationship was with Vietnam.

Our partnership with Vietnam began through a conversation at the Vietnamese embassy in Washington. My relationship with the Vietnamese ambassador, Ha Kim Ngoc, was excellent. We hit it off from our first meeting. Food diplomacy is one of my favorite strategies, and so early on, I invited Ambassador Ha to a kosher dinner at my home in Kalorama. It was a festive evening, with great food, drink, and company, joined by my good friends Bonnie Glick, then deputy administrator of USAID, and Brent McIntosh, then under secretary for international affairs at Treasury. The ambassador appreciated the effort, care, and attention that went into the meal and the experience, and he reciprocated by inviting me to a kosher meal at his embassy.

Serving a kosher meal at the Vietnamese embassy is no simple matter. I declined as politely as I could on several occasions, explaining how many restrictions our religion imposed, but he was not deterred. Thankfully, my senior assistant, Talia Rubin (also an Orthodox Jew), commenced a logistics exercise that would have made Secretary Mnuchin's advance team jealous. In addition to learning how many dietary restrictions there were to observe, the embassy staff discovered that preparation guidelines would also upend their normal process. To name some of the key intricacies of preparing a kosher meal, the embassy had to:

- buy new pots, pans, and utensils to be used in the meal;
- serve a dairy-free menu to avoid the issues of keeping meat and dairy strictly separate; and
- ensure that all ingredients were kosher and that the vegetables were free of bugs (per the Biblical prohibitions in Leviticus 11:20–23).

In addition to participating in the choice of ingredients and checking the vegetables, Talia or I had to have at least one role (per Jewish law) integral to the cooking process, such as lighting the stove. The staff invited us into the kitchen in advance to advise them on what to buy and to help to supervise the preparations.

No state secrets to hide! In the end, we kept it simple—a one-pot meal of Vietnamese beef noodles—but even that was a *potchke*, a hassle. The well-intentioned chef wanted to use a meat tenderizer that was kosher certified but had a dairy element. Disaster averted. *Oy ve*! And so our beef was not as tender as the chef would have liked, but it certainly was delicious.

It was a wonderful meal, made memorable by the care and generosity the kitchen staff showed in going out of their way to serve a special meal just for me. Treasury Deputy Assistant Secretary for Asia Robert Kaproth, a career civil servant and resident expert on Asia, joined me for the lunch. He has been around the block more than a few times, and he was blown away by the trouble that the embassy staff went through, as well as their genuine sincerity.

Ambassador Ha spent a lot of time understanding what we had to say, writing reports back to his country's leaders, and scheduling meetings with the right people. By the time we went to Vietnam for our first meetings there, the Vietnamese delegation had a firm grasp of the concept. But there were still political and diplomatic hurdles to clear.

Vietnam is an important US partner—for economic growth, trade, investment relations, and regional security and stability. Our embassy in Hanoi attracts the best and the brightest career diplomats who are closely attuned to the political, economic, and social issues of the day. Our in-country team at the embassy expressed preliminary concerns: How would this private capital infrastructure finance initiative fit in with other similar programs? Why was Treasury leading it? Which Vietnamese agency would be our key interlocutor and lead matters on the other side? Did we realize we'd come at a delicate time? The Vietnamese, we learned, were highly sensitive to increasing US pressure on several looming trade irritants, particularly currency manipulation and a growing trade deficit.

We had two action-packed days ahead of us, including meetings with the vice minister of finance, the chairman of Vietnam Electricity (EVN), the chairman of the State Securities Commission, the vice chair of the Commission for the Management of State Capital at Enterprises (CMSC), senior members of the World Bank in Vietnam, and the American Chamber of Commerce's Energy Group for the private-sector perspective. It was an opportunity to share our vision with key Vietnamese partners, especially the Ministry of Finance. I felt good about the meetings and potential programming. Despite the cautionary briefing from the US embassy, I was ever the optimist. I'd done a number of projects in Vietnam during my private practice years and could tangibly sense the opportunity.

The facial expressions during our first meeting with the CMSC reminded me of our first Panama meeting (and so many other first meetings, for that matter). Our colleagues from the embassy gave me the "I told you so" look, but I was not the least bit fazed. As we emerged from the CMCS, word arrived that we were confirmed to meet with one of the most important political figures covering economic matters: Nguyen Van Binh, chair of the Central Economic Commission of the Communist Party of Vietnam (CPV). Binh was also the former governor of the State Bank of Vietnam, the nation's central bank. I was pumped— finally, an audience with a key decision-maker! I was eager to talk infrastructure finance with him, and how we could assist Vietnam in achieving its growth goals.

Chairman Binh was a veteran, astute politician. He took the meeting because he had his own agenda that—surprise, surprise—did not revolve around infrastructure finance. This, too, was for the good, as the sages say, and quite familiar. I had by this time walked into many rooms with negotiators and political leaders in Asian cultures where the first order of business was to listen patiently and hold space for my counterparts to air frustrations or grievances.

It was full-on political theater. We met in an unmarked stately building, one of many in the CPV portfolio reserved for the reception of dignitaries. We entered a grand hall with a large, framed portrait of Ho Chi Minh. It had formal seating—two large seats at the top of a U shape with facing rows of seats on each side, one reserved for the US and the other for the hosts. The flower arrangements were numerous and bountiful. The displays of lotus, Vietnam's national flower and a symbol of strength, purity, and elegance, were most striking.

Silly me, I'd assumed the meeting was an exercise in political courtesy. I would tell Binh a little bit about the program, and then he'd pass me off to work out the details with his team. In reality, it was Chairman Binh's opportunity to show that he would not be intimidated by the United States. I suddenly recalled my East Asia colleagues at Treasury briefing me before my departure on the likelihood that Vietnam would be designated as a "currency manipulator" in the Treasury's foreign exchange report. Vietnam's foreign currency practices were exacerbating its trade deficit with the US, and the USTR had issued a number of stern pronouncements in response.

Chairman Binh was a gracious and kind host. He allowed me to get through my presentation on our proposed programming before he took me to task. The press was actively covering the flack the US was giving Vietnam about foreign currency manipulation and the trade imbalance. As an assistant secretary of the Treasury, I was an easy target. Chairman Binh, meanwhile, would be perceived as a hero in the press. Now, these issues were not my direct responsibility. A separate team of experts had compiled the foreign exchange report. I certainly hadn't been sent there to discuss these two weighty issues, much less negotiate them. But as the most senior representative of the US government, I had to answer.

I told Chairman Binh that I would dutifully pass his comments back to the Treasury secretary, and emphasized how important Vietnam was as a trade, investment, and security partner to the United States. I continued with an explanation of how my proposed programming would benefit our two countries and address the issues that concerned him. I pointed out that our programming would generate $10 billion or more in US energy commodity sales to Vietnam, and not less than $34 billion to $51 billion in US direct investment opportunities—both of which would address his two biggest headaches. The foreign currency and trade imbalance issues were irritants, but the solution for both sides was right before our eyes. Infrastructure works for everything.

Chairman Binh was pleased. He had his press moment, plus a feasible and intriguing solution. I managed to satisfy his desire to register his country's displeasure, while keeping our negotiations on track.

He instructed his people to work out the details and implement our framework.

Chairman Binh and I continued to correspond after I returned to the United States. We wrote about official business, as well as family—my Jewish culture, and his Vietnamese one. On the sidelines after our first meeting, we spoke on a more personal level. He spoke about his children, and I spoke about mine. After I returned to Washington, I wrote Chairman Binh to thank him for his warm reception and support for my programming. I added a personal note on his children referring to the line in Proverbs 17:6: "The crown of sages are their grandchildren, and the beauty of children their fathers." Chairman Binh wrote a very thoughtful message in response reminding me of the respect that both of our cultures place on the young and the old. There was a clear bond.

Chairman Binh came to America after that first meeting on an official business trip in December 2019. I wanted to do something special for his visit, so I organized a dinner at my home in Brooklyn. I planned to give Chairman Binh and his colleagues a good feel for our life, family, and customs. I live in one of the most densely populated Chassidic Jewish neighborhoods in the country, and on one of the busiest blocks in the neighborhood. There is plenty of culture where I live to facilitate "people's diplomacy."

I invited three business leaders, including two from our community, to talk about how we combine business with philanthropy and community. With us were Sol Werdiger, founder and CEO of Outerstuff, the preeminent global marketer of licensed sports apparel; Joel Epstein, founder and COO of Fabuwood, one of the top ten kitchen cabinet suppliers in the US; and Paul Freedman, general counsel at AES Corporation, one of the world's largest independent power producers. I also planned a special menu of Jewish "soul food," accompanied by pairings of my home-infused vodka (they loved the ginger—reminded them of home!) and the finest Israeli wines.

I arranged a U-shaped table in my dining room in, seating the chairman and myself at the head. In all, we had more than twenty guests—fifteen from his delegation, my three honored guests, and members of my team at Treasury. We had a savory corn and vegetable chowder to warm up—it was a freezing winter night—with a drop of balsamic vinegar, for a little taste to remind them of home. And what would a meal of Jewish soul food be without smoked fish, herring, and chopped liver? We had some of the most delicious cured- and smoked-fish appetizers—made with the choicest fish flown in from Hawaii and New Zealand and smoked by my dear friend Abraham Sieger—served on fresh baby peppers with nondairy cream cheese (it was kosher, after all, and meat was on the menu!). We also enjoyed homemade herring salad with Asian accents of ginger, coriander, and chili, along with craisins, bell pepper, and onions. As a second appetizer, we added chopped liver and *p'tcha* (calf's foot jelly, or *galareta*, as we call it in my neck of the woods) on crackers. I topped that off with cranberry-ginger-roasted chicken for the main course. I pulled out all the stops.

It was the perfect combination of business and pleasure. Chairman Binh made some official remarks, and I responded. We each emphasized friendship. We were able to squeeze in some discussion about infrastructure finance, but the highlight was hearing Sol, Joel, and Paul speak about commitments to community and charity. Sol regaled the group with his story of selling a multi-hundred-million-dollar stake in his company to Blackstone, on the condition that the buyer continued to give 10 percent of its profit to charity, with him as the head of charitable giving. Joel spoke about his multimillion-dollar program to assist the needy with wedding expenses. Paul talked about AES's exceptional work assisting communities with schools and medical facilities. The message was clear: Jewish business, and US business for that matter, stands on charity and community.

The dinner was a hit. The Vietnamese loved the introduction to Eastern European Jewish culture. They loved being hosted at somebody's home. They loved the house, the people, and the food. They loved my neighborhood in Brooklyn and seeing all the Chassidic people walking around. And, important for our work, they loved the programming.

The next time I visited Vietnam was in February 2020. Chairman Binh invited me to a very formal dinner in the Sofitel Legend Metropole Hanoi, a hundred-year-old landmark hotel in the heart of the city's French Quarter. He wanted to reciprocate, since I had entertained him. So he organized a grand room full of VIPs and a hearty menu, including a kosher option for me. Most important, he ensured that there was frozen vodka, so he could toast me in the same manner I had toasted him at my home in Brooklyn. And he toasted me more than once!

I was very pleased with how things were going with Vietnam, and yet we had our work cut out for us. Between August 2018 and December 2020, the US government entered into twenty agreements with countries in Latin America and Asia, representing $600 billion in potential investment opportunities.

One byproduct that emerged was teaching skills to our counterparts, the national governing authorities of partner countries. In any scenario where you're after long-term, lasting results, you must impart different ways of doing things. Our traditions may not have been new in the chronological sense, but they were new to the authorities we worked with, in terms of reforming policies and laws. We wanted—and achieved—sizeable progress in our partners' ability to attract funding, negotiate deals, conduct oversight, and recover from COVID-19 without losing their balance.

One key leg of the America Crecé stool was improving state-owned enterprises (SOEs), or what we called "capital enablers." If you picture the economy of an average Latin American country as a house under construction, SOEs are like the pillars that hold the structure upright. As a sturdy, well-constructed frame keeps a house upright during storms and earthquakes, SOEs with positive balance sheets work wonders, even during times of recession or crises like the pandemic. As homeowners know, once the building frames are built to code, they can add other elements that turn a house into a home. In the same way, US investors felt encouraged to take more risks when they could research and discover that the SOEs and public utilities had solid foundations. It led to a greater willingness to fund other projects.

By rolling up our sleeves and helping Panama's state-owned energy utility, ETESA, save $58 million on servicing its debt, we created a blueprint to set public utilities on a firm financial footing. By helping Ecuador find and monetize an additional $30 billion from its existing utilities, we taught the Ecuadorians a classic business principle: Use every part of the cow. This is standard practice among Fortune 500 companies—they shield themselves from recessions and global changes by creating as many revenue streams as they can, while slashing unnecessary costs. Every enterprise improves when it goes from a negative to a positive cash flow position. Best of all, in this case, the US private sector could finally let down its guard and fund the growth that America's partners badly needed.

As we worked to attract US investors, bundling loans—what we termed "capital bridges"—did more than anything else to achieve the goal. Now, before your mind goes to "mortgage-backed securities" and the subprime mess that led to the Great Recession of 2008, let me explain a few things. Bundling or packaging loans into a form of collateral isn't *always* a bad idea. It failed with residential mortgages for a variety of reasons, but none of those was present in our projects. To start, we used proven "templates" from the International Finance Corporation's Managed Co-Lending Portfolio Program and a private-sector counterpart from Bayshore

Capital. Unlike residential mortgages, these contracts require an old-fashioned approach to sharing risk. Borrowers must prove their profitability, fiscal discipline, and ability to repay the loan. If they fail to do any of those things, they don't qualify. This made it a shoo-in for institutional US investors, who are always in the market for big pools of the right kind of debt.

When institutional investors learned they could invest in these pooled debts held by financially sound public utilities, they didn't have to think twice. Particularly since public-sector utilities are normally off-limits to institutional investors! Unlike in the US, Latin American and Caribbean countries welcomed our investors with little to no reservations, including for energy and infrastructure debt to finance their cooperation with the global climate agenda.

A beauty of this programming is its enormous scalability. It can be adapted and applied to commercial bank emerging-market infrastructure debt, a market that presently stands at more than $1 trillion. That's plenty of institutional investor access and market creation.

Yet, we also live in a political world. Despite these incredible results, politics and political cycles got in our way and upended some of our work. The most disappointing example was with one of the first countries we reached out to: Mexico.

Mexico's under secretary of energy, Aldo Flores-Quiroga, ran the negotiations with my team as we attempted to construct a framework. Aldo came from impeccable lineage, held several senior energy positions for the Mexican government and international organizations, and he was a world-class concert pianist to boot! By the time we met, he'd already unlocked Mexico's vast upstream oil and gas resources through exploration and production auctions and liberalized its refined product and natural gas markets.

Aldo had a large and important buffet of initiatives to shepherd, but our offer was not on the menu. He was reluctant, apprehensive, and not the easiest to work with. He simply didn't want to do the deal. I suspect he didn't like the proposal because he perceived it as a distraction from the programming he'd already set in motion, when in fact it was intended to complement what he'd accomplished.

We had one challenging meeting after another. At one point, a huge US delegation flew down to Mexico. Besides me, there was John Rader on behalf of the White House; Kim Breier, assistant secretary for Western Hemisphere affairs at the State Department; Tim Fitzgerald, chief international economist at the Council of Economic Advisers; several people from the Department of Energy, and the ambassador to Mexico. The Mexican contingent included a very senior official from Mexico's government, as well as numerous under secretaries and assistant directors.

Aldo opened the meeting, someone from our delegation gave our formal opening, and then all eyes were on me. I was a deputy assistant secretary and one of the lower-ranking members of our delegation. Yet it was my programming, so I got the floor. I put our whole plan on the table. We offered a suite of initiatives covering anywhere from five to twelve areas of cooperation—upstream oil and gas exploration and production, oil and gas pipelines, LNG export terminals, cross-border sales of energy, fuel storage, conventional power generation, conversions of coal-fired plants to natural gas, geothermal, renewables, and more. We estimated as much as $75 billion in potential investment from the US private sector. We had a lively back-and-forth, but it was very clear that this under secretary was not having it.

To be honest, it was far from the hardest negotiation I've ever had. Even though I'd have preferred a more receptive and easier counterpart, it seemed like everything was going perfectly fine. But during our first break, I noticed several pairs of darting eyes from members of our team. One of my colleagues glared at me, and then out spewed, "What the f***? Why'd you screw that up? The guy's not ready to sign."

Now I had to manage both a reluctant under secretary from Mexico *and* a high-ranking representative from my own delegation. Was this deal destined for prime time, or the graveyard?

I still had an ace up my sleeve. I'd made a new friend at the negotiating table that day, who would be pivotal to pushing our framework through. Guillermo Turrent represented the Comisión Federal de Electricidad, Mexico's energy utility and energy trading company. Guillermo was born and raised in Mexico and had enjoyed a very successful career in the United States. He returned to Mexico, aiming to improve things in his home country. Eugenio Herrara, his general counsel, was also very helpful. They suggested we meet privately for dinner. Along with a few colleagues, I joined Guillermo and Eugenio at an exceptional kosher steak house in Mexico City's Polanco district. We ate and drank, and then drank some more. Suddenly, the barriers started to drop. We clearly spoke the same language, and Guillermo showed tremendous practicality and market orientation. Now all we had to do was get Aldo on board.

The US delegation came back from Mexico without having moved the ball forward, but we persevered. It took a lot of pressure from Mexico's president on Aldo and his team, but finally we made headway, with Guillermo serving as a counterpoint and an offset to Aldo.

One of our key delegation members was Dave Banks, head of energy and environment in the White House. He was very politically savvy and very effective. With just one final meeting in Washington to seal the deal, Dave invited everyone to the office he maintained at the Council on Environmental Quality, located in a lovely townhouse just across the street from the White House. We reviewed and reached agreement on the entire framework, settling all the details with Aldo and his team.

We celebrated the occasion over kosher chicken mole in honor of our friends from the Mexican delegation. I introduced it to them as "Holy Mole." As we drank my vodka and their Mexican tequila, I wondered if we had finally crossed the finish line.

We were scheduled to sign all twenty-three bilateral agreements with Mexico on a Thursday in February 2018. Two days before, President Trump called Enrique Peña Nieto, the president of Mexico, to say: "You've got to pay for the wall." The call didn't end well. As quickly as you could look around, Mexico canceled the bilaterals—including our infrastructure finance framework.

Politics, this time on the US side, derailed the last framework we negotiated as well. We had a hurried but highly fruitful engagement with Ecuador. We signed the agreement in February 2020, just before the pandemic. Ecuador's ambassador to the US, Ivonne Juez Abuchacra de Baki, was highly supportive of our engagement from day one. She facilitated and supported the negotiation and conclusion of our framework in record time. The pandemic slowed that project considerably, but we kept it alive through virtual conferencing.

The DFC led our Ecuador efforts, allocating more than $1 billion to spur Ecuadorian development and mobilize the private sector. Adam Boehler traveled to Ecuador for a meeting with President Lenín Moreno to take stock of our work. Shortly before he left, Ambassador Baki requested a meeting with me to present a new proposal under our framework. Several of her SOEs were burdened with unsustainable debt. The terms were onerous. Debt service was crippling them financially, and the collateral arrangements made messes of their balance sheets. It was an exciting challenge that America Crecé could certainly take on.

I set to work immediately. My team studied the balance sheets of some of Ecuador's largest SOEs. I had a hunch there was plenty of untapped cash that could reverse the current troubles. We raced against time, and my team pulled out all the stops. We crunched numbers and data on flights from Washington to Quito, and made one urgent phone call after another. Finally, the team took a breath—indeed, the Ecuadorian SOEs had plenty of buried treasure. The Ecuadorians simply didn't know where to look for it, or how to unlock it. By Sunday night, we'd found more than $30 billion on the balance sheets of eight Ecuadorean SOEs in the energy, telecoms, shipping, and water sectors.

And $30 billion was a number we could work with. Prior to our upcoming meetings with various Ecuadorian ministers, I'd prepared a one-sheet presentation of our proposal. The DFC would set up a short-term loan for Ecuador's Ministry of Finance, so the country could pay down burdensome debt and form a private-public partnership, which (in my world) is known as "asset recycling." It's a handy tool for strengthening a public entity, like a utility, without completely privatizing it. The goal of this program was to help SOEs stand on their own feet financially. This was *very* easy to do—but the previous terms that the Ecuadorians had negotiated expressly prohibited them from doing it.

Upon our return from Ecuador, the DFC hired outside counsel to flesh out the details and accelerate the transaction, alongside Ambassador Baki and colleagues from the Ministry of Finance. We completed documentation and negotiations in record time, and Adam hosted a virtual signing with President Moreno in January 2021. The transaction would have been transformative for the Ecuadorian economy, providing up to $2.8 billion in financing to help six of the country's state-owned utilities. If it produced the desired result, we would have proven the concept and replicated it elsewhere. Unfortunately, when President Joe Biden took office, he kiboshed not just this deal, but the entire America Crecé program.

Despite these setbacks, I remain enormously proud of our efforts to play the role America was destined to play in the world: the engine of peace, prosperity, and economic growth, and a nation that spreads the bounties of free enterprise to the entire world, making it more stable and more secure.

US leadership in driving capital and investment was essential to improving the lives of millions of people in smaller nations around the world. As you are about to read, our leadership was also critical to helping to chart a course for stability and growth during the financial revolution that was taking markets and economies by storm during Trump 45 as well.

CHAPTER 8

EMBRACING THE SPEED OF CHANGE: WALKING THE TIGHTROPE OF TECHNOLOGICAL BREAKTHROUGHS IN FINTECH

As a senior government official, you face a huge array of scenarios, each requiring a different solution, but all falling into four basic categories: (1) There are the clear and present dangers threatening our country that must be handled swiftly and confidently; (2) there are the meaty issues and imperatives that require leadership, diplomacy, and strong policy solutions; (3) sometimes you get whacked in the head with a baseball bat and have to respond to an unexpected crisis immediately; and (4) sometimes a brand-new issue unfolds that brings great promise for the future—and huge risk of the unknown.

The financial technology (fintech) revolution fell squarely into the last category. Massive upheaval in digital currency and transactions, and an almost incomprehensible increase in the volume of related global data flows, presented changes that were transforming the financial system almost overnight. To adapt to the dizzying implications of this new reality—never mind anticipate the implications and effects of those changes—was a mind-boggling assignment.

Ignoring threats to security, privacy, US market reliability, and global financial stability was unconscionable. Yet stifling the innovation and opportunity presented by the fintech revolution was equally problematic, especially to a president who understood the promise of the free market to lift every American's wealth and comfort.

Our task was stark: Protect consumers, companies, investors, and markets from disaster—while maximizing the opportunities for growth, efficiency, transparency, and productivity this technological revolution offered. We were stepping onto a tightrope between stability and growth.

As with all "category four" issues, the Trump administration had to study and take stock of the fintech revolution before crafting a sensible policy. The problem was, as with all revolutions, that the world was changing practically overnight. Previous administrations undoubtedly weathered significant threats to the US financial system—from stagecoach robberies to the 1987 savings and loan crisis. However, I doubt that any faced change at the furious speed of the fintech revolution during the Trump 45 years.

Contrast, for example, fintech's velocity of change with the historical narrative of the Cash Room—an architectural crown jewel within the halls of the Main Treasury Building in Washington. It fell into obsolescence just two years after President Richard Nixon left office in 1974. However, that only came after it had stood for nearly a century as a firm symbol and fixture of the republic it served.

The aesthetics, operations, functions, and safeguards of the Cash Room point to an era of history when transactions with the federal government, physical tendering, and storage of money meant physical bills, notes, and coins. Individuals and institutions alike (the Cash Room also functioned as a "bankers bank") literally walked up to the Treasury Building with wheelbarrows full of money. Can you imagine? In Nixon's final year, tellers at the Cash Room cashed almost eight million checks for local recipients. That's more than thirty thousand checks per business day! During the same time period, the Treasury processed more than $650 million in coins and $41 million in currency for local banks. That's more than $3 billon in today's terms—more than 100 million kilograms (220 million pounds) in coins. Think of the weight of more than 25,000 African elephants or more than 1,200 blue whales. That's a lot of blubber.

Today, bank branches sit as empty as the Cash Room. Digital currencies offer new, independent sources of money without the need of the Cash Room or the Federal Reserve. The Cash Room's 1974 processing rates resemble a snail with a blue whale on its back compared with the speed and accuracy of today's artificial intelligence, mobile applications, and machine learning. Money travels weightlessly, seamlessly, and instantaneously across countries, oceans, and borders, and transactions can be made without leaving one's office or home. You don't need a bank; you don't even need a wallet. Digital payment systems handle everything, and the money goes exactly where it needs to in seconds, sometime even nanoseconds. Citizens of Third World dictatorships run online businesses and trade in crypto rather than paper currency, while Americans transact with people around the world via PayPal, Venmo, CashApp, and more.

In many ways, the fintech revolution was the result, albeit unintended, of government's response to a previous crisis. In 2010, Congress passed a landmark financial services reform bill authored by Senator Chris Dodd and Representative Barney Frank (the Dodd-Frank Wall Street Reform and Consumer Protection Act), which President Barack Obama signed into law. The bill purported to protect consumers, investors, and the markets from the renegade behavior that led to the 2008 financial meltdown—the crisis that wiped out $2 trillion globally, along with legendary investment houses like Lehman Brothers and Bear Stearns. But as so often happens, the government's efforts to "protect" placed a huge new burden on companies large and small, burying them in an avalanche of red tape, paperwork, and regulation.

In the case of Dodd-Frank, the avalanche took the form of 4,537 new rules and 13,789 pages—written by more than ten agencies, in just three years after the law passed. As voluminous as a full twenty-eight copies of *War and Peace*, Dodd-Frank was enough to put Tolstoy to shame. While banks struggled to cope with the deluge of new and strict regulatory requirements and the attending costs of compliance, money did what it has since the beginning of time: It found the path of least resistance.

This time, that path "rerouted" money and data to hundreds of new "nonbank financial firms," which started leveraging rapid advances in technology to improve operational efficiencies and lower regulatory compliance costs. This new class of companies specializing in financial technology were called "fintechs." The corresponding explosion in global digital data flows greased their path, creating an amorphous electronic highway for value to travel across the world almost as fast as sunlight. Put all those circumstances together, and you had a fintech revolution.

This revolution, which caused a significant change in the financial services landscape, was made possible, among other factors, by three major advances:

- technology with unprecedented access to credit and financial services, as well as greater speed, convenience, and security than ever before;

- digitization of finance and the economy, which unleashed technological innovation through the use of data, speed of communication, expansion of information flows, and proliferation of mobile devices and applications; and
- massive flows of investment capital into fintech.

Almost overnight, nonbank financial firms began to offer back-end check processing, credit card issuance, processing, and network activities; customer-facing digital payment software; and financial advice and execution services to retail investors.

Until the fintech revolution came along, the financial services industry resembled many other traditional "siloed" business models. The rigid structure translated to slow process management, poor customer experience, failure to learn from mistakes, and a weighty, costly bureaucracy. Fintech firms torpedoed those silos.

Abandoning the traditional model allowed for specialization, enabling faster improvements and more nimble responses to market or transactional barriers. Smaller fintech firms focused on specific or customized products and offerings. New financial tools saved money for consumers and increased efficiency, driving additional capital formation and productivity gains. Cutting-edge advancements, such as back-end check processing and credit card issuance, accelerated the speed at which money flows through the marketplace. Checks that used to take three to five business days to clear now processed in milliseconds, while credit card applicants went from waiting two or three weeks to instant approval at the touch of a few buttons.

The growth in fintech was incredible as thousands of these small, entrepreneurial fintechs sprang up to fill the gap in financial services that banks and other traditional firms failed or refused to provide. From 2010 to mid-2017, more than 3,330 new tech firms sprang up, specifically to serve the financial services industry. A full 40 percent of them catered to banking and capital markets. By 2017, these fintechs had raised $22 billion globally, a thirteen-fold increase since 2010. In addition to the absence of federal interference, the velocity of money in the digital world held the promise of unprecedented profitability. Its automation would drastically reduce operational costs, while its precision and data-driven nature could sharply reduce the risk of fraud, tampering, or laundering.

By 2018, fintechs extended more than 36 percent of all US personal loans (compared to 1 percent in 2010). Digital fintechs reached more than 80 million consumers.

President Trump's first inauguration coincided with a tipping point in the fintech revolution. Up to that point, venture capital had provided the lion's share of seed money for research, development, and introduction of fintechs. Now, fintech was going mainstream. Many of these companies attained a new degree of financial and corporate maturity during President Trump's first year in office. Fintech became a favorite sector for mergers and acquisitions. Some fintechs were subsumed by larger ones, which monetized their shareholder value by taking the new acquisitions through initial public offerings. The traditional institutional world also caught on; brand-name financial groups like TD Bank Group and J. P. Morgan Chase bankrolled patent applications for start-ups, frequently without even requiring equity stakes.

Fintechs built strategic partnerships with e-retailers, financial infrastructure companies, social media platforms, startups, and information and communication technology companies. Practically, this meant that private companies from these varying sectors no longer bothered to use the traditional financial service system. Why should they? Compared to the speed, convenience, and efficiency of fintech, it was like continuing to use the horse and buggy when the automobile entered the mainstream.

For example, as Bitcoin surged into a worldwide phenomenon in 2017, the "blockchain" technology embedded in Bitcoins spun off and revolutionized finance in a myriad of ways. Companies like Rocket Mortgage, for example, seized on blockchain's attributes, such as real-time verification of financial documents, streamlined credit scoring and protection, and automated underwriting and distribution of funds. Blockchain technology reduced the timeline for securing a mortgage from between thirty and sixty days to minutes. It's little wonder that the real estate boom after COVID-19 reduced several cities' inventories to statistical zeroes! You could make an offer on a house with full confidence of financing on the same day you scheduled a tour to view the property.

Which, naturally, meant that consumer behavior transformed. Americans could apply for and receive approval for micro-loans, mortgages, and investment advice almost instantly, without ever visiting a bank branch or interacting with a human advisor. They could purchase products from overseas vendors that arrived on their doorstep within twenty-four to forty-eight hours. They could manage their finances entirely on handheld devices, transferring funds from one account to another without getting up from the sofa. They could deposit checks electronically, capturing the data with their smartphone cameras, and then promptly shred the paper. Bank branches sat empty for days, weeks, or months at a time without customer foot traffic.

Behind all these incredible accelerations in convenience, however, lies a web of complexity and sophistication that's something of a double-edged sword. The digital system, for all its merits, is predicated on the survival and sustainability of the "legacy" system. It is dependent, in other words, on age-old utilities like electricity, which is still vulnerable to failure, collapse, attack, or sabotage. It also relies on the value of fiat currency, at least relatively; you can't know what a Bitcoin is worth unless you know what a dollar is worth. And what if the dollar collapses?

The digital system is easily accessible from overseas, in far corners of the globe, where adversarial foreign powers can hack in and undermine its security. That leaves Americans exposed to robbery, violations of privacy, and theft of intellectual property, with limited or no recourse. Despite the supposed safety of certain technologies, such as stablecoins (which, as my friend and colleague then-Under Secretary Brent McIntosh used to remind us, were neither stable nor coins), fintechs are still prone to corrupt practices from human operators. Sam Bankman-Fried, for example, began spinning the web of the first Ponzi-like fraud scheme in cryptocurrency as we walked the tightrope between growth and stability. As oriented as the Trump 45 administration was toward free markets, this was no time for the government to look completely the other way.

Another facet of the fintech revolution involved not money but data. Until the past two decades, global trade and exchange had centered on tangibles like goods and services, and imports and exports. But then came an explosive growth of technology starting in 2005, and the world entered a genuinely new epoch in the categories of commerce and trade. By leaps and bounds, data overtook goods and services as the most frequently traded form of value in the world. Between 2005 and 2014, the total global value of data exchanged amounted to forty-five times the amount of goods and services.

The revolution in cross-border data flows accomplished something the traditional global market never could: It exported new levels of wealth and prosperity, for more people than ever before. According to a report from McKinsey in 2016, the ease and low cost of transactions in the global marketplace transcended traditional physical and legal barriers, which had kept people in Third World nations largely impoverished. With the advent of inexpensive and simple platforms and methods for people to exchange money for services, the world's GDP grew by 10 percent to $7.8 trillion in 2014. Of that total, $2.8 trillion of it came from cross-border data flows.

Thanks to this transformation in data flow, fintech soon reached the underbanked and unbanked; people in poor countries, such as Zimbabwe, suffering from hyperinflation and devalued currency, adopted it quickly. An entire new class of entrepreneurs sprang up across the undeveloped regions of Africa, southern and central Asia, and the Indian subcontinent, trading in cryptocurrency rather than paper or fiat money. The greater the percentage of unbanked people in a nation, the quicker financial technology solutions took off. Meanwhile, Americans eager to donate to less fortunate people in these regions sent payments to individuals or nongovernmental organizations, using apps like PayPal, Venmo, or CashApp—and the recipients received the money on the same day, often within an hour. Digital transactions on handheld mobile devices threw a lifeline to people who otherwise could not transact with the outside world, nor engage in meaningful commerce within their own borders.

The faster that human beings communicate, the more they buy, sell, and exchange. The easier it is to buy and sell, the more people get involved in the global economy, multiplying value and opportunity through their participation. Data runs rings around traditional goods and services by facilitating both; it speeds up the flow of money and exchange and allows more individuals to participate in the global economy more often.

But you can imagine the amount of bandwidth this requires. It's one reason the tech industry fanned out to smaller cities and regions across the US, purchasing large amounts of land to set up "data farms" to meet the demand for connectivity. Smaller metro regions like Salt Lake City, Utah, and rural states like Idaho suddenly flourished. New residents with disposable income and needs for housing, good schools, and safe communities poured in, and bingo—construction and real estate exploded, too. At the time of this writing, parts of the region traditionally known as the Rust Belt in Ohio and western Pennsylvania are undergoing a dramatic resurgence, despite languishing for decades. It's happening all over the world. Online giants like Google, Amazon, and Facebook drove many of these expansions. Soon, they discovered they could also monetize the bandwidth they'd developed, rather like leasing commercial real estate. Several tech giants, Amazon chief among them, turned their enormous data capacities into "leased space" where small retailers, manufacturers, and independent brokers could offer goods and services. Amazon's Web Services division is a prime example.

The Trump 45 administration faced this whirlwind of change head-on. Just weeks after taking office in 2017, President Trump issued Executive Order 13772. During the 2016 campaign, the president had argued vociferously against Dodd-Frank and vowed to dismantle it. This order represented his first step in that direction. Specifically, he assigned responsibility to Treasury to investigate and review the Obama-era Consumer Financial Protection Bureau and the Financial Stability Oversight Council. These two agencies sprang up because of Dodd-Frank and (as our reviews later confirmed) seriously undermined such traditional

American concepts as individual liberty, free-market capitalism, and government accountability. In addition to rethinking those agencies, Executive Order 13772 aimed to:

- empower Americans to make independent, informed choices and decisions in the marketplace, save for retirement, and build individual wealth;
- prevent more taxpayer-funded bailouts;
- foster growth and vibrant financial markets through:
  - ○ regulatory impact analysis
  - ○ addressing systemic risk and market failures, such as moral hazard and information asymmetry
- enable American companies to compete with foreign firms, at home and abroad;
- advance American interests in international negotiations; and
- restore public accountability and common sense to federal regulatory framework and agencies.

Considering the tidal wave of innovation sweeping financial institutions and systems, the path forward was far from clear. In many ways, the question we faced was: Did our goals of growth and stability require us, in the words of the Talmud, to take the "longer, shorter route," or the "shorter, longer route"? The Talmud's wisdom teaches that, sometimes, there are two ways to get from Point A to Point B. The first is by way of a longer, circuitous, but proven route. With time and grit, you will get there. The second option is a shorter route through treacherous territory and difficult, if not impossible, terrain. Some get there; most don't. We had to straddle this Talmudic wisdom. Our first instinct was to favor the shorter route—financial growth would benefit from speeding up to meet the pace of technology and innovation over a shorter route. And we wanted to encourage innovators who developed novel and disruptive technologies or business models. But to do that, we needed sound bases and thoughtful approaches to guide and regulate. Could we avoid a heavy-handed federal approach, favoring guidance over regulation and monitoring over micromanaging—and still fulfill our responsibility to defend and protect? This would require thought and study. As our forebears knew, taking time to build a solid foundation would mean smoother sailing, and faster advances down the road.

We quickly recognized that financial innovation, the explosion of data flow, and the rapid emergence of fintechs presented the Trump 45 administration, along with all international financial authorities, with a range of new challenges. The speed and velocity of money, the precise element that makes financial innovation so compelling, drove the change—and all the consumer benefits that came with it.

New challenges, however, don't automatically require new regulation. One key question we asked was how well the existing US regulatory system might serve to accomplish our goals of promoting innovation, protecting consumers, and ensuring market integrity in the context of this fintech revolution. We recognized that any changes must satisfy, as Brent McIntosh and former chair of the SEC Jay Clayton wrote in *The Wall Street Journal* in 2021, "the principal objectives underpinning existing financial regulations: financial stability, deep and efficient funding markets across the spectrum of debt and equity, and the prevention of fraud and illicit activity." The linchpin of this approach, McIntosh and Clayton continued, "is to identify the functions a new product or process is performing...and ask how a [new technology or instrument] is being used and what existing instrument or process the new technology competes with, complements or aims to replace—and then regulate it accordingly."

Jewish scholars have spent centuries navigating the delicate balance between Talmudic wisdom and practical requirements of daily life. As an observant Jew living for many years in non-Western cultures, I had many instances of doing my own balancing act. Perhaps the most memorable example is the weekend I got stuck at the Seoul airport.

I was on my way to Hong Kong for a Sunday meeting, and due to the flight time (which included a stopover in Vancouver), the only flight to arrive before Shabbos departed on a Wednesday night. All was going as planned. Takeoff was on time. Arrival in Vancouver was on time. The layover and takeoff from Vancouver were on time. The problems started when the flight was within striking distance of Hong Kong. A storm had picked up strength while we were in the air and turned into a major force, with the Hong Kong Observatory raising the Signal 8 warning, reserved for storms with winds above seventy-three miles per hour. In other words, it was a major typhoon, and the Hong Kong airport was closed. We were diverted to Seoul, and within an hour or two of landing, it became clear that continuing to Hong Kong would not be possible that day. I would be stuck at the Seoul airport for Shabbos.

My challenge was that I had no food, no supplies, and not enough time to make it to downtown Seoul before Shabbos. At least there was a hotel, if you can call it that, inside the terminal before Immigration. I checked in—my room had just enough space for a small bed and desk, with a separate small bathroom.

My next challenge was food. My wife had packed meals for my flight, and I still had one meal left. I had no rolls and no wine.

And so, I went scouting through the duty-free shops to see what was available. After reconnoitering every inch of them, I came up with only three kosher items—coffee, Pringles potato chips, and a bottle of vodka. Not a problem! I had the vodka for Kiddush; coffee for the morning, which I would drink cold; half a meal of meat and rice for the evening and half for the morning; and the Pringles *bim kom* the potato kugel! Well, at least I was not lacking in vodka! And so it went on Friday night. Vodka for Kiddush. *L'chaim*! Vodka *bim kom* the fish. *L'chaim*! Vodka *bim kom* the soup. *L'chaim*! Vodka *bim kom* the meat and kugel. *L'chaim*!

My Shabbos in the Seoul airport wasn't exactly classic, but it reminded me that Judaism's timeless traditions celebrate progress even when humans fall short of perfection.

As our team at Treasury surveyed the fintech revolution, we felt a similar challenge to use the best of tried-and-true guidelines, while being resourceful enough to develop some practical solutions.

Exciting revolutions in technology can also obscure gaps that bad actors can exploit, just as the internet's growth led to cybertheft, hacking, and the dark web. Financial innovations are famous for their association with financial disasters. We tried to keep a clear-eyed view of the upsides and the downsides as we wrapped our heads around this enormous, complex, and constantly evolving wave of change. As policymakers and regulators, our response to the cutting-edge developments in disruptive financial innovation had to support:

- healthy economic growth,
- appropriate access to new technologies,
- market stability and security, and
- consumer protection.

Some of the trickier regulatory challenges included:

- the role and regulation of digital currency and crypto-currencies within financial systems,
- the use of artificial intelligence (AI) in financial transactions,
- the use of AI to conduct financial regulation and supervision,
- the role of banks in this new world of finance aided by technology, and
- how to ensure free flows of global data across a landscape that included countries with restrictive data policies.

Cryptocurrencies (or stablecoins) have potential for widespread adoption, prompting concerns about their implications for financial institutions, central banks, and individual consumers. On the plus side, distributed-ledger stablecoins are virtually impossible to counterfeit because of the highly sophisticated technological foundation of their creation. Unregulated by governments, stablecoins are more difficult to manipulate through inflation or artificial devaluation. Provided that their data flows easily across borders, stablecoins can easily facilitate transactions between parties doing business. Every single activity on a Bitcoin ledger is recorded and can be traced to the IP address where it originated.

The advent of AI and machine learning posed novel questions about how to grapple with financial, regulatory, and supervision decisions made by machines. Taking nuanced and delicate decisions out of human hands could be a recipe for disaster. On the other hand, if the financial world adopts AI for supervisory purposes, it could free up trillions of dollars and incalculable hours of human capital, and simplify or ease regulation. The future of banks remains uncertain, as they face increased regulatory interference and compressed margins—not to mention added competition from startups and large technology companies. Even so, if they found ways to work with fintechs and big tech firms, they could survive the innovation, expand their reach, and access new markets.

Restrictive policies on free flows of data, particularly those requiring localization, presented serious obstacles to global growth. Data is integral to make the benefits of technology real. Limited data flows could still impede progress, given the gargantuan size and widespread adoption and commercialization of cross-border flows. Even as these flows promised to bring unimaginable improvements to the standards of living for the least fortunate people on the planet, noncooperation from certain nations threatened to interfere with the global market at large.

As we reviewed the unintended consequences of Dodd-Frank, we also studied the legacy of the Telecommunications Act of 1996, which kept the internet free from taxation and regulation. What extraordinary growth and opportunity it unleashed, by keeping government involvement to a minimum! Although the World Wide Web undoubtedly brought new, unpleasant realities that required laws and regulations to restrain people from injuring one another, no one today wants to return to life before the internet for the sake of safety—especially safety controlled by the government. With the Dodd-Frank law, we had a blueprint of what not to do; with the Telecommunications Act, we had an alternative—and much better—idea of how to proceed.

The approach we adopted was to "embrace, engage, examine, and enable." Specifically, we refused to remain in a defensive crouch, and instead *embraced* fintech by rolling with the changes.

We *engaged* by maximizing cooperation and collaboration with international authorities. We *examined* by engaging in research and study, keeping detailed records and monitoring the effects of each change. And, finally, we *enabled* through our global leadership in lobbying for data to move across borders without unnecessary restraint.

Some people wondered why the federal government should play any role at all. Why not allow this revolution to sweep across the economy freely, bringing new opportunities to innovators, entrepreneurs, and investors—and new conveniences to businesses and consumers? On the other hand, money is still money, no matter how fast or technologically advanced it becomes. It's still an expression of value between human beings, which makes it susceptible to abuse. One clear example of this is the 2022 collapse of crypto trading platform FTX, founded by Sam Bankman-Fried. Advanced as fintechs are, they are still overseen and run by human beings, who are prone to greed, poor decision-making, and dishonesty.

If we failed to anticipate bad actors and the ways they could meddle with the fintech phenomenon, we would probably end up back in 2008, with a fresh wave of national outrage, an endless chorus of media voices demanding to know why we were caught off guard, and a new wave of demand for even more federal intervention and red tape. If we heeded the pattern of the Telecommunications Act, however, we might just be able to usher in another wave of widespread success and prosperity.

Treasury spent the first eighteen months of President Trump's first term compiling a report titled *A Financial System That Creates Economic Opportunities: Nonbank Financials, Fintech, and Innovation*. It was both an assessment of issues and potential risks, as well as a blueprint for a streamlined regulatory environment to balance growth and stability. In the words of the July 2018 report, Treasury laid out recommendations and strategies for an "agile approach" to regulation that could evolve alongside innovation.

We took the "longer, shorter route" by gathering info and doing market soundings with our major international partners, by leading fintech policy and regulatory initiatives within international standard-setting bodies, and by designing the architecture that would guide all policy and regulatory work that would happen in countries around the world.

Our approach was rooted in a sense of responsibility for the leadership role the US financial system has taken in providing capital, credit, and stability for the entire global economy. Thus, we took the lead in monitoring the emerging world of digital currencies—for healthy growth, appropriate access, market stability and security, and consumer protection. Under Secretary McIntosh co-chaired the Financial Stability Board (FSB) working group on regulatory issues of stablecoins. This group produced the authoritative final report, *High-level Recommendations on the Regulation, Supervision and Oversight of Global Stablecoin Arrangements*, in October 2020. The report served as the foundation for thinking on the global regulation of digital currency. We also stood up a new G7 digital payments expert group. In addition, Treasury's Office of Terrorism and Financial Intelligence led the Financial Action Task Force (FATF). The FATF is the global standard-setter for combatting money laundering and the financing of terrorism.

In the FSB's Standing Committee on Assessment of Vulnerabilities, we also examined changes to the system as technology companies and new third-party service suppliers appeared. We assessed whether these changes in market structure could present new vulnerabilities. In the President's Interagency Working Group on Financial Markets, we prepared a report detailing all the risks we could foresee with the proliferation of stablecoins, as well as proposed legislation and oversight to protect citizens from harm stemming from:

- speculative digital asset trading and speculative platforms (such as FTX),
- compliance with laws concerning money laundering and the financing of terrorism,
- lack of legal tender status (the right of issuers to refuse to redeem a stablecoin), and
- gaps in authority over "payment with stablecoins"—safeguarding consumer expectations over redeeming a stablecoin on a one-to-one basis for fiat currency.

We stepped up engagement on data connectivity, using America's G7 presidency role to encourage cross-border data flows. Some countries maintain unnecessary restraints on financial institutions' ability to move data across borders, such as data localization requirements (China and Indonesia, to name just two). This remains a significant threat to both productivity growth and financial stability, like blood clots threatening an entire circulatory system, even though clots themselves are usually localized.

We also increased bilateral engagement on fintech-related issues with key jurisdictions worldwide. On a bilateral basis, we deepened cooperation with our friends in Europe, Asia, and across the globe to encourage the growth of fintech, while keeping a sharp eye trained for fraud, theft, money laundering, and financing of terrorism.

With major trading partners like the European Union, India, the United Kingdom, and Japan, with whom we had standing annual regulatory dialogues, we added fintech-related topics to the discussion. It might sound like standard procedure between friendly countries, until you consider the pressure from the speed of change and innovation. In many of these encounters, we negotiated and agreed on cooperative frameworks as quickly as Treasury later rescued industries from the pandemic. Negotiating under pressure and against time always subtracts foresight and adds the risk of mistakes. Fortunately, while our key trading partners wanted (just as much as we did) to seize the benefits of the fintech revolution, they also shared our concerns about foul players taking advantage of fintech's open-source nature. Some established online "sandboxes" as testing grounds for meaning-ful experimentation. We decided to follow their example, using the wisdom of software developers: We would proceed through "sprints" that matured our regulatory framework—stopping along the way to evaluate their efficacy.

These engagements yielded tangible results. When the US issued a joint statement with Singapore endorsing cross-border data transfers and opposing localized data requirements, that statement became a template for other, similar bilateral agree-ments. My group at Treasury began a stand-alone partnership on financial innovation with the UK and Israel, two countries with high concentrations of fintechs. I hosted a full-day fintech pro-gram with our Israeli counterparts and key members of the Israeli private sector to deepen cooperation and calibrate the regulatory environment to support growth and stability. We also convened private-sector programs with leading fintechs in Switzerland and Hong Kong.

When it came to committee assignments at Treasury, my bailiwick was in cross-border data flows. I spent significant amounts of time forging deep alliances with traditional allies like the UK, the EU, and Japan to reduce or eliminate unnecessary barriers. I also sparked dialogue with more hesitant countries, such as Indonesia, which were wary because of their preexisting, protectionist stances. Some countries simply needed detailed explanations of how localized data restrictions made their business climates unattractive to the nimble nature of fintechs. I'd made cases like that to foreign counterparts many times.

Between my adventures in Hong Kong and China in the late 1990s, the challenges of negotiating with the Chinese Communist Party, and the renewal of friendships through America Crecé, I had all the experience I needed to persuade foreign governments to move into the new technological frontier. Did they need funding for infrastructure and growth? You bet they did, which meant that joining the fintech revolution would be as helpful to them as it was when Washington created the FedNow Service, the Federal Reserve's fintech-driven payment system that replaced the Automated Clearing House system from the 1970s. Why would you want to wait months or years when you can have the money you need—on the day you need it?

Was it in these countries' interest to drop their protectionist stance against cross-border data flows? Of course it was, and we could show them why, just like when we showed the Chinese the folly of their World War II–era credit rating system. We created a color-coded heat map to show the differences in GDP between countries that opened their borders to data versus nations that closed them (hint: in the billions). They didn't take long to warm to the idea when those kinds of figures popped up.

Would adopting fintech make these countries more bankable from the point of view of international markets and investors? Of course it would, just like when we disrupted Panama's participation in China's Belt and Road Initiative. We helped them to build meaningful, lower-cost infrastructure that solidified and bolstered their domestic economy. A financial infrastructure capable of moving at twenty-first-century speed is, by definition, more attractive to investors than one that continues to use antiquated technology.

Until March 2020, I moved across Europe and the Middle East at the nonstop pace of fintech growth. In late February, I journeyed to Rome, Amsterdam, Jerusalem, Tel Aviv, and Brussels in a span of nine days, furthering the fintech dialogue with our trading partners. Those trips took an immense amount of planning, in terms of building proposals for cooperation as well as anticipating and preparing contingencies we could offer when we encountered obstacles.

My last stop was in Brussels on March 3 to deliver a keynote at the fourth annual Afore Conference on Fintech and Digital Innovation, where I outlined Treasury's vision and consideration of the threats and risks we faced from the spread of fintech. In hindsight, it was a suitable precursor for the mammoth changes that awaited when my Treasury delegation returned to Washington a few days later. If we'd already led the charge to fundamentally alter the world's systems of trading and exchanging currency, at breakneck speed, we were about to go through a crucible of even faster change, which nobody could have anticipated.

I walked off the plane at Dulles International Airport and headed to my office at Treasury, ready to roll up my sleeves and get to work on the massive list of next steps from the trip. But before I could even begin, a new specter arose. On the first day

I showed up at the office, Brent McIntosh walked in and said, a little sheepishly, "I'm sorry, but you must leave. You're going to have to work from home for at least two weeks." I went (as did all my colleagues who'd traveled with me) straight home into quarantine, followed by a marathon of phone calls and video conferences as we braced for impact from a national—and indeed global—shutdown.

If there is such a thing as jumping from the frying pan and into the fire, I challenge you to find a more accurate example than responding, as a member of a key federal cabinet like Treasury, to a crisis like COVID-19. Secretary Steven Mnuchin was already working on the CARES Act, which President Trump signed into law a mere three weeks later. Treasury leaders told us to think about which industrial sectors we'd prefer to work on; I chose the committee to save the airline industry, since it was so transaction-oriented. The committee broke us up into teams to administer the rescue bailouts (so much for the "no more federal bailouts, period" part of Executive Order 13772), and we hunkered down for a ride that made negotiating with China seem like a walk in the park.

The Trump 45 presidency would end on an even greater note of tension, it turned out, than the one on which it began. A climate of tumult, fear, and uncertainty dominated the year 2020. Its legacy of widespread panic and massive social unrest easily overshadow the legacy of fintech growth, but the truth in totality is more complex. Fintech's speed, accuracy, and data-driven nature facilitated several rescue packages during the pandemic and allowed a great many businesses and individuals to continue to earn revenue and income. As the Chassidic masters say, "The brightness of light is a function of the darkness that preceded it."

Fintech may have started as a revolution in the financial services industry, but that's not where it ended. It soon spread to the concept of earning a living itself. Though there's no doubt that post-2020 workforce phenomena like "quiet quitting" and "the Great Resignation" had plenty to do with employee frustration and burnout, encouraging news came alongside the tight labor market: More and more Americans turned to self-employment, particularly as content creators. Drawn by the speed and simplicity of creating homemade videos and earning a living from the sale of information products and advertising space, many who formerly earned their living by working for companies now earn it for themselves, without leaving their homes or giving hours of their lives to lengthy commutes. If there was an idea that most of us in the Trump 45 administration supported, it was a society where an increasing number of Americans achieved a greater-than-ever degree of financial independence, in every sense of the word.

At the time of this writing, fintech continues to rewrite the rules of financial services. Most of the large traditional institutions are shuttering their local branches and retraining employees as "problem-solvers"—comprehensive account executives, if you will. Traditional calculations and bank labor no longer require bankers and tellers; AI can handle it. Negotiating and proliferating fintech turned out to be ideal advance training for 2020, given the speed and grace under pressure it took to react to COVID-19. But more than that, the development we worked to keep pace with turned out to be essential to surviving the effects of the shutdown. Today, people think nothing of making friends, generating business, conducting international commerce, and transmitting huge amounts of data and currency to people on the other side of the world. They do it without nanny-state supervision, as if they've come to embody the science fiction worlds once imagined in movies.

While COVID-19 materially redirected the fintech revolution, the more immediate imperative for the Trump Treasury as the pandemic swept the globe was to save the American economy—and the global economy—from complete and devastating collapse. And, as you are about to read, we had ten days to do it.

CHAPTER 9

THE CARES ACT:
THE TEN DAYS THAT SAVED AMERICA

The day is short, and the task is great...
and the master of the house is insistent.

—*Ethics of Our Fathers*, chapter 2, verse 15

In March 2020, the economy—which had enjoyed record-breaking growth for three consecutive years—went off a cliff. Borders closed, passenger transportation ground to a halt, stores and restaurants shuttered, production facilities shut down, and global supply chains froze. Schools closed. Layoffs went through the roof. Cities emptied, and fear spread faster than sickness. Major grocers and wholesalers sold every last inch of toilet paper and ounce of hand sanitizer the market could manufacture.

In a matter of weeks, a worldwide pandemic froze the entire social order, and millions of Americans hid in their homes, with no idea how long it would last.

I arrived home from my whirlwind mission to Rome, Amsterdam, Tel Aviv, Jerusalem, and Brussels, only to find the country in lockdown and myself in quarantine. I went from a fast-paced series of engagements on export credits and fintech and an important session before the Financial Stability Board to a screeching halt.

As I waited for permission to return to work, I began to see the writing on the wall. Without some kind of stopgap action, I realized, the shelter-in-place orders and extreme prevention measures would lead to economic conditions that would make the Great Depression seem bullish. We had to figure out how to keep two hundred million working adults "paid" during a crisis with an indefinite timeline. Treasury had just days to come up with a rescue plan before the US economy collapsed.

The word "unprecedented" was used a lot during 2020, and it was appropriate for what we were about to do. No one had ever tried to rescue an entire economy—especially the world's largest, with a multitrillion-dollar GDP. At any other time in history, no one would have even thought to attempt it; the technology necessary for these levels of communication and cooperation simply didn't exist. And it all had to come together in fewer than fourteen days.

As I look back on this time now, I struggle to recall how we maintained our focus on the economy's fundamentals. Unlike previous government actions, such as the 2008 mortgage or auto industry rescue programs, the Coronavirus Aid, Relief, and Economic Security (CARES) Act of 2020 targeted every single level and sector of the economy. This was not a single-dimensional issue—*every* industry, not just lending or manufacturing, was affected. We had to allocate emergency funds for individuals, small businesses, state governments, the transportation industry, and many more. Millions of people were suddenly unemployed or unable to work because of lockdowns. Small businesses were unable to make payroll and overhead. State, local, and tribal governments could not meet budgets because their tax revenues plunged through the floor while their costs of coping with the pandemic skyrocketed. Airline traffic plummeted by 98 percent in a few short weeks, sending the industry into a tailspin. Working-class neighborhoods and communities needed low-cost loans to stay afloat and grow, and creditors urgently needed cash to continue lending to individuals, businesses, nonprofits, and governments.

Something told me, however, that we at Treasury would get a chance to do something truly extraordinary and impactful in response. As consensus spread through Congress and the White House that we must act quickly, I began to see recognizable "pattern points" from my experience with international finance and law. Each year, when the Jewish people celebrate the High Holy Days, we're reminded that one door closes while another one opens. Bleak as the pandemic seemed at the time, Americans had to look for that one door that was cracked open just a bit—and my senses told me it was right in front of us.

During the late 1990s, when I worked at Allen & Overy, I played a key role in restructuring many large projects with upside-down finances, none bigger than Guangdong Enterprises (GDE). As the largest public-owned finance firm in China, its primary role in Guangdong province—China's growth engine and largest sub-sovereign economy—was to act as a transactional and finance bridge to facilitate trade and investment between China and the outside world. Much of this finance activity took place in Hong Kong. Think of GDE as Guangdong province's finance window to the international markets. By the time my firm was called in, GDE had become the largest debt sinkhole in the entire People's Republic of China—more than $6 billion in the hole when the restructuring started and "too big to fail." GDE turned to Western firms, including Goldman Sachs, for help. My law firm represented the creditors committee on the other side of the table.

A centerpiece of the rescue focused on essentially privatizing the Dongshen Water Supply Project, one of the province's crown jewels supporting its economic growth. The Dongshen project supplied 75 percent of the raw water needs for the island of Hong Kong. It took two years and, at times, as many as two hundred lawyers from our firm, to put together the structure, consents, government approvals, and documentation to complete the restructuring, including the reorganization and privatization of Dongshen. The water project was integral to the whole process because its revenue stream provided the collateral that GDE used to support the massive amount of new debt that it needed to create to pay off the sinkhole of debt that it had created and defaulted on. There were an overwhelming number of moving parts, and the challenge sometimes felt like we were playing bumper cars with monster trucks.

The background and context of rescuing the US airline industry had features that I recognized from GDE. In both situations, collapse would have sent shockwaves throughout the US, Chinese, and global economies. Both cases presented a looming deadline; we completed each one in the nick of time, before a financial pressure cooker exploded and scalded everyone involved. Both cases demanded that we weave a thin cord of agreement between myriad stakeholder groups, including powerful bureaucracy chiefs and industry leaders. And in each case, the gigantic size of the enterprise at hand produced a staggering level of complexity and documentation, requiring both visionary thinking, a grueling attention to detail, a mountain of paperwork, and a Herculean level of transaction management.

I remembered something else from the blueprint for rescuing GDE: compartmentalization—the practice of separating wide amounts of work into narrow areas of focus—and staying on task. If confronted with the impossible task of climbing to heaven, well, then, get your ladder out and take it rung by rung. And remember: There are no shortcuts, just deliberate, steady, and determined steps. I recalled the teaching of the great medieval commentator Rashi, who reminded us of what the good Lord told Moses when tasking him with the impossible ordeal of staring down Pharoah and freeing the Israelite slaves: "You do yours and I will do Mine." This is a staple of Ancient Jewish wisdom that always pushed me forward, rung by rung.

It's too much to ask one single person to tackle an enormous project in a short period of time. But in both Guangdong and during COVID-19, I was hardly alone. For GDE, we created multiple teams around work verticals—the Water Project, Capital Markets, Credit, Corporate, Trusts, Asset Management and Real Property—that divided and further subdivided the workload among hundreds of sharp and detailed minds. When Treasury got the call to rescue the airlines, I knew we could pull it off. We had some of the best and brightest minds in the world working with us, and more besides if we needed them. No matter how complex a problem came our way, I believed we could overcome it if we remembered the practice of breaking it into manageable pieces.

So as the groundswell of demand and support for federal intervention grew, I suppose you could say I saw the "trees for the forest" a little clearer than most. I felt confident that Treasury could rescue any industry in an effective, efficient, and responsible manner that looked after the taxpayers' interests. All I needed was an opportunity to test, in a domestic situation, what had already succeeded in China, Southeast Asia, and the entire Western Hemisphere.

In the meantime, however, I had to watch helplessly, like any other American, as the entire social order buckled under a tsunami of fear. It took me back to the time I'd lived through a real-life tsunami, the one that struck Indonesia and the South Pacific in December 2004.

That fateful day began with an uneventful speedboat transfer across calm waters to the idyllic Similan Islands, off the coast of Phuket, Thailand, which offers some of the finest scuba diving and snorkeling in the world. Flying across the water for just under an hour at speeds up to a hundred miles per hour, our charter tour arrived around 9:00 a.m.—but as we approached the islands, we could sense that something wasn't right. The waterline was rising and falling at a blurring ten feet *per second*, and our guide told us the levels were ninety feet lower than normal. The fish, which were usually everywhere, had vanished. We later understood that the tsunami had traveled right under us in stealth mode, and that we were so far offshore in such deep water that the only sign of its passing was the erratic shifts in water level caused when it approached the islands.

As information trickled down, we found ourselves in a lock-down of sorts. There had indeed been an earthquake that triggered a tsunami, and as a result, the authorities would not let anyone move. So we sat and waited, overexposed to the sun and breathing a steady diet of exhaust fumes from the boat's motor, for several hours.

Eventually, the boat was permitted to return to the mainland, where we immediately entered a quarantine. The Thai navy dispatched a frigate to the coast, and its crew herded together everyone from all the returning vessels. The waters were calm and there were no signs of tidal waves—but no one was allowed to go ashore.

When we were finally allowed off our boat, we were horrified. The tsunami had struck the Thap Lamu Pier, from which our pleasure boat had left that morning. It was utterly devastated—entire structures wiped out, reduced to piles of wood, leaving only cement foundations and walls. Cars were upside down in the streets; some hung suspended in large trees. An entire Thai naval vessel had beached—two hundred feet of gray steel washed up on the land like a whale. You can imagine the disruption and dismemberment of the local economy this caused.

To compound matters for me personally, my hotel was seventy miles away. There were no taxis or transports to be hailed. I did manage to get in touch with the manager of my hotel, who said he would send a car—but he also warned me that he had no idea how soon it could get there. The roads were congested, bridges were closed, and it could take days. The entire chain of supplies and services had been severed, and no one knew how long it would take to get it back to working order.

And then, just as I thought the worst was over, the authorities hit the panic button again. They'd detected an aftershock and scrambled a military truck to evacuate everyone to high ground. This provoked pandemonium—people running in every direction, trying to jump onto moving vehicles, screaming and crying. A truck took us to a shelter in the hills, where we crowded in with hundreds of other people.

In the nick of time, before my cell phone's battery died, I reached the hotel manager again. The car he'd sent finally made it to Thap Lamu, and after twenty hours of adventure, I returned to my hotel room at 1:00 a.m. Exhausted and overwhelmed, I took a few days to process and unwind from the entire affair.

The time I spent in reflection sums up a key Jewish principle: The greater the darkness, the brighter the light that follows it. Of all the questions I could ask and opinions I could form about the tsunami, one thing hadn't changed: Life goes on. We can ask *why* during extraordinary and terrible events. But once we survive them, the question should shift to *what*. As in, "What do I do now?" Or more specifically, "What do I do now, *to bring light to the darkness?*"

Once the initial tsunami of COVID-19 had struck and passed, we were faced with a similar question: What do we do now? If the darkest shadows eventually give way to the brightest light, how could we align ourselves to cooperate, facilitate, and let the light in?

I had a feeling I already knew some of the answers, and in just a few days, my suspicions were confirmed.

Treasury Secretary Steve Mnuchin oversaw the design and negotiations for the $2.2 trillion CARES Act. The secretary and his very tight and elite SWAT team spent five days designing the statutory program, and an additional five days (and nights) on Capitol Hill negotiating the legislation. The secretary and a handful of unsung heroes from Treasury who supported him did not leave the Hill for those last five days and nights. They held one meeting, discussion, haggle session, negotiation, and revision after another. And just when they thought they'd reached agreement, they went back for more, literally without sleeping, until they had a bill Congress would approve.

President Trump signed the CARES Act into law on the sixth day, and it took force on March 27, 2020. It was the largest economic relief package in history, dwarfing anything the US government had ever done before.

I couldn't help but reflect on the forty days and forty nights that it took Moses to bring the Law down from Mount Sinai. It took the Treasury secretary only five days and five nights to bring the CARES Act down from Capitol Hill. At a moment of such profound consequence, Steven Mnuchin was indeed the lawgiver.

Amid all the scrambling we did to keep the economy afloat, I was also well aware that US history was replete with financial relief programs in moments of crisis. Treasury Secretary Alexander Hamilton led the nation's first government-funded financial rescue, in response to the Panic of 1792. At the time, the United States' fledgling securities market was as vulnerable as the ones we'd been trying to spur throughout the Western Hemisphere. Since then, Treasury has intervened on numerous occasions to prevent total market collapses. The Great Depression comes to mind, beginning in 1933 with enormous amounts of direct federal aid flowing from President Roosevelt's New Deal.

Then there was the savings and loan rescue of 1989, where taxpayers spent somewhere between $105 billion and $132 billion on failed financial institutions. In more recent times, Treasury acted to help the market absorb the fallout from the collapse of Fannie Mae and Freddie Mac in 2008—the subprime mortgage crisis.

The COVID-19 pandemic was different, however. It was the first time in our lives that a massive health scare would cause global financial disruption, and no one knew how soon it would subside. However, we did know that our existing emergency relief plans might easily run out of funds before the disease finished wreaking havoc. To sit back and rely on what we already had was like trusting the pre-2005 levees built to protect New Orleans from flooding, with Hurricane Katrina just a few miles from shore. Our best estimates suggested—and our worst ones demanded—that we act. Whatever was about to happen, we were going to need a lot of cash to withstand it. We'd also need to exercise restraint, objectivity, and fiscal discipline to deploy the resources, assess progress, and adjust the strategy as circumstances evolved.

Another novelty of the pandemic was the sheer velocity of our response. There was no time to make advance plans, develop ideas, or craft rules. When President Obama signed the Dodd-Frank Wall Street Reform and Consumer Protection Act in 2010, it was the broadest and most sweeping financial regulatory reform in decades. The entire bill was 848 pages long. *Two years* after its passage, ten regulatory agencies had generated 8,843 pages of rules and regulations. That figure represented just 30 percent of rulemaking contemplated under the act. Moreover, that entire process was still unfolding four years after the crisis that triggered it.

In stark contrast, we had less than *two weeks* before, for all we knew, the US economy would be dead in the water. At Treasury during those days, it often felt like we didn't even have two hours.

Before the law went to Congress, we'd already divided into emergency response teams around each of the Treasury programs in the CARES Act. My division, Treasury International Affairs, took charge of aviation and national security relief. With little rhyme or reason, I spent the last ten months of my government service—the most disruptive, stressful, and indeed rewarding period in my career—preventing the airline industry from cratering.

The law required Treasury to publish procedures within ten days of its enactment, and make our first payment within ten days of approving the first application. Just to make things even more interesting, the deadline coincided with the first days of Passover on the Jewish calendar. After sunset on April 8, I would be offline for religious observances in line with Jewish law.

As soon as President Trump signed the bill, Treasury was inundated with phone calls and correspondence from the press. There were congressional requests for formal and informal briefings, which meant that, in addition to designing, building, and running a mammoth infrastructure, I conducted at least one briefing every week for bipartisan members of Senate and congressional committees. This went on for the better part of two months until our colleagues in Legislative Affairs took over this function.

Complications arose overnight. Due to the pandemic, Washington, DC was on lockdown. Treasury mandated a remote work policy, with only senior officials coming to the office and operating under strict protocols. This meant running the show and managing each case of the program by phone and video, often using teleconferencing platforms that many people had never used before.

At the same time, the nation, and particularly the nation's capital, convulsed through a period of intense and serious civil unrest, stemming mainly from the death of George Floyd at the hands of the Minneapolis police. The ensuing protests interfered with simply getting in and out of the Treasury Building so the core team could do its work. On May 29, amid of one of the most complex and intense phases of work, protesters occupied Lafayette Square in front of the White House. They attempted to breach the White House gate, and then proceeded to vandalize, graffiti, burn, break windows, and loot stores and buildings in the area. On the stretch of Fifteenth Street that includes the east wall of the Treasury Building, protesters smashed the storefront windows of virtually every store and commercial space. They burned outdoor furniture and left vulgar, obscene, and offensive graffiti on every surface they could find, including all over the walls of the beautiful and majestic Treasury Building—the Fortress of Finance. They hurled bricks, rocks, and bottles of urine and alcohol. The Secret Service raised the alert level to red.

It felt like I was working in a war zone. Mayor Muriel Bowser imposed curfews. The Secret Service erected a ten-foot-high protective fence around the entire White House and Lafayette Park, including Main Treasury. Battalions of armed Secret Service and police surrounded the White House complex. On some days, they gathered just under my window, which overlooked the Bell Entrance of Main Treasury. I entered work through high gates and checkpoints, walking in between armed troops. The Secret Service frequently sent early warnings about security threats anticipated during the day, such as roaming groups of rioters. The Secret Service told us to keep our ID cards out of sight until we had to present them to enter the complex. Combined with my overt appearance as an Orthodox Jew, I felt particularly exposed. I thought of how my grandfather must have felt in the old country in the times of pogroms.

We'd grown up hearing two terrible stories from the Ukrainian village where my grandfather was born. He spoke about how Cossacks brutally killed his grandfather—they'd put him in a burlap bag and beat him until blood ran through the fabric, then they picked him up and threw him, bag and all, into his burning house. The Cossacks killed another relative by tying his beard to the back of a wagon that dragged him to his death through the streets of the village. Jews in Eastern Europe were always dreading the next attack, never knowing where it might come from but certain that it would. Was Washington, DC headed for a similar reign of terror?

Beyond the tense environment, Treasury now operated with *very* limited resources. Prior to the pandemic, the head count for the entire Main Treasury staff, including everyone in Domestic Finance, International Affairs, and Terrorism and Financial Intelligence, was around three hundred. All of us worked at full tilt. We didn't have extra hands, and there was no reserve staff available from elsewhere. We were already used to a demanding job, but now the job had to be done with the building mostly empty. More than half the people were working from home, only available via phone or videoconference. If you needed face time to discuss something, it was unlikely you could get it.

And yet the work got done, to the immense credit of the Treasury's dedicated employees, the secretary first and foremost. I have been blessed to work with some great commercial and financial minds in the course of my thirty-year law practice, and Secretary Mnuchin certainly took the cake when it came to projecting down the road and identifying holes and solutions. His uncanny ability to filter out the immense chatter when presented with and considering a complex issue and to remain laser-focused on the path forward and the solution, his exceptional ability to process facts and analysis in a virtual nanosecond, and his extremely sound decision-making were invaluable in saving not only the airline industry, but the entire economy. Despite the obstacles, the CARES Act successfully tackled *all* the challenges identified by the act's framers, and in record time. Consider its achievements:

- It offered a lifeline to millions of Americans faced with losing their jobs, by paying their salaries and spiking their benefits via the Payroll Support Program (PSP). Treasury originally estimated $32 billion for program and expanded it by an additional $15 billion when all was said and done.
- The Paycheck Protection Program (PPP) granted more than 5.2 million loans and protected small businesses with more than $525 billion. A full quarter of those loans

went to "historically underutilized business zones" and supported more than fifty-one million jobs. Latest estimates calculate that the PPP supported more than sixty million jobs and saved more than thirteen million jobs.

- Programs for state, local, and tribal governments provided almost $150 million to bolster their financial response to their residents, including rental and utilities assistance.
- The Emergency Capital Protection Program granted $9 billion in loans to small businesses, including minority-owned businesses, and individuals primarily in low-income and underserved communities. Using the Federal Reserve Act, Treasury and the Fed unleashed $454 billion of loans in record time.
- My role was with the $76 billion Airline and National Security Relief Programs, which helped to protect more than seven hundred thousand jobs and rescued the airline industry from insolvency and bankruptcy. Without our action, an entire industry would have collapsed like a house of cards.

By the end of March, we had passed a momentous bill and marshaled our resources to begin administering aid. But challenges aplenty remained. And they began with saving the most vulnerable industry: the airline industry.

CHAPTER 10

SAVING THE AIRLINE INDUSTRY

Saving the airline sector's seven hundred thousand jobs, as well as the millions of jobs in related or dependent sectors—not to mention preserving a vitally strategic industry—was a tour de force of triage, dedication, and clinical expertise that rivaled any Level I trauma hospital in the world. In fact, it's probably fair to say that it matched several of those trauma hospitals working simultaneously on the same patient. As though the patient had broken both legs and gone into cardiac arrest at the same time.

But if anyone could save the airlines, Treasury staff had the pedigrees. We were all seasoned dealmakers. Secretary Steve Mnuchin knew markets and finance, inside and out. Brent McIntosh, under secretary for international affairs, was a recognized national security law expert. He'd served in senior positions in the George W. Bush White House and cut his teeth on large crisis management litigation cases as a partner of the venerable Sullivan & Cromwell law firm. We also had Eric Froman, an old colleague from Allen & Overy; Gary Grippo, longtime Treasury official and federal finance pro; and Dan Katz, an experienced lawyer and former Goldman Sachs investment banker. As for me, I brought thirty years of making complex, billion-dollar deals across borders, with multiple parties, often under hair-raising deadlines, to the table.

If you noticed foreign banks, such as HSBC, Mitsubishi, and TD, proliferating in the US, that's the kind of work I did for a considerable part of my career. I spent several of my thirty years as an attorney assisting foreign financial institutions to expand into the US, in addition to helping US investors, mainly in the energy sector, to enter the China market. When they needed help with financing to penetrate a market that was foreign and seemingly unnecessarily complex, I helped them to find their way through the administrative thicket. Like a courier who gets to know the streets of a busy downtown by name, I found "traffic jams" exciting—because I learned so much about finance laws that I knew the alternate routes. So, if the job we were about to do called for moving enormous amounts of money from Treasury to an industry that was on life support, I felt like a lone motorcyclist weaving cheerfully through a sea of car traffic, with red brake lights everywhere and horns honking nonstop.

Ironically, the expertise I found most useful for the airline rescue was the same strategy we'd used for America Crecé, the growth initiative we'd shared with our neighbors in the Western Hemisphere. "Project financing," as the method is known, often helps fledgling countries industrialize their most basic necessities—energy and infrastructure. It was not apparent at the outset that project financing techniques would be helpful in rescuing the US aviation sector. But the more we analyzed the airlines' numbers—particularly their sources of cash flow and value—the clearer it became that we already had a tourniquet to stop the bleeding and prevent their demise.

Make no mistake—this was still a leviathan of a task. There was no "Airline Rescue Bank" operating in the United States in March 2020, which means that we had all of fourteen days to make one appear. Moreover, this nonexistent "bank" needed an injection of $76 billion to prevent nearly three-quarters of a million people from losing their jobs. If that wasn't enough, it also needed an administrative machine to make it effective. If you've ever gone through the process of getting a mortgage, you've probably dealt with tellers, loan officers, underwriters, title companies, and their pages (and pages and pages) of procedures and legal considerations. We didn't have any of this structure built. Not one sheet of paper.

And the clock was ticking.

The CARES Act finally took effect on March 27, 2020. It felt a bit like being on the Allied ships that sailed for northern France on D-Day. The good news was that the rescue was on its way. The not-so-good news was the enormous effort it would take, across miles of unforgiving terrain, with plenty of opposition and obstacles impeding our success. On top of that, the law required Treasury to make the first payments within ten days of accepting the first application for relief.

The CARES Act divided relief for the airline industry into two major "buckets": (1) Payroll Support Program (PSP) payments, which provided a six-month runway for the airlines to pay their debts and keep their employees on staff, and which meant that wages, salaries, and benefits were at the very front of the line; and (2) loans, which gave them the funds necessary to stay in business, even though the pandemic caused air traffic to plummet by 98 percent.

Each bucket was a distinct program with congressionally determined allocations. Based on those congressional stipulations and the figures we obtained from the airlines, we were looking at payroll support budgets of $25 billion for passenger air carriers, $4 billion for cargo air carriers, and $3 billion for air carrier contractors. This would give each of them nine months of breathing room, and then we'd review in December to see if they needed further assistance. On the loan side, we allocated $25 billion for passenger air carriers and $4 billion for cargo air carriers.

Normally, a federal loan or grant program like this would be implemented over the course of months or years. There would be detailed consideration of several angles and issues before we opened ourselves to receive applications, to say nothing of distributing funds. What would normally take place over ninety to 180 days, in other words, was suddenly crammed into ten.

You could say we pulled some overtime shifts. Remember, this was nothing like going to your local bank to set up a wire transfer. These were legal decisions, as well as financial ones. That meant we had to spend a lot of time thinking about the basic legal requirements of the CARES Act, which portions required formal actions, such as an application and the content of that application; which sections required guidance and the timing of any such action; and which sections would present challenges in implementation. To receive support at this scale, the airlines would have their own legal teams review, understand, and negotiate their obligations, which would complicate and lengthen the process.

I honestly don't know how we got through the application intake work, when I reflect on it. I felt like Nehemiah, the biblical figure who oversaw the record-breaking, fifty-two-day reconstruction of the wall of Jerusalem, circa 444 BCE. By the time the application periods closed, we'd received more than a thousand applications for the Payroll Support Program, and hundreds of applications for loans.

At this stage, and throughout the CARES marathon, Dan Katz played a pivotal role, from assisting with application intake and underwriting to running quants at bullet train speed to inform our critical decision-making on PSP loan allocations and sizing and structuring of taxpayer protection, to fielding a deluge of inquiries from applicants, and everything in between. It's not an overstatement to say the airline industry owed much of its survival to Dan.

How, exactly, did the rescue operation proceed? In several phases.

Phase 1: Emergency Response Program and Infrastructure Design

The hasty assembly of this "Airline Rescue Bank" and its loan application process was a mere first step. The global economy was still in freefall, the pandemic was still open-ended, and we had no time to waste. The first two weeks, from March 27 to April 11, were devoted to designing and establishing the infrastructure.

We managed to settle the terms of the PSP. We knew it would have the greatest effect by focusing on applicants with the largest numbers of workers in the shortest amount of time—the major carriers Delta, American, United, and Alaska. Now that we knew which companies to start with, we could study their size and scope in much more detail, and arrange our programs into categories of scale. Through one conference call after another with airline executives, I learned more about the aviation industry in those ten days than I had in the previous ten years.

The first thing we did was to publish the application processes and procedures. The law gave us a handful of days to do it, and we beat the deadline by two days. The documents went live on April 3, 2020. I'm at a loss to describe how detailed, painstaking, and challenging this process was, from the standpoint of critiquing and revising procedures—and that's not to mention the clearance process!

Our CARES Act website required significant design and engineering before it could begin to receive applications. David Eisner, assistant secretary for management, pulled the first of many rabbits out of his hat and came up with a workaround. His work was just one example of a lesson we learned many times: People with deep experience in building practical, real-world solutions to complex problems are essential when confronting a crisis.

Now we could add definition and create distinctions for this "Airline Rescue Bank." If you want to reduce confusion and offer something that's helpful and efficient, make it as simple and direct as possible. We parsed our way through the back-office departments: legal, financial advisory, communications, compliance/anti-fraud, conflicts, reporting, and IT. Then we arranged the "storefront," which included six Operational Pillars: Applications, Decision-Making/Credit, Documentation/Closing, Payment Systems, Asset Management/Servicing, and the Department of Transportation's coordination mechanism. Each of these areas needed rules, procedures, policies, forms, documents, and operational guidelines.

I knew Legal would apply to every aspect of the program. They'd want oversight on program eligibility, compliance with the law, and documentation of transactions, to name just a few. Eric Froman, an unsung star of this program, was our guardian angel in legal support. Eric supported Secretary Mnuchin throughout the framing, structuring, negotiation, and documentation of the CARES Act on the Hill. He was trained by two leading global firms (including my former firm, Allen & Overy), and was a Treasury Legal team veteran. We also got support from a few sister agencies, mainly the SEC, as well as from three excellent outside law firms: Cleary Gottlieb, Davis Polk, and Sullivan & Cromwell. Jay Clayton, then chairman of the SEC, was most generous in lending legal and other resources under interagency secondments. If it hadn't been for their help, the massive job of documenting PSP and loan transactions would have been a nonstarter.

Both programs relied heavily on outside financial advisors to answer questions about how the funds were allocated, the size of Taxpayer Protection Instruments, pricing of loans, acceptable collateral, financial cover tests, and much more. We got a ton of support from the excellent teams at PJT Partners, Moelis & Company, and Perella Weinberg Partners. Our Public Affairs and Legislative Affairs Departments assisted with the communications function, including liaising with stakeholders, the press, and Congress.

David Eisner worked tirelessly to ensure that the two of the most challenging areas—reporting and IT—never held us up. It was an impossible job. The program had myriad layers of reporting to Congress and the Office of Management and Budget, as well as at the transactional level. The entire project was automated and hosted on the internet; it took an army of web designers and coders to handle the workload. David ensured that the web designers kept pace with the rollout's breakneck speed, so that the web-based portal could absorb the influx of applications.

Last but not least, existing teams within Treasury addressed compliance and anti-fraud issues, to ensure the program maintained modern standards and expectations. The last thing we wanted was for negligence, corruption, or graft to pounce on this days-old organism and undermine the trust of the airline industry or the public.

As for the six Operational Pillars, we started from scratch. In record time, we created standards for intake, cataloging, verification, and eligibility review, so our Applications group could do their jobs according to the law. Going deeper, we cleared the road for the decision-making group, the people who would decide which loans were processed and which were denied. Gary Grippo, deputy assistant secretary for public finance, played a pivotal role laying out the process for budget-scoring each transaction and building out the program's payment systems.

With the blurry, frenetic pace we kept, there's no way we could have documented everything without assistance. Outside law firms stepped forward to help keep track of the flood of transactions. Borrowing from standard-form loan documentation, which I'd set up for banking clients over the years, I worked with external counsel to prepare and settle suites of transaction documents, framed in plain English to expedite review.

There were internal resources and tools we could put to good use for the program's basic operations. For example, we borrowed from the existing systems for fund disbursement and custodial bank services. In addition, existing Treasury staff filled posts for our asset management, accounting, loan management, and servicing functions until we could hire new employees.

Finally, there was coordination with the Department of Transportation (DOT). As the primary regulator of more than 90 percent of program recipients, the DOT held huge sway over eligibility. We needed a channel for communicating with DOT in real time so we could make decisions and take action without running afoul of their authority or standards. When you're trying to rescue an airline that's one week from collapse, the last thing you need is a six-month holdup while another cabinet department forms a committee to study the implications of saying yes.

We needed nothing less than direct, linear access to qualified DOT decision-makers.

When the need is high and time is short, it's amazing how you can marshal resources to solve a problem. As we scrambled to pull every lever we could to put our rescue plan into action, I was reminded of a family crisis of almost equally epic proportions.

When my oldest son, Meshulam, celebrated his bar mitzvah, we had festivities planned for the entire week, both in New York and in Israel. All went beautifully—until it came time for the Kiddush and meal in our New York shul on Shabbos day. I had called and organized a caterer a good three months in advance of the event. Disaster, however, hit less than an hour before candle lighting: We were still at home when the *rebbetzin* (wife of the rabbi) called to ask where the caterer was since he had not shown up to drop off any of the food and put up what needed to be kept warm. I immediately called the caterer, who didn't pick up at first. When we finally got him on the phone, he swore up and down that the bar mitzvah was the following week.

There we were, less than an hour before Shabbos, expecting more than a hundred people for Kiddush and more than twenty for lunch, with no food. The machinery kicked in. The rebbetzin took four kugels she had in the freezer, my mother-in-law ran to Schick's to get fish, and I ran to Ateres Chaya, the hall across from shul, to see if they could assist with cakes and cholent. In the end, we got by. I won't say that we had an overwhelming quantity or variety of food, but it was more than sufficient. More important, Meshulam felt like a million bucks, the show went on, and no one was left hungry. It was a beautiful *simcha*, and I am still immensely indebted to everyone who pitched in to help. We would not have been able to pull it off without them.

We had similar unexpected surprises as we scrambled to get CARES money into the right hands. Most carriers, for example, are required to report their employment levels to the DOT at regular intervals, but there were some who were exempt, as well as many who used contractors. For these carriers, we required certified statements of employment. It added another layer of complexity to their workload, as well as to ours. When it came to interpreting the data to decide how much money to award, evaluating carriers who were exempt from reporting required even more time, which we already didn't have.

In other instances, of course, the bad apples floated to the surface easily enough. Several applications failed to pass even the basic smell test, including a clearly non-US applicant seeking more than $1 billion in PSP payments. Treasury's anti-fraud unit stayed very busy during this time, but, thankfully, not on cases like that one.

Most of the applicants wanted more money than we were prepared to pay out. But now that we had categories and general guidelines, it was easier to determine which "box" an airline belonged to—and offer it prorated support based on the severity of its shortfall. For example, if we received two applications, one from a major carrier with twenty thousand employees and the other from a small regional operation, we would settle both, one in proportion to the other. We did not, in other words, write blanket checks of equal amounts to anyone and everyone who applied.

Phase 2: Rushing Aid to Major Airline Carriers

It was finally time to get money into the right hands, and fast. We focused on the largest passenger airlines first.

During the weeks of April 12 to 25, 2020, we embarked on a "marathon sprint" of approvals and payments. The PSP decision committee met every day to review and approve applications. Of the funds we set aside for PSP payments, we reached decisions for 90 percent in just two weeks. By April 25, we'd awarded $12 billion and approved $24.5 billion of our allocation, representing 196 applications. If you average that out, that means we processed loans worth more than $61 million to nearly two hundred different companies in just thirteen days. I challenge you to find a lending institution willing to lend that amount of money to that many applicants in such a short space of time without enormous and costly errors, or collapse.

Then there was the speed with which we disbursed the funds. By the end of Phase 2—less than a month after the CARES Act went into effect—we'd approved agreements for 98 percent of the funds available for passenger carriers. That number also represented 85 percent of the program's total funds. Phase 2 protected more than 434,000 American jobs within four weeks of the law's passage, and just six or seven weeks since the shutdowns began. For the top thirteen US passenger carriers, we paid out more than $23 billion in payroll support.

These payments kept American airline workers on the job. They stabilized the airlines' financial position and prevented huge numbers of furloughs and layoffs.

As April gave way to May, the weeds began to sprout. Difficult issues of law, fact, and policy emerged, in cases presented by smaller applicants. So we shifted our focus to solving the issues that required more nuance and fewer broad strokes. On balance, however, the crisis had at least been stalled. Time would tell if we had truly averted it.

Phase 3: Turning Attention to Air Cargo and Contractors

The passenger carriers taught us some of what we needed to know for our next job: the cargo and contractor PSP applications we processed between April 26 and May 7. But there were learning curves, and we could only discover them the hard way.

These industries were distinguished from the air carriers in two fundamental ways. First, the pandemic spiked demand for emergency response equipment and supplies. It disrupted supply chains and shipping routes. This benefited the air cargo sector, rather than threatening it. Once this became clear, leading cargo firms like FedEx and DHL withdrew their applications. For the carriers that remained, however, eligibility was much more challenging. It involved complex factual investigation and analysis.

The contractor classes were much harder to quantify and define. Passenger carriers were more straightforward—the cost of travel prohibition was equal to the debts, payroll, and operations of the airline. They're easier to approve or deny as a category—either you are a passenger airline, or you're not. The danger to taxpayers was a clear and present one, in view of the program's potential impact on so many other industries. Contractors were much more case by case. We went through several revisions of a supplemental application they had to complete before we could even consider them for the program.

Phase 4: Resolving a Mountain of Thorny Problems

The situation reached a fever pitch between May and June. The remaining PSP applications presented difficult questions of law, complex facts, and nuanced policy. Even so, Treasury continued to process all three categories of PSP applications, issuing major cargo and contractor approvals and payments at a rapid clip.

More than one thousand problematic PSP applications were still left to resolve. Each one needed to be done by hand, so to speak, carefully evaluated by human beings. We could not automate, delegate, or outsource the minutiae. We had to dig for the information we needed through complex corporate organization charts, detailed tax filings, and other documents. We identified nearly twenty bottlenecks in three basic categories: (1) basic issues that could easily be corrected, (2) eligibility, and (3) complex corporate matters.

The basic correctable issues mainly consisted of clerical mistakes and mathematical errors. Resolutions were straightforward, if still labor-intensive. Fixes frequently depended on timely responses from applicants; in many cases, they took longer than the emergency circumstances of the program would allow.

Eligibility, meanwhile, depended on answering some extremely difficult questions of law, fact, and policy. For example, defining "contractor" for eligibility was complicated, and obtaining background evidence and information to support defining a carrier as a contractor took a lot of time. We also struggled with the term "'air carrier"; simply checking the DOT's records was insufficient. After several exhausting rounds of back-and-forth, we finally agreed on a framework to evaluate the eligibility of air carrier and contractor applicants alike.

We still weren't finished, though. Now that we had a framework, it was time to apply it to the carriers that sought our help. You can imagine, in many cases, that we required significant additional information, materials, documents, and follow-up. You can also imagine how the applicants reacted to those second and third phone calls.

Eligibility often hinged on applicants' underlying corporate structures—which presented some unforeseen complications. The scope and speed at which the CARES Act was created and passed made it impossible to include provisions for every instance. For example, when the framers of the CARES Act needed to define "air carriers," the best shorthand they could reference was the definition found in other statutes and DOT rules.

However, we subsequently discovered that "air carrier," within the meaning of the statute, meant *inter*state air carriers but not *intra*state air carriers. This distinction was not a problem for the continental US, but it posed a significant challenge to many small companies operating in Alaska that were classified as "intrastate" carriers because they only flew within Alaska's massive expanse. This was not a mere technicality. Treasury had no legal authority to provide funds to these carriers, meaning that it would have been illegal for Treasury to approve their applications.

The Alaskan congressional delegation was predictably very unhappy with this situation, but Congress took no action to fix the problem. Treasury and the DOT got creative and devised a solution: an expedited process that would allow intrastate air carriers to apply to become interstate air carriers—and therefore become eligible for relief. With significant outreach to the Alaskan community through the Alaskan trade organization and the Alaskan congressional delegation, we succeeded in ensuring that this backbone of the state's economy was able to survive the pandemic.

On balance, despite the obstacles and the odds, we reached a critical mass of cargo agreements, representing 70 percent of all PSP funds approved for cargo carriers, and 80 percent of all PSP funds approved for contractors. We'd passed by Nehemiah's fifty-two-day mark; the pandemic was moving into its third month. The airline industry had lived to fight another day.

Phase 5: Final Application Review and Remediation

The final three months of work, from June 7 to August 31, moved slowly and painfully. It was like running a four-hour marathon, except that you sprinted the first twenty-six miles in an hour and then crawled over hot coals for the remainder.

The unresolved remnant of applications presented the most complex issues of law, fact, and policy. In contrast to overall program applications approved (652), we approved a small number of applications during this last stretch. And each project was long and tedious.

Even simple communication was a major drag on progress. Many applicants were unresponsive, others were slow to respond, and many provided incorrect information. It was shocking to me that companies that applied for emergency relief were unable or could not be bothered to respond to intensive personal outreach— by email and phone—by our dedicated team. Our team was much smaller during this period, having lost several of our members. When it was over, we handed off day-to-day operations for approved applicants to the Treasury Coordination Team, Summit Consulting, the Office of General Counsel, and the Office of the Assistant Secretary for Management. They would handle future compliance, reporting, approvals and award revisions.

With the PSP behind us, we turned our full attention to the task of administering $25 billion in loans.

The Loan Program

Not all borrowers were created equal. There was a balance to strike between keeping the airline industry alive and managing the risks of lending billions of dollars to cash-strapped companies. The CARES Act required us to administer the loan program in a way that would protect US taxpayers, as much as possible, from long-term harm. But of course, if government loans were made purely on market terms, there would be no need for them! Our job was to provide capital that the private market was not prepared to offer.

The first thing this program needed, therefore, was flexible credit and collateral tests for the various groups of borrowers. The Airline Rescue Team designed algorithms to help to make quick credit decisions, and tests to ensure that we received appropriate collateral in line with the requirements of the law. We had a process to set money aside for the large carriers, since they usually requested more than we were prepared to offer (such as their payroll support requests).

By July 2, we'd signed agreements with five major airlines for loan commitments of more than $10 billion. The COVID-19 pandemic was still just four months old.

A few days later, on July 7, we finished the deals with the remaining five major carriers. We closed on seven of these loans on September 29. A byproduct of the process was the creation of a new collateral class for airline lending, which gave rise to a whole new aircraft finance market.

One of the distinctive characteristics of the CARES Act was its heavy emphasis on taxpayer protection. In effect, it was designed to function like a business loan. Any airline that applied for financial support had to put something valuable on the line as collateral. In the event a carrier folded despite federal intervention, the government could recoup some of its losses by selling the collateral—warrants, options, stocks, or notes.

At some point, like any bank or mortgage company, we also wanted the loans to be repaid in full. We didn't want the airlines, whose stock prices had fallen to historic lows, to end up as one more burden on the taxpayers' balance sheet. Everyone agreed: If we could backstop them from going under, they could eventually regain their financial health when the crisis ended. When that happened, we expected a timely repayment of the loans.

Thinking it through with our financial brain trust, we decided that certain companies would have collateral requirements. If a passenger airline applied for more than $100 million in PSP payments, that would trigger the collateral requirement. The same went for a cargo carrier seeking more than $50 million, and a contractor who wanted more than $37.5 million. Anyone seeking less than those numbers would not be subject to the collateral requirement.

As of this writing, the warrants granted in PSP1, PSP2, and the loan program have appreciated in value by roughly $200 million. Of course, the point of the program was not to make money; it was to stabilize the airline industry at the lowest possible cost to taxpayers. And that's what we did, learning a lot about the airline industry as we went along.

Like the value of loyalty programs.

Consider this: Commercial airlines rely on loans to purchase new aircraft. Prior to the pandemic, they mainly offered their existing equipment (airplanes and parts inventory) and real estate, and pledged economic rights in slots, gates, and routes (SG&R) that they owned, as collateral. All that changed with the CARES

Act loan program. Our program pursued a new approach, one that has revolutionized airline financing.

Loyalty programs are some of the most valuable assets that airlines own today, in addition to aircraft, real estate, and liquid financial assets. These loyalty programs are cash cows that airlines generate from selling travel and marketing services to loyalty program partners, the majority of which are financial institutions. Loyalty revenues account, at the low end, for more than 10 percent of a commercial airline's revenues, and often exceed 20 percent.

Almost no one had ever used loyalty programs as finance collateral. There were significant legal risks involved, and their complex nature made them cumbersome. Only a handful of loyalty programs featured prominently in airline financial transactions prior to the pandemic. Virtually all of them were monetization transactions, with mixed results. None were in the United States.

When we surveyed these transactions, we discovered that they'd been invaluable in helping airlines monetize value, especially when strapped for cash. In many instances, the sponsor airlines bought back the programs to enjoy their ongoing financial benefits. Some of the transactions failed, but primarily due to the financial condition of the airline, rather than the loyalty program. I noticed that each transaction was heavily tailored and structured, which made them costly and time-consuming to execute. Based on my experience in the financial world, I knew it would be an uphill battle to persuade lenders to accept these programs as collateral.

But then, in July 2020, United Airlines completed a $6.8 billion loan using MileagePlus, its loyalty program, as collateral. If United could do it, perhaps our idea wasn't so crazy after all.

At first, we weren't sure. This would present significant challenges. We could foresee real risks of bankruptcy, and there was little in the way of legal guidance or precedent to follow. It would take a lot of focus to nail down the value of these programs, including their underlying contracts and intellectual property. Implementing loyalty program security was highly technical, tedious, and time-consuming, and we weren't sure that we had the time. Besides, we would have to spend even more hours debating the precise value of the programs and how much collateral they counted for in any given contract. But of paramount importance was the taxpayer. We simply could not consider a structure that would fall like a house of cards in bankruptcy. The political and financial accountability was just too great.

That didn't mean, however, that loyalty programs were out of the question as collateral. Moments of crisis and transition often surprise, with the innovations they force to the surface. Closed-circuit TV and ammonia-based refrigeration, for example, were products of the development of the atomic bomb in World War II. So we took more than a month to explore these questions, peeling back layer after layer. The airlines were happy to help us understand how their programs worked; many were already maxed out on collateral to other financiers. The issues were complex, the decisions consequential, and time was not on our side. Ultimately, Secretary Mnuchin approved a highly structured and secure approach to accepting loyalty collateral, one that was structurally far more sound than the United Airlines collateral program.

Loyalty collateral eventually became a foundation of the CARES loan program. Six of the largest borrowers used their programs as collateral, and three others offered theirs in negotiations. The introduction of this collateral signaled to the market that loyalty programs were now an acceptable collateral class in airline finance, and in turn, a new, deep market was created. Creation of this collateral class catalyzed an additional $12 billion in airline finance during the crisis.

Since July 2020, major US carriers have raised more than $40 billion in financing using this approach. I am very proud of our team for having paved the way for the creation of this financing market.

Just when we thought we were done, on December 27, Congress passed an additional $18 billion in relief for the airline industry under the Coronavirus Response and Consolidated Appropriations Act of 2021. We had only one alternative: After nine months of nonstop work, we put the pedal to the metal and pulled out all stops in order to pump out an additional $18 billion in the last three weeks of the term.

I think about those hectic weeks a lot. I fly routinely for my work these days, and every time I board a flight, I wonder whether some of the pilots and crew I encounter are still on the job today because of what we accomplished, under the most trying of circumstances. I couldn't be more proud of what we've done.

EPILOGUE

With an end date in sight for the first Trump administration, the tone at Treasury shifted. I could feel a palpable sense of urgency. To borrow again from the *Mishna*, the day was indeed short, and the task was overwhelmingly great. While some people in the administration had resigned, I felt honor bound to stay and do as much as possible in the time we had left. My team and I were on the same page—we just wanted to get the job done. Our work was important.

Aside from the urgency of our work, we all knew that it would take the Biden administration a long time to get up to speed. It would be an unfair burden to ask others to hit the ground running at the same speed at which we were working.

Particularly with CARES and America Crecé, we felt responsible to get funds out the door. It wasn't just our dignity in doing a job well that was on the line; the beneficiaries of these programs were in immediate need. The more progress we could make on these projects, the more benefits we could bring to the American economy and other countries as well.

There was also the looming worry that the next administration would likely have different priorities. They could shut down our projects as soon as they entered the building. We were wholly focused on accomplishing as much as possible before January 20.

One of the biggest tasks to complete was an implementation of CARES II. The original CARES Act had been designed to provide businesses nine months of runway to recover and resume operations. That in itself had been a gargantuan task, standing up an entire financial institution; creating from the ground up all the necessary rules, procedures, policies, and paperwork; and then managing the intake, oversight, underwriting, risk management, and implementation of actually distributing the money. But in the fall of 2020, we recognized that businesses and employees were still perilously vulnerable. After considerable debate, Congress authorized an additional $18 billion in PSPs. Known as CARES II, these funds would provide another three months of runway to employees. Our beneficiaries needed these funds immediately, and now they were reliant on a lame-duck administration to make sure they got it. With determination, our team committed to getting all the money out the door before we left, knowing hundreds of thousands of airline and aviation industry workers were depending on us to save their jobs, even as we were about to lose ours.

Many of the America Crecé infrastructure projects were highly time sensitive as well. We were not simply working with our own deadlines and multilayered approval process, but with a variety of political cycles in other countries that affected project negotiations and implementation.

Our goal with all of these infrastructure projects was to enable other countries to stand on their own two feet. A key facet was helping to finance, strengthen, and modernize state-owned enterprises (SOEs), which dominate the energy and infrastructure sectors in virtually every country in the world. One of the biggest burdens for so many SOEs is the debt they carry on their balance sheets. Some SOEs are better than others at managing the levels and terms of that debt. We found that most in the emerging markets were carrying unsustainable levels at debilitating terms, in many, if not most, instances imposed by countries frequently engaged in predatory lending practices. Our approach was to find creative and sophisticated ways for them to stand on their own by optimizing their balance sheets, reducing their debt service costs, and generally making them more creditworthy. Doing so would free up more capital for improvements and growth, as well as make the SOEs more attractive to better lenders for future financing—at much more manageable interest rates and terms.

We had been working for some time on a program for Ecuador. It was very big and specific. Ecuador was operating under a crippling amount of sovereign debt, mostly owed to China, that it had been unable to resolve. Debt service was so high that many of Ecuador's natural resources were going to China to help make payments. In one case, the Ecuadorians were forced to ship 60 percent of their shrimp to China just to service their debt. Ultimately, I hatched a plan that would allow Ecuador to achieve self-sufficiency without giving away all of its valuable natural resources and agricultural production at a discount. On the plane ride down, I studied the Ecuadorians' balance sheets. I identified eight SOEs that had a total net asset value of $30 billion sitting idly on their combined balance sheets—surely there was a better way to leverage this money. So I devised a program that would provide the means for Ecuador to get out from under a good piece of its debt to China by conducting a series of privatization transactions via bridge loans provided by the DFC. Essentially, we were showing Ecuador how to free up liquid capital which it could then use to enhance operations, reduce debt, and spend on new capital-intensive construction projects.

Just to do one of these transactions could take up to two years, as any transaction like this required thoughtful structuring and many regulatory approvals. However, I knew this program could change Ecuador for the better—and I doubted the next guy in my job would pursue it. We worked tirelessly, going through five agencies to finalize the project. It was a labor of passion, and I pushed my team to make it happen, knowing it would significantly improve the lives of an entire country. (We finally got it approved, but sadly, like so many of our programs, President Biden chose to kibosh it.)

I remember getting the White House memo with specific instructions on the end-of-term submission of resignation letters to the president from political appointees like myself in the normal course. It would have been easy to exit a few weeks early and start the next phase of life. But for me, my heart was in my work. In our tenure together, our team would show up at 8:00 a.m. or earlier, often not leaving the office until 8:00 or 9:00 p.m., or even later. We stayed in the administration until virtually the last day, choosing not to jump to greener pastures.

No matter how dedicated we were, the end date was certain. A new president would be sworn into office on January 20. And so, it came time to say goodbye. I had such a long list: fellow members of senior leadership, the teams that ran my portfolios at Treasury, friends and colleagues at so many other Federal agencies, interlocutors from so many foreign governments, and many more.

My friend Thomas Storch, then in charge of international economics and trade at the NEC, invited me over to the White House for my last visit on the Monday of our last week. The Eisenhower Executive Office Building was like a ghost town, but Tom and I had a nice walk down memory lane as we went through the East and West Wings, reminiscing about our various eventful meetings in those halls of grandeur and power.

For a number of my friends and colleagues in the administration, including many of my dedicated career staff and senior officials, I prepared a very special parting gift, presented with a personal note to each person. The gift was my way to honor them and the consequential time we had together. On the wall in my office was a piece of art from the national collection: an original 1863 etching of Abraham Lincoln, his cabinet, and generals with the Emancipation Proclamation. I considered it one of the best works of art in the US Treasury Building. I had reproductions made (at my own expense) in various sizes, which I had matted and framed as mementos and tokens of my esteem.

Due to COVID restrictions, many could not meet in person, so I organized Zoom calls with all of my Treasury teams and was able to bid farewell to each person virtually. I valued all of my team members—political and career alike. It did not matter to me how my team was hired, all that mattered was that we pulled together and served well when we were needed by our nation. (Little did I know that as soon as I exited the building, career staffers would be warned not to communicate with me, a sad reality of the political world.)

We had one final all-hands meeting for Treasury International Affairs, one last opportunity to issue farewells. Unbeknownst to me, each of the under secretaries and assistant secretaries got their own tailored farewell. Mine was delivered by Lailee Moghtader, an extraordinary career official who led our international trade portfolio. I was extremely touched by her words—not just the recap of my work at Treasury, but perhaps even more when she said this:

What Mitch has demonstrated through all this is his keen ability to make a personal connection with others through stories, food, and frequently humor...and this goes to whether he is speaking to an ambassador, a CEO, or a desk officer.... Despite Mitch's hard-driving persistence at work, he also understands the importance of putting family first. I personally am grateful for his complete support for taking the time I needed to care for my ailing father. And I'm sure Amtrak appreciates his many trips up to New York each week to be with his family on the weekends. So, Mitch, thanks for the leadership and support, and we wish you all the best in wherever your ideas and talents take you next.

Even with those warm words, I left the Treasury Building on January 19 with an exceptionally heavy heart. It was tough to say goodbye to so many trusted colleagues and good friends that I had cultivated over my three-plus years. I had a lump in my throat when I handed in my PIV card and left the building for the last time.

The ride from Treasury to Union Station was not a long one, though it was not easy with all of the fences and barricades that had been erected. I made some chitchat with my faithful driver from the Treasury pool. Through the car window, I scanned the scenery during the ride I had come to know so well. I tried to reflect on my journey of the past three years and also think about the road ahead, but my mind was a bit numb. I bid the driver goodbye upon my arrival at the station—or as close as I could get dropped off due to enhanced security—and schlepped my luggage across the streets and into the train station.

———

For three and a half years, I had dutifully ridden that train, week in and week out. Every Sunday afternoon, as my wife and I would pull out of the driveway to head for Penn Station and my train to Washington, the rhythm of my home and Borough Park faded behind me. I traded the cacophony of Yiddish conversations, squealing school buses, the creak of strollers navigating uneven sidewalks, and the screeching of the subway overhead—its sharp cry dulled only by the not infrequent blare of the volunteer ambulance service, Hatzolah, manned by a veritable army of volunteer EMTs who provide among the fastest response times in the nation—for the sterile calm of Washington, DC. In the halls of the Treasury Department, the work was urgent, weighty, and filled with purpose, but it was far removed from the tapestry of sounds and scents of my neighborhood.

I missed the sound of life spilling out of Borough Park's streets—the laughter of children darting between mothers with their arms full of groceries, the clamor of car horns in the endless dance of traffic, and the sweet aroma of challah, cakes, cookies, bagels—you name it—wafting from corner bakeries, mingling with the distinct scent of the neighborhood's bookstores brimming with *seforim*.

More than the streets, I missed the familiar sights and sounds of home. My devoted wife, who was left to look after the three of our eight children still at home while also tirelessly serving the community as a physician assistant, was my greatest partner and my deepest longing during the week. I missed the pitter-patter—and sometimes thuds—of our children's feet racing through the house, their giggles and occasional screams filling the air as they played and, of course, fought together, and the soft murmur of our older boys as they studied our holy texts, their voices rising and falling like a melody from another time. The house itself seemed to hold its own rhythm, from the warm smells of my wife's home-cooked meals to the gentle hum of family life, its love and devotion palpable in every corner. It was this warmth, this wholeness, that lingered in my mind when the quiet of Washington or weightiness of work seemed too much to bear.

The abundance of shuls in Borough Park, at least one and up to three or five on nearly every block, was another luxury I only truly appreciated in its absence. In Borough Park, you never need to search for a minyan; if anything, people grew restless if they had to wait more than five minutes for one to start. The ease of stepping into a *shtiebel*, or study hall, greeted by the distinct sounds of Torah learning—sometimes a soft murmur and not infrequently an all-out argument in the name of getting to the bottom and truth of a sage's message in, say, the Talmud—or the rustle of a siddur being opened, was an anchor of daily life that I could only yearn for during the week. And the life cycles, sometimes experienced in one short day! The steady hum of milestones—*brisim* in the early mornings, funerals in the mid-mornings, engagement parties and weddings in the evenings—kept the pulse of the community beating strong. Each event was a reminder of the unbroken chain of tradition, an eternal dance of joy and sorrow, faith and resilience. In Washington, the absence of a family simcha a few nights a week was deafening.

Then, Thursday evening would arrive, and with it, the commute home. The train ride back to Borough Park felt like an ascent—not just geographically but spiritually. As my neighborhood and family drew closer, the air seemed to shift, buzzing with the urgency of preparation.

The first thing that would greet me when I returned home was the symphony of familiar scents that filled the air, each one a note in a melody of love and tradition. The caramelized sweetness of onions browned to perfection—the way my grandmother had taught, a recipe passed down like a sacred heirloom—wafted from the chicken soup simmering gently on the stove, its warmth embracing the house like a promise of comfort. The delicate aroma of lightly glazed gefilte fish mingled with the briny, smoky scent of my famous grilled sardines. The earthiness of potato kugel, crisped golden at the edges, mingled with the char of grilled vegetables and the savory richness of roasted chicken. Each smell carried its own story, a memory preserved in the air, reminding me of the sanctity of home, the sanctity of Shabbos, and the sanctity of love poured into every dish. Every street corner, every store bustled with families completing last-minute errands, their movements an intricate choreography of devotion and care. As my wife always says, "Shabbos waits for no man!"

As the sun dipped lower, the sirens would blare—sharp and unmistakable, announcing the imminent arrival of Shabbos. Fifteen minutes later, they would blare again, and with them came the final flurry before Shabbos descended, wrapping the neighborhood in a sacred stillness.

Returning to Borough Park for Shabbos was not just coming home—it was being restored. The streets, so alive with the measured footsteps of men in *shtreimels* and women in elegant Shabbos finery, became a refuge. The hum of weekday traffic gave way to the soft strains of *zemiros* floating from open windows, mingling with the quiet rustle of leaves. The density of life that had felt overwhelming on Thursday became the source of my strength by Friday evening. Multi-generational families gathered around dining tables, grandparents sharing stories, children laughing, and the warmth of tradition filling every corner. By Shabbos morning, walking to the shul a mere few steps from home, the scent of kugels wafting from nearby kitchens, I was reconnected to what truly mattered: a life of faith, family, and community.

When Sunday evening arrived and the Amtrak train once again pulled away from Penn Station, I would take one last glance at the streets of Borough Park, holding onto the sound of those sirens and the feeling of Shabbos to carry me through the week ahead. It was my wife, my children, and the Borough Park streets that gave me life, and each week, they were there, waiting, ready to welcome me back into their embrace.

After three and a half years of this weekly commute, my Trump 45 chapter was finished, and it was time to reorient and focus on my family, my community, and my own self. My wife and our three youngest children had only seen me two to three days per week the entire time I worked at Treasury. I had paused most of my pro bono work during my time in government as well, stepping back from my role as chairman of Agudath Israel of America's pro bono legal services network, and leaving some large pro bono projects unfinished. After putting so many personal priorities on hold, I badly needed to recharge and take stock.

Returning to the daily rhythms of family and community life was a blessing that felt both restorative and overdue. To wake up each morning and see my children off to school, to daven in my own shul surrounded by familiar faces, and to resume my daily learning program with my rebbe was to reconnect with the foundation of who I am. The simple joys of sitting at the supper table with my family in the evenings, hearing about their day, or attending parent-teacher conferences were reminders of the beauty of being present. I was once again available not just for my own family's milestones but also for the seemingly endless simchas of my wife's large extended family and our community generally. After three and a half years of commuting and missing these moments, reintegrating into the daily life of Borough Park felt like stepping back into a well-worn, cherished garment. To mark this new chapter, my wife and I took a brief but much-needed vacation to recharge and reconnect. It was a time to reflect, to exhale, and to prepare for what was next. My priority became serving my community and addressing projects that had been waiting far too long. One of these was completing some writing projects that had been sitting unfinished for thirty years, their detailed editing requiring far more time and energy than I had in Washington, and their ideas lingering in the back of my mind through countless late nights and busy days. Though there was the inevitable concern about finding a job, I knew that the first step was to rebuild my foundation, re-center my life around family, learning, and service, and trust that the next opportunity would present itself in due time.

I had no problem filling my time. The pro bono matter I left when I joined Treasury was still incomplete and demanded my attention. The case involved restructuring and implementing a compliance program for fourteen not-for-profit and religious corporations and nineteen unincorporated entities and community engagement programs that housed the whole of the Brooklyn school system for the Satmar Chassidic group, one of the largest in the world. The group was subject to criminal proceedings relating to allegations of defrauding government programs. Pre-Treasury, I had streamlined their corporate structure and drafted and put into place a compliance system for all aspects of the yeshiva system's operations. It was easily a thousand-hour project that I completed on a pro bono basis with a team of ten lawyers.

However, the proceedings dragged on and the compliance system I had introduced had not yet been fully implemented. And so, like Nachshon ben Aminadav, who was the first to jump in the Red Sea just before it parted, I jumped right back into the deep end, spending many painstaking hours of technical legal and compliance work to establish a compliance order that would reflect best practices and satisfy the government.

As we approached the finish line on settling matters with the Department of Justice on the Satmar matter, the community had a bomb dropped on it. In September 2022, the State of New York took aim at the Chassidic community with a well-orchestrated, unprecedented, and multifaceted attack on our community, values, way of life, and, most alarmingly, our children. For months, random violence against Chassidic Jews had been occurring in New York on an almost daily basis. Indeed, for the period around the time of these incidents, New York City witnessed more hate crimes against Jews than against all other vulnerable groups combined. But the state's attack was even more concerning. On September 11, *The New York Times* published a report of a yearlong investigation into New York's yeshiva school system. Twisting facts, misrepresenting data, and—when all else failed—inventing stories whole cloth, the *Times* painted a picture of our schools and our community as corrupt, illiterate, and abusive. The content of the report was noxious, and the timing was malicious. Two days later, the New York State Board of Regents was due to vote on regulations that threatened to shut down our community's schools entirely.

My community sprang into action, and I took a leading role. Recognizing the urgency of the moment, Agudath Israel of America launched KnowUs, a strategic initiative designed to correct the record, promote understanding, and shift the public

narrative. One of our first salvos was a September 23, 2022 op-ed
I penned, published in *The Federalist*. I explained that the *Times'*
front-page hit piece was designed to bolster a narrative that
paints Orthodox Jews as corrupt and unworthy of equal societal
standing. "Rather than feature even one story of success within
our system," I wrote, "the *Times* chose to push a dehumanizing
narrative of ethnic stereotyping. Their 275 interviews conducted
over more than a year did not yield even one single voice among
the tens of thousands of families touched by our yeshivas in profoundly positive ways."

The *Times'* mischaracterization came as New York State
proposed the Substantial Equivalency Regulations, an unprecedented attempt to exert control over nonpublic schools, including yeshivas. In a May 30, 2022, letter of opposition to these regulations, I argued against the "unprecedented requirement that
yeshivas obtain a state license to operate, with the issuance of the
license wholly dependent on the state's approval of the yeshiva's
curriculum and faculty."

This intrusion, I stated, failed to recognize the proven success
of the yeshiva system, which has consistently cultivated students
who excel in critical thinking, values-based education, and civic
contributions. While the powers that be in New York accused us
of mistreating our children, the truth is that yeshiva students and
graduates enjoy greater happiness, greater safety, greater emotional health, greater critical thinking skills, greater language
skills, deeper historical knowledge, greater success, greater family
stability, and greater life achievements than their public school
counterparts in the state. In addition to the shameful fact that
about 25 percent of public school graduates are functionally
illiterate, public school students are frequent victims of alcohol
abuse, drug abuse, suicide, gun violence, and rape—threats virtu-

ally nonexistent at yeshiva schools. All of this at parents' expense, to the tune of $2 billion in annual private tuition and contributions, while these same parents also gladly paid their taxes to support the public schools they did not use. Why do parents make this expensive choice?

"When you compare the harmony and hope in yeshiva schools," I wrote in *The Federalist*, "to the public school landscape of drugs, alcohol, depression, suicide, violence, dismal literacy rates, and despair, our choice was easy."

Even more troubling was the reality that New York State policymakers and regulators could not possibly judge a system that they simply did not understand. As I pointed out: "With respect, when the Regents, their deputies and the local school authorities have been through the 2,711 folios of the Talmud, the Code of Jewish Law, the Scripture, with all of its voluminous commentary that our children learn with the hermeneutic rigor of critical textual analysis that our system teaches and nurtures, then we could perhaps have a sensible conversation about 'substantial equivalency.'"

My writings were just part of the campaign organized by KnowUs. Our goal: to counter this false narrative, protect yeshiva autonomy, and promote understanding of the Orthodox community's values and achievements. It combined public education campaigns, such as prominent Midtown Manhattan billboards, with in-depth publications like a one-hundred-page white paper prepared with painstaking detail by the indefatigable Rabbi Avrohom Weinstock that debunked the inaccuracies perpetuated by the *Times*. Additionally, through a detailed thirty-page, well-documented letter (again, through the immense efforts of Rabbi Weinstock), KnowUs alerted the Pulitzer Prize board to the *Times*' journalistic failings. Ultimately, the Pulitzer board decided to exclude the *Times* series from the prestigious awards—a significant victory for fairness and truth.

Through KnowUs, we sought to move beyond defense and foster a broader appreciation of yeshiva education and Orthodox life. KnowUs stands as a testament to the resilience and dignity of our community, ensuring that the truth about yeshivas and Orthodox life is not only defended but celebrated.

Yet the campaign was not merely about protecting the Orthodox Jewish community; it was about preserving religious liberty and countering a dangerous trend of hostility toward faith. As I warned in my op-ed: "The Chassidic-American community is the target today, but expect these attacks to come soon to a church, mosque, synagogue, or meditation retreat near you."

———

After three intense years of service in Washington, DC, I also needed some quiet time. I found solace and renewal in writing. It became a much-needed balm for my recovery from the pressures of navigating high-stakes government roles, a global pandemic, and the demands of international diplomacy. Writing allowed me to reconnect with myself and my deepest values. Among my long-standing projects was the first complete English translation of the *Kedushas Levi*, one of the most widely studied Chassidic commentaries on the Bible. For over thirty years, this endeavor lingered as an unfinished dream, often shelved due to the pressures of my work as a Big Law partner, my tenure as an assistant secretary of the Treasury, and the fulfilling yet demanding life of raising eight children with a healthy dose of communal responsibilities. Now it was time to complete the task.

My journey into the world of the *Kedushas Levi* began in the summer of 1995 with a trip to Ukraine, initially undertaken to visit my maternal grandfather's ancestral hometown of Nadvorna. After an arduous thirty-hour drive over Ukrainian roads— crammed into the backseat of a tiny Soviet-made Lada sedan— we arrived in Berditchev, the resting place of the revered Rabbi Levi Yitzchak, better known as the Kedushas Levi.

The Kedushas Levi's *ohel* (tomb structure) was stark and quiet, largely untouched by the throngs of pilgrims it sees today. Inside, the space bore the familiar elements of such holy sites: a box of unused candles for lighting, remnants of many others left behind, and a small shelf with a large glass container of olive oil and a wick for an eternal flame—unlit.

I was deeply unsettled. How could the flame behind the grave of this monumental Chassidic master not be burning? I tried again and again to light it, contorting myself to avoid stepping on the *matzeva* (gravestone) or losing my balance. Match after match failed, and I burned my fingers more than once. Was this a test? A message from above? Or was it simply poor design, with the wick unable to draw enough oxygen to sustain the flame?

Reflecting on that trip in the days that followed, I saw the extinguished flame as a metaphor for the underappreciation of the Kedushas Levi's profound contributions to Jewish thought. It became clear to me that a greater effort was needed to illuminate his works for a broader audience. What better way to cast light on the Kedushas Levi than to make his Torah commentary available in clear, elegant, and accessible English?

Throughout my life, the *Kedushas Levi* has served as a trusted guide, particularly during moments of professional and personal challenge. During my tenure at the Treasury Department, I often turned to the *Kedushas Levi* for wisdom. Upon my confirmation as assistant secretary, I searched for a source of timeless guidance and inspiration, and, just as in my law practice, the *Kedushas Levi*, my superpower, "found me."

Unlike typical political treatises, the *Kedushas Levi* offers keen insights into human behavior, psychology, and resilience. Its teachings guided me in high-pressure situations, from negotiating the $4.6 billion restructuring of a Chinese corporation controlling Hong Kong's water supply to managing the $94 billion CARES Act relief for the airline industry during the COVID-19 pandemic.

One of the Kedushas Levi's bountiful teachings particularly resonated during trade negotiations with senior Chinese officials. The *Kedushas Levi* recounts how God cast the attribute of Truth from heaven to earth, embedding it in the fabric of society. Drawing from this, I emphasized the undeniable truth of the disparity in market access between US banks in China and Chinese banks in the US, the latter of which had enjoyed double-digit and, in one year, even triple-digit growth in loan assets in the decade from 2005 to 2015. As the Yiddish saying goes, "*Di beste ligent iz di rayne emes*" (The best lie is the absolute truth). Truth, wielded effectively, carried the day.

By the Fall of 2023, I proudly held in my hands the fruits of this journey: a three-volume, nearly two-thousand-page set of the complete *Kedushas Levi*, translated and annotated to make its timeless lessons accessible to all. This work, I hope, will light the flame of inspiration for others as the Kedushas Levi did for me.

As I reflected on the ohel in Berditchev and the unlit oil lamp that first sparked this project, I felt profound gratitude for the opportunity to bring this cultural and spiritual treasure to light. What began as a mission to honor the Kedushas Levi has transformed into a testament to the enduring relevance of

Chassidic wisdom in guiding us through the challenges of our modern world.

Four years after taking that fateful call from Eli Miller that led me to Washington, I am thankfully and happily reintegrated back into my family and community. I have published the *Kedushas Levi*, and the two books I have written on the Nadvorna Chassidic dynasty are in the publication process. I have devoted thousands of hours to supporting my Chassidic community and providing much-needed legal services and support. And now, we have a new administration. Time to come full circle, to take stock of the policy work discussed above and review what happened in the four years since I left Treasury.

———

Good policy is never the result of one smart person exerting his or her will. It's the product of months and years of painstaking negotiations between many interested parties—one part persuasion and one part sparring match. In the end, this book is not just my story; it is the story of a dedicated team of patriots as we tried to grapple with many giant, complex, and life-changing challenges. While I am immensely proud of the accomplishments of Trump 45 Treasury, I also feel a duty to document the contrasts between that administration and the one that followed. The decisions and policies of the Biden administration took this country in a decidedly different direction, and I believe it's constructive, even vital, to assess those differences as we embark on yet another new chapter in economic policy.

There was—and still is—no bigger challenge facing this country than China. Trump 45 marked a fundamental departure from decades of US policy toward China. Where past administrations had hoped that economic engagement would encourage China to adopt fairer trade practices and integrate into a rules-based international order, the Trump 45 administration recognized that approach had failed. China had consistently exploited global norms to further its own interests while systematically undermining US economic and strategic security. Trump 45 took the crucial step of recognizing China not as a partner in global prosperity but as a strategic competitor whose predatory behaviors demanded a recalibrated approach.

This recalibration manifested in a comprehensive set of policies aimed at addressing the long-standing imbalances in the US-China relationship. The administration's strategy was clear: Force China to play by the same rules as other nations or face concrete consequences. Through tariffs, restrictions on investments in sensitive sectors, export credit reforms, and enhanced protections for US intellectual property, the Trump 45 administration brought pressure to bear on Beijing in a way that previous administrations had not dared. Those efforts culminated in the Phase 1 trade deal of 2019, a landmark agreement in which China committed to purchasing more US goods and services, improving protections for intellectual property, removing non-tariff barriers, and reforming aspects of its technology transfer practices.

The road to this agreement was fraught with challenges; however, it signaled a new era in US-China relations. Trump proved that a firm and results-oriented stance could yield progress, even when dealing with a rival as adept at stonewalling as China. By holding the line against endless meetings and meaningless commitments, the administration demonstrated to China that the United States was serious about rebalancing the relationship and protecting our economic and strategic interests.

The Biden administration entered office inheriting the tools and frameworks necessary to continue the progress made under its predecessor. They acknowledged some of the Trump administration's achievements and retained some key measures, such as the tariffs imposed on Chinese goods. Those tariffs remained a crucial source of leverage, signaling to Beijing that the United States would not tolerate continued violations of international trading norms.

However, the Biden administration reversed course on many critical issues, surrendering much of the progress we had made. When President Biden began his term, he and his administration chided the Trump economic team for fixating on the trade deficit. A better approach, they argued, was to work with G7 allies, as well as other nations such as Australia and India, to engage China in a multilateral fashion while simultaneously striving to outcompete China by strengthening our economy at home. The policy hit a wall, however, when the Indo-Pacific Economic Framework for Prosperity, the Biden administration's flagship project of bringing together all of America's trading partners in Asia, fizzled and died, with even congressional Democrats voicing their concerns. Among the factors plaguing the Biden administration's efforts were, as always, an excessive ideological insistence on prioritizing environmental concerns, as well as an adherence to the importance of interaction, which meant much time squandered on meetings that produced very little of any real value.

The Biden administration also lacked the resolve to enforce the commitments China made under the Phase 1 trade agreement. China's failure to meet its purchase targets or implement promised reforms went largely unchallenged, sending a message that the Biden administration was unwilling to hold Beijing accountable.

Instead of pressing China for tangible results, the Biden administration reverted to the ineffective strategies of the past, prioritizing talk over substantive action. Starting in 2023, a series of Biden cabinet officials visited China, including Secretary of State Antony Blinken, Commerce Secretary Gina Raimondo, and Treasury Secretary Janet Yellen. These visits culminated in the establishment of two dialogues—the Economic Working Group and the Financial Working Group—launched by Secretary Yellen. These groups met at least six times during the Biden administration but achieved virtually no progress. Back to meetings for the sake of meetings.

These vague and unfocused dialogues signaled weakness to Beijing, which respects and responds only to strength. The Biden administration's approach—characterized by an emphasis on meetings and discussions devoid of real consequences—failed to counter China's aggressive economic policies. Instead, it emboldened China to continue its behavior, secure in the knowledge that the United States was unwilling to escalate. This pattern highlights a critical miscalculation: When dealing with China, any perception of softness is interpreted as an invitation to push boundaries further.

With a combined GDP of more than $47 billion, the US and China are the world's two largest economies. That provides forty-seven billion reasons why we need to work toward a robust collaboration with Beijing with one very big caveat: It must be fair. As in any relationship, the US-China economic relations must be balanced, equal, reciprocal, balanced, non-discriminatory, and predicated on respect for intellectual property and all other legal rights.

The second Trump administration has an unparalleled opportunity to reorient the US-China relationship once again and reclaim the strategic momentum lost under the Biden administration. While the United States and China are deeply intertwined economically, finding a way to coexist does not mean tolerating unfair practices or strategic vulnerabilities. Instead, the United States must prioritize its own interests and address China's persistent violations of trade norms and global rules.

Central to this effort will be addressing key areas of Chinese misconduct. Currency manipulation, unfair credit subsidies, material misrepresentation or failures to disclose material information by public company issuers that seek to tap the US capital markets, forced technology transfers, and tariff and non-tariff market barriers must be met with firm resistance, particularly those that serve to increase the trade deficit. US businesses, workers, and investors cannot afford another era of unchecked Chinese behavior that undermines innovation, fairness, economic growth, and market stability. The entire world will benefit from President Trump's commitment to maintaining and escalating tariffs as necessary, strengthening investment screening mechanisms, and pursuing broader export credit reforms to neutralize unfair or undesirable practices.

These measures will make it unequivocally clear that further infractions will result in tangible and costly consequences. Beijing's past behavior has shown that it responds to power dynamics rather than diplomatic niceties. Therein lies the importance of a willingness to sustain and escalate economic measures, as well as leverage multilateral partnerships to isolate China diplomatically when necessary.

With President Trump back in office, we can be confident that all engagement with China will be results oriented. Symbolic summits and working groups are meaningless unless they yield substantive outcomes. Hollow dialogues cannot stand in place of verifiable, time-bound commitments from Beijing.

Rebalancing the US-China relationship is not just a matter of economic policy; it is a strategic imperative. A strong and fair economic partnership with China will not only benefit American workers and businesses but also reinforce the United States' position as a global leader. By standing firm and demanding accountability, the US can demonstrate to the world that it will not be bullied or undermined, even by its most formidable competitors.

Through strength, clarity, and an unwavering commitment to fairness, the US can compel China to respect international norms and engage in a relationship that benefits both nations. The tools and frameworks are already in place; the challenge lies in having the vision and determination to use them. By doing so, the United States can secure a prosperous and equitable future while reasserting its leadership on the world stage.

———

One of the China problems Trump 45 grappled with happened right in our own backyard. In 2017, President Trump inherited a Western Hemisphere that felt all but abandoned by its big brother to the north and was welcoming China with open arms. The most consistent question I received from partners throughout the Western Hemisphere and the Caribbean on my earliest official visits was, "Where have you been?" Enter our hallmark infrastructure finance program, America Crecé.

The Trump administration's infrastructure finance initiatives represented a triumph of vision, strategy, and execution. The America Crecé initiative and related efforts succeeded in addressing one of the most pressing global challenges—the gargantuan infrastructure funding gap—through disciplined, private-capital-driven solutions. These programs were not only innovative in their approach but transformative in their impact, delivering tangible benefits for both partner countries and the United States.

By February 2020, we had delivered America Crecé infrastructure finance frameworks to nearly half of the governments in Latin America that identified over $300 billion in transactable projects. The mutual economic growth opportunities contributed demonstrably to our national security.

The power of the program spoke for itself. Take small but high strategically important Panama. By the end of 2020, our infrastructure finance work with Panama yielded $2.455 billion in accretive private capital infrastructure investment in Panama, all with lower carbon footprints, a utility balance sheet refinancing that saved $60 million in debt service costs, and the successful tendering of Panama's backbone power transmission line. Two of these projects displaced Chinese projects criticized for predatory and unfair debt and procurement practices.

Across the region, and indeed throughout the world, the approach and tools of the initiative demonstrated how private capital, paired with US expertise, could meet infrastructure demands while reducing carbon emissions and promoting economic growth. Its success was a testament to disciplined planning, innovative financing, and the unyielding pursuit of mutually beneficial partnerships.

The Biden administration inherited this promising legacy but chose to chart a different course. Instead of building upon the tested and proven strategies of America Crecé, it pivoted to initiatives like the Build Back Better World (B3W) and the Partnership for Global Infrastructure and Investment (PGII). These programs emphasized noneconomic projects, heavily shaped by a singular focus on climate change, and failed to achieve comparable results. They also served to open the door and invite Chinese influence and predatory financing practices back in.

B3W, launched in 2021 as part of the G7's efforts to counter China's Belt and Road Initiative, aimed to advance infrastructure development in low- and middle-income countries. However, its focus on "climate-aligned" infrastructure often came at the expense of practical economic growth opportunities. Similarly, PGII, introduced in 2022, sought to leverage $600 billion in infrastructure investment globally but prioritized projects with lofty environmental and social goals over actionable economic results. Unlike America Crecé, neither initiative offered a clear mechanism to attract significant private capital, leaving them reliant on public funds and bogged down by bureaucratic inefficiencies.

These programs' shortcomings are evident in their limited uptake and muted outcomes. While America Crecé delivered measurable results in terms of investment, job creation, and energy security, B3W and PGII have struggled to move beyond the conceptual stage in many regions. Their lack of focus on economic fundamentals and private sector engagement has left them ill-equipped to compete with China's Belt and Road Initiative, which continues to expand its influence unabated.

When President Xi Jinping traveled to Latin America in November 2024, he celebrated nearly $300 billion of Chinese projects in the region, including a megaport in Peru, as well as leading trade relationships with virtually every Latin American country, notably in lithium, crude oil, iron ore, and soybeans. This is on top of the alarming levels of public debt to China as a percentage of GDP of countries like Suriname, Guyana, Jamaica, and Ecuador.

For example, just before President Trump left office in 2021, we had completed building, negotiating, and approving a massive framework for Ecuador, as mentioned above. The Biden administration's cancelation of that program had dire consequences for Ecuador and its people. Once the US had slammed the door in their face, Ecuador had no choice but to turn back to China for "help." The result has been a massive and devastating new debt burden on the country, backstopped by pledging to pay onerous levels of Ecuador's natural resources to China. By September 2024, Ecuador's debt to China was an alarming $3 billion.

The decision to abandon America Crecé imposed grave harm on many smaller countries, relinquishing an opportunity to strengthen US global leadership in infrastructure finance. By prioritizing ideology over pragmatism, the Biden administration left partner countries with fewer viable alternatives to China and Russia, and jeopardized the progress made under the first Trump administration.

President Trump's second term provides a historic opportunity to reclaim the mantle of global infrastructure leadership and build upon the successes of its earlier initiatives. The need for reliable infrastructure—particularly in energy generation and transmission—has never been greater. The next industrial revolution will demand unprecedented power generation and connectivity, and the United States must be at the forefront of enabling this transition.

I was delighted to see President Trump announce his intentions to pursue America Crecé 2.0 less than a month after taking office. I'd like to see an infrastructure finance czar within the White House, or elsewhere within the US government, to oversee and coordinate a revitalized global infrastructure strategy. This leader would spearhead the creation of a comprehensive global map of infrastructure opportunities, modeled on the original América Crecé framework, and integrate efforts across the ten federal agencies that participated in the first Trump administration's initiatives.

The policy prescription is simple but powerful: Focus on the fundamentals of building energy and infrastructure systems that support economic growth. By leveraging private capital and unleashing American energy, the administration can close the global infrastructure funding gap while advancing US interests and promoting healthy development. Just like the original program, America Crecé 2.0 can counteract the influence of adversarial powers by offering partner countries superior alternatives rooted in transparency, efficiency, and mutual benefit.

A revitalized infrastructure finance program should take several steps to build upon the successes of the first Trump administration. First, the administrations should expand the geographic scope of America Crecé 2.0 beyond the Western Hemisphere. The infrastructure finance component of the initiative should extend to Asia, the Middle East, Central and Eastern Europe, Africa, and elsewhere. By broadening the program's reach, the United States can unlock new opportunities for American private-sector investment in these regions while simultaneously fostering economic growth in partner countries.

At the heart of this programming must be large-scale energy infrastructure projects that unleash American energy and strengthen US energy independence. These transformative projects would serve as strategic anchors—providing opportunities to deploy US private capital and US natural resources by expanding access to affordable and reliable power. We delivered two such successes in Panama and Vietnam under Trump 45. These initiatives validated the development model and have proven their value with the potential to maximize impact across diverse markets.

In parallel, the programming also must actively advance small and medium-sized energy solutions that complement and accelerate the broader strategy. Projects such as micro- and mini-grid systems, energy-efficient multi-modal municipal lighting systems, energy efficient smart building refurbishments, and renewable energy installations—including hydropower, geothermal power, and small modular nuclear reactors—can be deployed far more rapidly than large, capital-intensive projects. By increasing deal velocity and delivering quick, visible wins, these smaller-scale projects enhance the credibility and momentum of US engagement while laying the groundwork for deeper, long-term partnerships utilizing US private capital, equipment, and know-how. Together, large and small-scale efforts form a comprehensive, high-impact energy strategy rooted in American strength and leadership throughout the globe.

Another highly critical programming element involves strengthening state-owned utilities in partner countries, which was a key focus of the first America Crecé. Providing technical assistance to improve the financial health and operational efficiency of these utilities will not only make them more attractive to private investors but will also create the foundation for sustainable, long-term economic growth. The Panama ETESA refinancing and DFC Ecuador facility were demonstrable wins in this area, proving the high impact of this programming.

Moreover, enhancing procurement practices is essential. The United States must promote transparency, competition, and life-cycle cost analysis in project procurement to ensure that outcomes are appropriately sized and sited, of the highest quality, and free from corruption. These practices will reinforce the credibility of the United States as a partner and differentiate its approach from that of predatory actors like China.

Finally, the program must harness the potential of the AI revolution. This means developing infrastructure to support the widespread adoption of AI technologies, such as building data centers, expanding broadband networks, and creating advanced manufacturing facilities. These investments will provide the technological backbone for the next industrial revolution and further cement the United States as a leader in global innovation.

By pursuing these objectives, I fully expect President Trump to position the United States as the global leader in infrastructure finance, addressing critical needs while driving economic growth and stability.

————

While the Biden administration's lack of will served to unravel much of the progress made by Trump 45 in international finance, both with China and with our America Crecé partners, the Biden team moved aggressively on the domestic front. Unfortunately, those changes in fiscal policy, particularly in fintech, shifted in a direction that undermined both economic growth and stability. Trump's bold, pragmatic solutions were replaced with a landscape marked by excessive regulation and a stifling of innovation, reminiscent of the challenges we sought to overcome. Furthermore, the Biden team's obsession with climate change dramatically colored all economic policy and severely undermined our economic growth and security—without, sadly, any appreciable benefit to the climate.

The Biden administration pursued a regulatory agenda that paradoxically made the capital markets and the financial services industry more fragile. Their focus on increasing regulation, much of it driven by climate alarmism, has resulted in greater concentration within the industry, as smaller players struggle to comply with the ever-growing complexity of rules. For instance, the Biden SEC's climate disclosure requirements imposed significant burdens on all issuers, with nearly no impact on climate. Similarly, bank regulators forced climate risk monitoring on financial institutions, diverting resources from core risk management activities. The Federal Reserve's push to raise capital requirements further strained the industry's ability to innovate and grow. These measures, while well-intentioned, created a labyrinthine regulatory environment that favors incumbents and increases systemic fragility.

Moreover, as regulators embarked on a dogmatic quest to regulate everything that moves, they neglected their core responsibilities. The failure of Silicon Valley Bank is a glaring example. By the Federal Reserve's own admission, supervisors were completely asleep at the wheel, failing to identify and mitigate the accretion of interest rate risk within the regional banking system. In the words of Michael S. Barr, vice chair for supervision of the Board of Governors of the Federal Reserve System, "Supervisors did not fully appreciate the extent of the vulnerabilities as Silicon Valley Bank grew in size and complexity. When supervisors did identify vulnerabilities, they did not take sufficient steps to ensure that Silicon Valley Bank fixed those problems quickly enough." The Financial Stability Oversight Council (FSOC), preoccupied with climate-related financial risks, neglected to address more immediate and tangible threats. Indeed FSOC, on which sits the Fed chair, listed climate change as its leading priority just a month before the failure of SVB. Fed focus on the basics of interest rate risk, instead of climate risk, would certainly have mitigated the impact of Silicon Valley Bank's failure on the system. This lack of fundamental oversight led to a catastrophic collapse that could have been prevented with prudent, focused supervision.

The FTX debacle further illustrates the Biden administration's regulatory shortcomings. Despite active engagement with FTX, regulators completely missed the rampant fraud within the company. This failure not only highlights the inadequacies of the Biden regulatory framework but also underscores the dangers of misdirected regulatory priorities.

Nowhere was the Biden administration's outright hostility toward financial innovation more evident than in the crackdown on the crypto industry. The Securities and Exchange Commission under Biden took an aggressive stance against cryptocurrencies. High-profile actions against major crypto exchanges and block-chain-based projects created an environment of uncertainty and fear. The SEC's enforcement actions, ostensibly aimed at protecting investors, have instead stifled innovation and driven many promising fintech enterprises overseas.

Thankfully, President Trump has already signaled his clear intent to recalibrate our approach to financial regulation, prioritizing responsible innovation that bolsters economic growth and stability. This marks the start of a transformative era for fintech, digital assets, and financial innovation. Unlike the regulation and enforcement-heavy stance of prior years, the new administration gives us clarity, market stability, and global leadership in digital finance.

From the outset, President Trump made fintech a priority. One of his first bold moves (among many) was to issue an Executive Order "Strengthening American Leadership in Digital Financial Technology," which established a strategic framework for digital assets and prohibited a US central bank digital currency (CBDC). He further cemented America's stake in the digital economy by creating the Strategic Bitcoin Reserve and the US Digital Asset Stockpile, positioning our country as a key player in global crypto markets.

In addition to redirecting our focus to "promote United States leadership in digital assets and financial technology while protecting economic liberty," and revoking Biden's fintech policies, President Trump established a President's Working Group on Digital Assets Markets. This working group was charged with quickly assessing all existing regulation and rules affecting the digital asset sector and making recommendations on a wide range of digital and fintech issues.

One of the most important elements of President Trump's Executive Order is "providing regulatory clarity and certainty built on technology-neutral regulations, frameworks that account for emerging technologies, transparent decision making, and well-defined jurisdictional regulatory boundaries." By creating rules and frameworks that focus on the functionality, risks, and outcomes of financial technologies rather than the specific tools, platforms, or systems used, we can ensure that regulations apply equally to all technologies with similar purposes, avoiding favoring or restricting a financial service or transaction based solely on the type of technology. "Let one hundred flowers bloom," so says conventional Chinese wisdom. In this vein, it is wholly possible to allow innovation to thrive in a technology-neutral manner while still addressing core concerns such as security, consumer protection, and financial stability.

The President's EO clearly signals a return to the basics of financial regulation. By reorienting regulation to its proper focus, rather than advancing politicized goals like climate change (addressing the environment is important, but it should not come at the expense of core financial stability), regulators can ensure the safety and soundness of financial institutions and protect consumers from fraud and abuse.

At the regulatory level, change has been swift and sweeping. The SEC, under new leadership, has reversed its adversarial posture toward crypto, rolling back burdensome policies such as SAB 121 and the ambiguous "investment contract" framework. A newly-formed Crypto Task Force, headed by veteran commissioner Hester Peirce, is working to establish a more rational, transparent regulatory approach, while the agency has halted indiscriminate enforcement actions against intermediaries and fast-tracked long-delayed crypto IPOs. Additionally, the SEC's acknowledgement of Bitcoin and Ether as non-securities marks a pivotal shift, injecting long-overdue clarity into the market.

Taken together, these developments represent a fundamental recalibration of US fintech policy. Instead of regulatory uncertainty and litigation battles, the Trump administration has set fintech on a course toward responsible innovation, legal clarity, and global competitiveness. The message is clear: Under Trump, America is open for business in the digital financial age.

———

Of course, sometimes government intervention is necessary. The significant government intervention in the economy during the COVID-19 pandemic was not only justified but essential. The pandemic was akin to a natural disaster—an exogenous event that required decisive action from the government to stabilize an otherwise healthy economy. The government, having mandated shutdowns in the name of public health, had a responsibility to provide economic support. Never before had the country, or the world, confronted a dual crisis—a financial market melt-down with a concurrent health pandemic. The CARES Act was designed to preserve the productive capacity of the economy, ensuring that businesses and workers could weather the storm until the public health emergency abated and normal economic activity could resume.

This intervention was calibrated to the nature of the crisis. The CARES Act was time-limited, focused on providing immedi-ate relief and bridging the gap until the economy could stand on its own again. As 2020 progressed, the balance of risks between additional economic support and over-intervention began to shift. By December 2020, the economy was starting to show signs of recovery. However, the nation faced the peak of the winter COVID season without widespread vaccine availability. Thus, the CARES II relief package signed by President Trump at the end of 2020 was a reasonable response given the uncertainties at the time.

In contrast, the Biden administration's approach was marked by an opportunistic expansion of government intervention under the guise of crisis management. To a hammer, everything looks like a nail, and to big spenders, COVID-19 represented the ulti-mate justification for expanding the reach of government. The massive spending contained in Biden's American Rescue Plan poured gasoline on the flames of an already recovering economy, leading to demand-driven inflation. At the same time, the Biden administration's regulatory zeal hindered the supply side of the economy from responding effectively to the increased demand. The result was the highest inflation in forty years, which eroded Americans' standard of living and highlighted the pitfalls of excessive government intervention.

The Biden administration's priorities continued to focus on ideological projects rather than ensuring smooth market functioning. The Inflation Reduction Act, for example, funneled billions into green technologies without regard for the actual environmental impact. The supply chains for these technologies often rely on dirty materials and coal-generated electricity, undermining their purported environmental benefits. Additionally, the administration's resistance to expanding natural gas infrastructure, including blocking LNG export permits, constrained one of the most effective means of reducing carbon emissions.

The CARES Act was a necessary and effective response to an extraordinary crisis, aimed at preserving the economy's productive capacity. However, the subsequent policy choices under the Biden Administration have highlighted the dangers of using crises as a pretext for expanding government reach. Crisis policies must be reserved for actual crises. The overuse of such measures not only strains government resources but also distorts economic signals and incentives. The lessons from the COVID-19 pandemic and the subsequent policy responses are clear: Targeted, temporary interventions can stabilize the economy during unprecedented disruptions, but prolonged and expansive government intervention can lead to unintended consequences.

Under President Trump, we can expect a private-sector-led economy. This means removing distortionary subsidies and spending on inefficient green technologies that do more harm than good. It also involves a reduction in regulation to allow the private sector to innovate and expand the supply side of the economy, fostering noninflationary growth. A return to a private-sector-led approach, with reduced regulation and a focus on genuine innovation, is essential for sustaining economic growth and stability. The path to a resilient economy lies in empowering the private sector, fostering innovation, and reserving crisis measures for true emergencies.

———

This book, I hope, is a testament to the fact that when common sense, moral clarity, and grit lead the way, with more than a little help from divine providence, there is no limit to the good we can do in the world.

From October 2017 to January 2021, I had the greatest honor of my life in serving my country at the US Department of the Treasury, first as a deputy assistant secretary and then as a Senate-confirmed assistant secretary for international markets. My office was in the Main Treasury Building, which is technically on the White House compound, and overlooked the East Gate of the White House. I was regularly in meetings at the White House, sometimes every day of the week.

That's a far cry from my humble beginnings. Although I was not born in the shtetl of Nadvorna, in many ways my roots are in this small city in Southwest Ukraine. In Nadvorna's heyday, Jews were integral to the town's social fabric and central to its economic development. Nadvorna was an important Jewish religious center, home to many important rabbinic leaders and an important Chassidic dynasty.[1] From the 1800s until World War II, Jewish residents dominated the population, representing 64 percent of its 1880 population of 6,552, 50 percent of its 1890 population of 7,227, and 34 percent of its 1921 population of 6,062.[2] Today, no Jews remain.

---

1 *See* Moyshe Silk, *Upwards: In Heaven and On Earth – The Rebbe R' Mordchele of Nadvorna* (with an Introduction by Liel Leibovitz), Hidden Light Press 2025.

2 *Encyclopaedia Judaica*, 2nd ed. (Detroit: Macmillan Reference USA, 2007), 7:566.

My maternal grandfather was born and grew up there before coming to our great country in 1920. I am aligned with the Chassidic dynasty that took root there. The lessons of Nadvorna have guided much of my life and can be summarized in what I've come to call the Four P's: Providence, Personal touch, Perseverance, and Progress over perfection.

What do I mean by *divine Providence*? Perhaps because of my alignment with Chassidism, I can best relate to the Baal Shem Tov's explanation of the concept. He taught:

> Divine providence governs every minute creation... [even] a fallen leaf that has been tossed over and over by the wind...or a bit of straw which someone used when thatching a roof some years ago.... To move them from one place to another a storm wind breaks out, shaking heaven and earth in the middle of a warm sunny day and brings to fulfillment the Divine providence that governs this small stray leaf and old wisp of straw.[3]

> The movement of a single blade of grass in the depths of a forest, on a stately mountain, or in a deep valley where man has never passed...to its right or to its left...is determined according to Divine providence....

> Furthermore, the movement of this particular blade of grass affects...the creation in its entirety... [allowing] G-d's intent in the creation to come to fulfillment.[4]

3   *Likkutei Dibburim, vol. 1, p. 164, p. 177 in English.*
4   *Sefer HaMaamarim Kentreisim, vol. 2, p. 740.*

This is a view that I strongly believe in and have seen time and again in my life—both in good times and bad. In fact, I have no explanation whatsoever for many things that have occurred in my life, other than divine providence.

My life has also been a testament to the power of personal connection and concern—which I tend to express through humor, and food. My colleagues throughout the world have enjoyed (or endured) my homemade vodka, my roasted sardines, and, of course, my wife's honey cakes as we struggled through challenges that seemed insurmountable. I have had the pleasure and the honor of hosting diplomats, world leaders, rabbis, students, friends, and fellow travelers around my dinner table. I never cease to be amazed at the power of food shared with love to bridge the most daunting gaps.

Meanwhile, one of the easiest (or perhaps hardest) challenges of working with me is suffering through my sense of humor. Injecting humor into the equation, even with senior people and in serious circumstances, is a part of my nature. Like Rabbah, the great Babylonian Talmudist who lived over two thousand years ago, who would "warm up" his crowd with a joke or humorous statement before every one of his Talmudic lectures, I use humor to encourage others to embark upon weighty subjects with an open mind. Each joke is meant to prepare those around me for the analytical and mental challenges ahead of us.

When it comes to the other two P's—Perseverance and Progress over perfection—I hope the stories I have shared in this book fully demonstrate the value I place on practical, hard work. I have learned the lesson, many times over, that progress is made incrementally, and that nothing truly meaningful is accomplished without steadfast determination, plenty of hard work, and a good dose of common sense to remind us that perfect can be the enemy of good.

Over the years, I have endeavored to share these lessons with those in our community, particularly the younger generation, who desire to make a difference. I urge them to focus on the sky and on limits in two ways: First, I promise the younger crowd that the sky is indeed the limit and that they could have a role in changing the course of history, just like anyone else. Second, I remind them to appreciate that the sky, the heavens, imposes limits on us through our holy sources that apply to our thoughts, speech, and actions. We should really seek to achieve the fullest of everything, and while we're doing that, we should be mindful of our "limits" dictated from upstairs.

I have frequently been asked how my Judaism or the fact that I was the first Chassidic person to hold a senior position in a presidential administration impacted my work. The truth is, I do not compartmentalize myself into lawyer, government official, Jew, Chassidish, or whatever. Certainly, I have been blessed with certain skills and capabilities. I have taken those skills and capabilities, built up my expertise, and gained considerable market experience with these technical skills over the course of my career. At the same time, the values and traditions of my faith inform my thought, speech, and actions in a way that I believe positively impacts the way I approach my work. The way I conduct myself in the workplace and with my colleagues up and down the chain is influenced heavily and guided completely by our traditions and laws. In short, I believe that, to the extent that I have been successful, I had *siyata dishmaya* (heavenly assistance) from the beginning. I can also say that I have never been in a situation where I felt a need to compromise my values. To the contrary, I feel strongly that my values assisted me every step of the way.

I like to think that I was also able to make my faith accessible to those around me. Rather than viewing my tradition as something to overcome, it sometimes weaved its way into the fabric of our daily work. For instance, early in my tenure, Under Secretary David Malpass and Sigal Mandelker, then under secretary of the Office of Terrorism and Financial Intelligence (TFI), sought my input on a major sanctions action that TFI was considering. I was called into a meeting the day before Rosh Hashana and sat through a discussion of the facts and circumstances relating to the proposed action and discussion with Secretary Mnuchin. The legal issues presented were complicated, but I saw the semblance of a way forward. I boarded the train back to New York on the eve of Rosh Hashana. I was relieved that meetings on the issue would not reconvene until after yontif.

I had a long train ride home and two days of intense introspection and repentance ahead of me during Rosh Hashana observances, most of which take place in synagogue. The davening in my shul is exceptionally beautiful and moving, but the facts of this particular case kept nagging me. And so my mind wandered—perhaps just a bit. As it turned out, during the morning services of the first day of Rosh Hashanah, I came up with what I thought was a novel, simple, and elegant solution to the issue. It borrowed from an approach I had used in a highly complex, multibillion-dollar cross-border restructuring when I was in law practice.

On the one hand, I was elated that I'd come up with a solution. On the other hand, I was terrified that I would forget the details and concepts I'd conceived because I could not write them down. We do not use electricity or write on the Sabbath or during major festivals. The good Lord must have been with me, because I retained my thoughts and was ready to present them at an early morning meeting the day after Rosh Hashana. I took a very early train down to Washington and ran into Sigal in the hallway before we entered the secure room in which we were meeting with the secretary.

"Sigal, I figured it out!" I exclaimed and proceeded to explain my idea to her. She seemed to like it. We went into the secure room and waited for Secretary Mnuchin to arrive. Brent McIntosh, then Treasury general counsel, was also there, so I explained my idea to Brent, and he liked it as well. The rubber hit the road when the secretary arrived. After brief initial discussion, Sigal indicated to the secretary that I had an idea that she thought might be helpful, and she invited me to present it to him.

Within minutes, I could tell he was not on board. I gave a quick wink to Sigal and sat through my grilling. All was good. We served at the pleasure of the secretary. He was our principal, final arbiter, and decision-maker. But Sigal felt bad nonetheless as she had brought me into this issue, which was outside my International Affairs portfolio. Part of the way through the interrogation, Sigal attempted to intervene on my behalf. She pointed out the positive aspects of the approach and even went as far to say that I had spent two full days in synagogue over Rosh Hashana thinking through this considered approach. The secretary's immediate response: "If that's the case, then he needs to repent!"

It was my greatest honor to have served as assistant secretary for international markets at the US Department of the Treasury—my most rewarding and fulfilling position ever. My three-plus-year journey at Treasury was glorious and exciting and allowed me to leverage my expertise in energy and infrastructure, financial services, and disruptive technology to advance US financial growth and stability globally.

I look back fondly and with immense gratitude to the leadership at the department, particularly Secretary Steven Mnuchin, my great friends David Malpass and Heath P. Tarbert, all my fellow political appointees, my front-office counselor Daniel Katz and Special Assistant Talia Rubin, and my trusted friends and valued colleagues in the White House and across the interagency, not to mention the most impressive, intelligent, hardworking, and dedicated corps of career experts that I have ever had the pleasure to work with across so many offices—far too many to name.

I still miss walking into the Treasury compound and serving our great country, sitting under the watchful gaze of that extraordinary etching of President Lincoln, and looking out at the East Gate of the White House just a short thirty yards from my window. Even more, I miss the stimulation of grappling with a pressing issue and coming up with a solution and implementation in service to the United States of America.

To the extent that I have achieved any success, whether in the private sector or in government service, I attribute that to the blessings the good Lord has showered on me, the incredible support of my extraordinary family, a ton of really hard work, and the unique opportunities that our great country offers.

Only a country that adopts a national motto of "In G-d We Trust" and advertises it on all of its currency would support the freedom to serve in the government and stay guided by my faith, honoring tradition while advancing a better world for the future. And so, how apt it was that I could say the Mourner's Kaddish with a minyan in my regal office at the Main Treasury Building to recognize my father's *yartzeit*. It was 2020, and we wore our masks and maintained social distancing as we prayed and recited the Kaddish. And yet we had our great country's motto, "In G-d We Trust," in mind as we prayed, just as I shared that trust in G-d with my fellow workers as we toiled day and night to serve our country and help make the world a better place for all of us.

ACKNOWLEDGMENTS

At the onset, I am compelled and obliged to "[g]ive thanks to the Lord, for He is good; His steadfast love endures forever." (*Psalms* 136:1) In every chapter of this journey—whether in private practice or public service, in moments of clarity or uncertainty—I have seen the quiet, steady hand of Divine kindness guiding my steps. This book is a reflection of that providence and an expression of gratitude for the privilege to serve, to build, and to strive toward good.

As *Genesis* recounts, "And the earth was without form and void, and darkness was upon the face of the deep,"—or, rather, to paraphrase, In the beginning, there was darkness and confusion!— ". . . And God saw the light, that it was good." (*Genesis* 1:2-4) Much like the story of creation, this book emerged from a place of complexity and uncertainty. It was born out of an effort to give shape and permanence to a singular experience: the privilege of serving my country at a time of global upheaval, economic uncertainty, and historic opportunity. It began as a policy project, one that sought to distill the major initiatives we undertook at the Treasury Department into a volume of practical value. Yet, as the work deepened, I found that the road that led me to public service—and the personal convictions and professional experiences that anchored my time in office—needed to be described too. The result is this hybrid: part personal history, part professional growth, part roadmap.

To bring this book to life took a kind of collaboration that deserves its own place at the table. That effort was led with wisdom, grace, and brilliance by the inimitable Marji Ross, whose ability to extract structure from chaos and elevate substance to story knows no equal. Marji was ably assisted by Julie Stewart, whose care and precision shaped many chapters, and Paul Edwards. I owe deep thanks to my dear brother and co-conspirator in ideas Liel Leibovitz. His gift for capturing the spirit behind the substance and for translating policy into poetry is truly singular. And to the extraordinary folks at Bombardier Books—led by the visionary Adam Bellow, whose editorial courage, intellectual breadth, and instinct for timely ideas have shaped a generation of consequential books—thank you. Adam saw the potential of this story—part history, part policy, threaded with personal narrative—and recognized how it could cut across genres to reach both heart and mind. He was supported with creativity, precision, and dedication by Aleigha Koss, who saw the process through from inception to completion with grace and skill, and by Cody Corcoran, who aptly captured my and Marji's vision of "The Table," that stately table in the Secretary's Diplomatic Reception Room, home to so many consequential meetings, including parts of the China trade talks. Together, they stewarded this book from vision to finished product with a level of care and commitment for which I am deeply grateful.

Drawing on the teaching of *Avos*, "Who is wise? One who learns from all people." (4:1), my service at Treasury was built on the foundation of a thirty-five-year career in international law and finance. I am indebted to the many mentors, partners, clients, colleagues, and friends across the private sector who shaped my thinking, challenged my assumptions, and supported my work—especially those in the energy, infrastructure, and financial services sectors who entrusted me with high-stakes matters across Asia, the Americas, and beyond. They taught me how to analyze, synthesize, communicate with clarity, identify and mitigate risk, build, negotiate, lead, and deliver. These skills, refined in private practice, became essential tools in public service.

In government, I was fortunate to work alongside deeply dedicated professionals—both political appointees and career staff. To my dedicated colleagues at Treasury and across the interagency, thank you for your wisdom, resolve, and relentless pursuit of excellence. Together, we advanced a vision of economic strength grounded in fairness, security, and real-world outcomes. Special thanks to the teams behind América Crecé, AsiaEDGE, the $94 billion CARES Act airline rescue, our strategic initiatives countering China's economic coercion and work at the Financial Stability Board. I hope these pages reflect the quality and courage of your work.

Rabbi Yose taught, "A good neighbor" is among the straight paths to which a person should cleave (*Avos* 2:9). To the communities I've called home, from the bustling Chassidic enclaves of Borough Park to the skyscrapers of Hong Kong, to the brownstones of the Upper West Side and Upper East Sides of Manhattan, to the corridors of Washington, D.C., and the minyan rooms in between, thank you for anchoring me. Your faith, friendship, and support have enriched my life and fueled my purpose. Your voices walked with me into every negotiation room, and your stories kept me grounded. You reminded me, always, of what I was advocating for.

"Appoint for yourself a teacher. . .." (*Avos* 1:6)—My deepest gratitude to the many Rabbinic leaders and spiritual mentors who have guided me with wisdom and compassion. Your insights and encouragement—always attuned to the eternal amid the urgent—helped me keep my footing and direction.

As *Proverbs* teaches, "Children's children are the crown of the elderly, and the glory of children is their parents." (17:6) Family is both legacy and promise—the sacred chain that binds generations. Though words fall short, I give thanks for the strength of the family that preceded me and the blessing of those who follow.

To my grandparents and parents (all sorely missed), and the entire Silk and Friend families, thank you for the strength of family bonds and for believing in me—quietly, constantly, and completely. To my exceptional in-laws, and to the extended Orlander, Teitelbaum, and Halberstam families, thank you for your steadfast support, for your loyalty to family and values, and for the mantle of sacred legacy you carry.

To my children and grandchildren, who challenge me to be better and remind me why this work matters, you inspire me with your questions, convictions, and courage and keep me going with your unconditional love.

Especially, to my wife, Yocheved Rikva, who has been my partner not only in life but in every ideal I have ever pursued. As the Talmud teaches, "A person's home is his wife" (*Yevamos 62b*), and in her, I have found a home of grace, strength, loyalty, and depth. Your presence is my sanctuary, and your sacrifices made this service possible.

To President Donald J. Trump and Secretary Steven T. Mnuchin, my sincerest gratitude for your trust and confidence in me.

And finally, to the great people of the United States: I am deeply grateful for the honor to serve you. I hope these pages give voice to that service, in all its complexity and with all its heart. May it reflect a faithful accounting of service, and may it contribute, in some small way, to our ongoing pursuit of peace, prosperity, and purpose.

With gratitude to the following:

NB: In most instances, if you appear in the book, your name will not likely be here. If your name isn't here or in the book, please assume it was redacted for national security reasons, buried in a FOIA backlog, misplaced in the ruthless formatting of this section, or—most likely—truly inadvertently forgotten, somewhere between memory, margin notes, and the merciless final draft. The order reflects no formal hierarchy, only the ungovernable logic of a deadline-driven sprint to the finish. I had a genuine desire to acknowledge all who contributed to so many events over such a long period of time—and never, ever to slight anyone. Please forgive me if I fell short of the mark. If you're still offended, consider this your official invitation to ask nicely for (1) inclusion or upgrade in the second edition or (2) my editor's great list of therapists.

Legal Career

Coudert Brothers: Owen Nee, David Halperin, Lucille Barale, Thomas E. Jones and Norman Givant; Hughes Hubbard & Reed: Yasuo Okamoto, Michael Iovenko, David Tillinghast, Beverly Miller, Lydia Tugendrajch, Merrikay Hall, Christoher P. Reynolds, Hazen Moore, Michael RL Hooton and Paul Hanau; Chadbourne & Parke: Rigdon Boykin, Peter D. Cleary, Chaim Wachsberger, Robert Bohme, Kerin Cantwell, Marc Alpert, Martin Bashall,

Lester Ross, Zhang Yi, George Zhu, Xiaowei Ma, Olivia Cheung, Marianna Chan, Lulu Luk, Mei Chuang, Yvonne Hu, Lewis Man, Helen Cheung and Anna Lee; Allen & Overy (all of my former partners, far too many to name; in alphabetical order): Thomas Abbondante, Andrew Ballheimer, Anne Baldock, Shaun Beaton, Simon Black, Charles Borden, Jonathan Brayne, Thomas Brown, Kenneth Chan, Pamela Chepiga, Ernie Chung, Peter Curley, Aled Davies, Wim Dejonghe, Bimal Desai, Andrew Digges, Erwin Dweck, David Esseks, Michael Feldberg, Todd Fishman, Matthew Gearing, Yassir Ghorbal, Jas Gillar, Jim Grandolfo, Paul Griffin, Dan Guyder, Andrew Harrow, Peter Harwich, Jack Heinberg, Victor Ho, Yvonne Ho, Matt Huggett, Jason Humphreys, John Hwang, Stephen Jaggs, Jane Jiang, Julian Johansen, Thomas Jones, Etay Katz, Robert Kartheiser, Richard Kim, Benno Kimmelman, Bernadine Lam, Elizabeth Leckie, Jean Lee, Dave Lewis, Ling Li, Vicki Liu, Roger Lui, Cindy Lo, Simon Makinson, Will McAuliffe, Cathleen McLaughlin, Gary McLean, David Miles, Sami Mir, Adam Moncreiff, Paul Monk, David Morley, Sidney Myers, Scott Neilson, Deborah North, Kevin O'Shea, Gareth Price, Jay Pultman, Alan Rae-Smith, Andrew Rhys-Davies, John Richards, Ken Rivlin, Kent Rowey, Chris Rushton, Kayal Sachi, Chris Salter, Bill Satchell, Christian Saunders, Eric Shube, David Slade, Bruno Soares, Joseph Stefano, Mark Sterling, Barbara Stettner, Heath Tarbert, Andrew Trahair, Graham Vinter, Matthias Voss, David Wainer, Nick Wall, Philip R. Wood, Dorina Yessios, Ji Zou, plus the many, many counsel, associates and members of the marketing, finance, human resources, admin and support teams with whom I had the pleasure of working. And a special thanks to my friends and the members of the team that I built, who helped build/carry on the work of the U.S. China Group, including Jillian Ashley, Gary Lazarus, Yanmei Wei, Mingzhang Zeng, Victoria

Guo, and Niso Matari. Olivia Cheung was my executive assistant for a number of years, first at Chadbourne and later at A&O. Carrie Ng, Dawn France-Somersel and Roselyn Montero ably followed her.

Lasting friends (and clients) who offered wise counsel, unwavering support, and deep insights: Isser Elishis, Christopher P. Reynolds, James Wood, Ashley Wilkins, Paul Freedman, Steven Greenspan, Neil Z. Auerbach, Dr. Junyuan Gu and Ed Kania.

Agudath Israel of America Pro Bono Legal Services network: Rabbi Chaim Dovid Zwiebel, Shlomo Werdiger, Howard Tzvi Friedman, Ralph Reider, Mordy Herzog, Bruce Listhaus, Steven Mostofsky (before he was appointed to the bench), Rabbi Mordechai Biser *a"h,* Yitzchok Ehrman, A.D. Motzen, Abba Cohen, Yehuda Braunstein, Avrohom Weinstock, Leah Zagelbaum, Eugene Balloun, Dr. Chaim Shine, Eric Stern, Elliot Moskowitz, Avi Schick, Moshe Kurzmann, and all of my great pro bono clients.

Government[1]

Key Treasury Advisors and Policy Partners: David R. Malpass, Under Secretary of International Affairs and later President of the World Bank; Heath Tarbert Assistant Secretary of International Markets at Treasury and later Chairman of the Commodities and Futures Trading Commission; Justin Muzinich, Deputy Secretary; Sigal Mandelker, Under Secretary for Terrorism and Financial Intelligence; Brent McIntosh, General Counsel and later Under Secretary of International Affairs; Mauricio Claver-

---

1   All titles as of the time of our service together.

Carone, Counsellor to the Under Secretary and later Special Assistant to the President and Senior Director of the United States National Security Council's Western Hemisphere Affairs directorate; Brian Callanan, General Counsel; Adam Lerrick, Counselor to the Secretary; Geoffrey Okamoto, Acting Assistant Secretary for International Development David Eisner, Assistant Secretary for Management; Thomas Feddo, Assistant Secretary for Investment Security; Judy Shelton, U.S. Executive Director to the Board of the European Bank for Reconstruction and Development; J. Steven Dowd, U.S. Executive Director to the Board of the African Development Bank and then to the Board of the European Bank for Reconstruction and Development; DJ Nordquist, U.S. Executive Director to the Board of the World Bank; and Jason Chung, U.S. Executive Director to the Board of the Asian Development Bank.

My Exceptional Front Office: Daniel Katz, my Counselor Talia Rubin, my Special Assistant, and Jake Gerber.

Key Interagency Advisors and Policy Partners (by agency): White House: Jared Kushner, Senior Advisor to the President; Jason Greenblatt, Assistant to the President and Special Representative for International Negotiations; Avi Berkowitz, Assistant to the President and Special Representative for International Negotiations; Thomas Storch, Deputy Director of the National Economic Council and Deputy Assistant to the President for International Economic Affairs; Richard Goldberg, Director, National Security Council; State Department: David Friedman, Ambassador to Israel; Michael G. DeSombre, U.S. Ambassador to the Kingdom of Thailand; Keith Krach, Under Secretary of State for Economic Growth, Energy, and the Environment, Department of State; Aryeh Lightstone, U.S. Special Envoy for Economic Normalization; Roxanne J Cabral, Chargé d'Affaires,

U.S. Embassy in Panama; Joseph P. Schmelzeis, Jr., Senior Advisor to the Ambassador, U.S. Embassy in Tokyo; Julie Chung, Principal Deputy Assistant Secretary; David Feith, Deputy Assistant Secretary, East Asian and Pacific Affairs; Dan Negrea, Special Representative for Commercial and Business Affairs, Department of State; David Peyman, Deputy Assistant Secretary. Department of Energy: Joseph F. Uddo III, Deputy Assistant Secretary for Market Development and Energy Innovation. Department of the Interior: Katharine MacGregor, Deputy Secretary. Department of Transportation: Diana Furchtgott-Roth, Acting Assistant Secretary for Research and Technology, and before that, Acting Assistant Secretary for Macroeconomic Analysis, Department of the Treasury. Department of Commerce: Wendy Teramoto, Chief of Staff. U.S. International Development Finance Corporation: Adam Boehler, Chief Executive Officer; Will Doffermyre, General Counsel (OPIC); David Penna, Senior Vice President, Office of Strategic Initiatives; David Glaccum, General Counsel. Export-Import Bank of the United States: Kimberly Reed, President and Chairman of the Board of Directors; David Slade, General Counsel; David Fogel, Chief of Staff and after that Senior Advisor and Chief Business Development Officer, Department of State. Trade and Development Agency: Thomas R. Hardy; Nathan Young; Keith Eischeid; U.S. Agency for International Development: Bonnie Glick, Deputy Administrator; Dore Feith, Special Assistant to the Deputy Administrator. U.S. Commission for the Preservation of America's Heritage Abroad: Paul Packer, Chairman.

Colleagues Across Treasury: Eli Miller, Chief of Staff; Dan Kowalski, Counselor to the Secretary; Michael Faulkender, Assistant Secretary for Economic Policy; Monica Crowley, Assistant Secretary, Public Affairs; Drew Malone, Assistant Secretary, Legislative Affairs; Dave Kautter, Assistant Secretary for Tax; Baylor Myers, Deputy

Chief of Staff; Zac McEntee, Deputy Chief of Staff; John Morrissey, Deputy General Counsel; Kipp Kranbuhl, PDAS, Financial Markets; Fritz Vaughn, PDAS for Legislative Affairs; David Lacquement, Deputy Assistant Secretary, Cybersecurity and Critical Infrastructure Protection, Financial Institutions; Peter Phelan, Deputy Assistant Secretary, Capital Markets; Rebecca Miller, Deputy Assistant Secretary, Public Affairs; Devesh Ashra, Deputy Assistant Secretary for Investment, Energy, and Infrastructure; Brian Morgenstern, Deputy Assistant Secretary for External Affairs and later White House, Deputy Press Secretary and Deputy Communications Director; Jon Blum, Deputy Assistant Secretary for Banking, Finance & Terrorist Finance; Steve Miran, Senior Advisor, Economic Policy; Tom Dans, Counselor to the Under Secretary for International Affairs; Max Raskin; Ben Joseloff; Sean Rushton, Deputy Assistant Secretary for Public Affairs IA; Michael DiRoma, Deputy Assistant Secretary, Public Affairs David Dwyer, Counselor to the Under Secretary for International Affairs; Aharon Friedman, Senior Advisor, Tax Policy; Alexandra Gaiser, Executive Secretary; Trevor Kellogg, Cooper Godfrey, Joey Smith, Director of Operations; Kelsey Kats, Senior Advisor, Office of the Treasurer; Brady Howell, Senior Advisor, Legislative Affairs; Zach Isakowitz, Director, Public Affairs (Terrorism and Financial Intelligence); Jackson Miles, Special Assistant; Shirley E. Gathers; Karen DeLaBarre Chase.

Career Deputy Assistant Secretaries in International Markets: Larry McDonald, Robert Kaproth, Michael Kaplan, Lailee Moghtader, Eric Meyers, Lida Fitts, Matt Swinehart and Sharon Yang, and all of their teams.

Partners in Infrastructure and Energy Initiatives: USG: DJ Gribbin, Special Assistant to the President for Infrastructure; Jessica Bodoya, Deputy Senior Director for Western Hemisphere

Affairs, National Security Council and Managing Director, Western Hemisphere, US International Development Finance Corporation; Dave Banks, Special Assistant to the President for International Energy and Environment, National Economic Council and National Security Council; John Rader, Deputy Assistant to the President and Advisor for Policy and Strategy; Timothy Fitzgerald, Chief International Economist for the Council of Economic Advisors; Frank Fannon, Assistant Secretary for Energy Resources, Department of State; Wells Griffith, Senior Advisor to the Secretary of Energy for International Energy and Environment and after that Senior Director for International Energy and Environment, National Security Council; Landon Derentz, Director for International Energy and Environment, National Security Council; Theodore Garrish, Assistant Secretary for International Affairs, Department of Energy; Sandra Oudkirk, Deputy Assistant Secretary for Energy Diplomacy, Department of State; Catherine Hein, Office of the General Counsel; Isabella Rioja-Scott, Economic Counsellor, U.S. Embassy in Panama; Rachael Baitel, Deputy Chief of Staff, US International Development Finance Corporation. Brazil: Erivaldo Alfredo Gomes, Secretary for International Economic Affairs, Ministry of Economy; Ambassador Nestor Forster. Chile: Minister Ignacio Briones Rojas; Ambassador Alfonso Silva Navarro. Colombia: Vice Minister of Foreign Affairs Francisco Javier Echeverri; Ambassador Francisco Santos Calderon. Ecuador: Minister of Economy and Finance Mauricio Pozo Crespo and Ambassador Ivonne A-Baki. Guyana: President Irfaan Ali and Vice President Bharrat Jagdeo. Israel: Minister of Finance Moshe Kahlon; Minister of Finance Israel Katz; Ministry of Finance Accountant General Ronny Hizkiyahu. Jamaica: Prime Minister Andrew Holness; Minister of Finance Nigel Clarke;

Ambassador Audrey Marks. Panama: President Laurentino Nito Cortizo; Minister of Economy and Finance Hector Alexander; Secretary of Energy Jorge Rivera; Banco Nacional de Panama, Gerente General Javier Enrique Carrizo Esquivel; Minister Jose-Alejandro Rojas; Secretariat for Public-Private Partnerships Saleh Asvat; Ambassador Juan De Dianous; Jennifer La Rocca. Indonesia: Ministry of Finance, Director General Luky Alfirman; Ministry of Finance, Head, Fiscal Policy Agency Febrio Nathan Kacaribu. Singapore: Deputy Minister of Finance Yee Ping Yi; Executive Director, Infrastructure Asia, Seth Tan. Japan: Deputy Vice Minister for International Affairs Yasuhisa Nakao; Ministry of Economy, Trade and Industry Deputy Director General Kohei Okada; South Korea: Deputy Prime Minister and Minister of Economy and Finance Hong Nam-ki; Deputy Minister for International Affairs Kim Hoe Jeong; KEXIM Chairman Sun-soo Eun; Ministry of Economy and Finance Director General Chung-Keun Park; MOTIE Deputy Minister Young-joon Joo. Taiwan: Minister of Finance Jain-Rong Su; Minister without Portfolio John Deng; Bank of Taiwan Chairman Joseph Jye-cherng Lyu (former Minister of Finance) and Ambassador Bi-Khim Hsiao. Thailand: Ministry of Finance, Director-General of Fiscal Policy Kulaya Tantitemit; Charge d'Affaires Boosara Kanchanalai. Vietnam: Central Economic Commission Chair, Nguyen Van Binh; Vice Minister of Finance Tran Xuan Ha; Ambassador Ha Kim Ngoc. Philippines: Department of Finance Undersecretary Mark Joven. Suriname: President Chan Santokhi.

China Trade: USTR: Amb. Robert Lighthizer, USTR; Amb. Jeffrey Gerrish, Deputy USTR; Amb. Greg Doud, Deputy USTR; Jamieson Greer, Chief of Staff; Stephen P. Vaughn, General Counsel; Terry McCartin, Acting Assistant USTR for China; Department of Agriculture, Ted McKinney, Under Secretary of Agriculture for Trade and Foreign Agricultural Affairs; Department of Commerce: Secretary Wilbur Ross; Alan Turley, Deputy Assistant Secretary; Department of Energy: Steve Winberg, Assistant Secretary for Fossil Fuels; Helena Fu; Nina Palmer; Everett Eissenstat, Deputy Assistant to the President for International Economic Affairs, National Economic Council; Clete Willems, Deputy Assistant to the President for International Economic Affairs, National Economic Council; Treasury: Albert Lee; Matthew Sullivan; Bill Block, Financial Attaché.

CARES Act: Eric Froman, Assistant General Counsel; Gary Grippo, Deputy Assistant Secretary for Public Finance; Jacob Loshin and Joe Clark, Office of the General Counsel; Steven G. Bradbury, Acting Deputy Secretary and General Counsel, Department of Transportation.

Finreg and Fintech: Jay Clayton, Chairman, U.S. Securities and Exchange Commission; Hester M. Peirce, Commissioner, U.S. Securities and Exchange Commission; Andrew Olmem, Deputy Assistant to the President for Economic Policy and Deputy Director, National Economic Council; Rebeka Jurata, Treasury, Deputy Assistant Secretary, International Financial Markets, later Special Assistant to the President for Financial Policy, National Economic Council and later Board Member, Public Company Accounting Oversight Board; Craig Phillips, Counsellor to the Secretary; Bimal Patel, Assistant Secretary for Domestic Finance; Francis Brooke, Deputy Assistant to the President for Economic Policy and Deputy Director of the National Economic Council; Jonathan Greenstein, Deputy Assistant Secretary, Financial Institutions; Robert Greene, Senior Advisor, Domestic Finance - Financial Institutions; Israel Ministry of Finance, Deputy Minister Yitzchak Cohen, Director General Shai Babad and Chief

Economist Shira Greenberg; Israel Ministry of Foreign Affairs, Director General Yael Ravia-Zadok.

Those Who I Cannot Name: The dedicated members of our intelligence community and secret service to whom I owe a deep debt of gratitude.

Rabbis

Grand Rabbi Shloime Leifer, the Nadvorna Rebbe shlita; Grand Rabbi Yehoshua Heschel Eichenstein, the Zidichover Rebbe *zt"l*; Grand Rabbi Yakov Perlow, the Novominsker Rebbe *zt"l*; Rabbi Chaskel Besser *zt"l*; Rabbi Aaron D. Twerski shlita; Rabbi Michel Twerski, the Milwaukee Rebbe shlita; Rabbi Adin Steinsaltz *zt"l*; Rabbi Yitzchok Singer *zt"l*; Rabbi Avrum Leifer; Rabbi Yitzchok Breitowitz; Rabbi Shlomo Porter; Rabbi Moshe Rappaport; Rabbi Avrohom Steinberg; Rabbi Mordechai Avtzon; and Rabbi Levi Shemtov; and all of their families.

Community

All of my fellow congregants and friends at Tiferes Shulem d'Nadvorna in Borough Park, as well as Congregation Yetev Lev d'Satmar, Congregation Zichron Chaim Shia Sorvosh and Congregation Shomrei Shabbos; Congregation B'Nai Israel Chaim, Rabbi Besser's shtiebl on the Upper West Side, the Mincha Minyan at the offices of Allen & Overy in New York, Congregation Bnai Israel, Rabbi Ralbag's shtiebl on the Upper East Side; Chabad Lubavitch of Hong Kong; Shuva Israel; Ohel Leah; TheShul of the Nation's Capitol; and Kesher Israel. In particular, Rabbi Berish Leifer *zt"l*, Rabbi Yisroel Chaim Leifer *zt"l*, Rabbi Yisumer Leifer, Yitzchok Rutner, Sumi Leifer, Rabbi Yitzchok Twersky, Alan and Joan Fuchs, Rabbi Zalman Leib

Meisels, Avrumie Sieger, Naftuli Brachfeld, Isaac and Freida Kamhin, David and Ruthie Schreiber, Reuven Mandelcorn, Morty Stern, Isaac and Leah Gniwish, Rabbi Akiva Osher Padwa, the Kamhazi family, the Seidenfeld family, the Salzberg family, the Schor family, Rabbi Sinai Moliwitsky, Nachman Elbaum a"h, Isa "Doc" Goldman a"h, Rabbi Amram Kass, Paul Rubin, Sander Gerber, Paul (Pinky) Schwartz, Philippe Benedict, Ari Cohen, Rabbi Zalman Leib Meisels, Rabbi Yehoshua Hecht, Rabbi Menachem Shemtov, Rabbi Yitzchok Zeitlin, Menachem Mendel Amar, Menny Feldman, Todd Schwartz, Moshe Gano, Avi Ben Haroush, Vito and Milly Arbib, Isaac and Betty Btesh, Allan and Rosalind Baitel, David Harari, Jeffrey and NaTang Schwartz, and all of their families.

Family

Uncle Leon and Aunt Rose; Leeny (and Mike, Lauren and Pemma) and Ronda; Cousins Nancey and Stu, Minnie and Ben and their families; our beloved and exceptional Orlander, Teitelbaum, Halberstam, Gantzvi, Thaler and Lieber aunts and uncles and all their families; Naftuli Chaim Halberstam and Mendel Tetitelbaum and their families; valued and cherished Gross, Orlander, Pshemish and Friedman brothers- and sisters-in-law and their families; Meir and Malka Aidel (and Toivy, Raizy, Tzvi and Hadassah), Moishie Yitzchok and Dina (and Zishe and Sruli), Meshulam and Noga (and Shira), Raphy and Bella, Chavi, Naftuli Chaim, Mordechai Dov and Tauba Raitza.